DICTIONARY OF SCOTTISH BIOGRAPHY

Volume I
1971-75

Dictionary of Scottish Biography

Volume I
1971-75

Edited by Kenneth Roy

Carrick Media

Published by Carrick Media
2/1 Galt House, 31 Bank Street, Irvine KA12 0LL
01294 311322

Copyright 1999 Carrick Media

Series editor: Kenneth Roy
Deputy editor: Fiona MacDonald

Printed in Great Britain by Redwood Books

All rights reserved. No part of this publication may be reproduced, stored in a retrieval system, or transmitted in any form or by any means – electronic, mechanical, photocopying, recording or otherwise – without the prior permission of the publisher.

British Library Cataloguing-in-Publication Data
A catalogue record for this book is available from the British Library

ISBN 0 946724 41 5

Foreword

On a summer's day in 1998, in the newly-established "International Book Town" of Dalmellington, Ayrshire, I came across a complete eight-volume set of Robert Chambers's A Biographical Dictionary of Eminent Scotsmen (1832-34). The first thought that occurred to me was how odd it was that no one had made a serious effort to emulate Chambers's achievement for the modern era; how surprising that a small country which had given so many outstanding people to the world had done such a poor job of commemorating their lives and accomplishments for posterity. The second thought came with the force of inspiration: it should be done; it should be done at once.

After I lugged the books home I realised that it would be impossible to emulate Chambers's achievement. Some of the essays in that incomparable work amount to 30,000 words. Even relatively minor personalities are dealt with at a length daunting to the modern eye. Yet, in spirit if not to the same formidable extent, the idea was possibly capable of adaptation. The question was how.

After toying with various schemes and methods, I settled on the manageable principle of a series of volumes each looking at a selection of prominent men and women, Scottish by birth or residence, who had died within a half-decade. The period covered by this first volume is 1971-75 – a minimum of 24 years since the date of death. I judged that this was long enough to lend detachment, but close enough for many readers to remember the personalities – with affection or otherwise.

Today's broadsheet newspaper, with so much space at its disposal, is profligate in its devotion to obituaries. Both *The Herald* and *The Scotsman* actively solicit "appreciations" and the like, as a result of which people of the slightest importance acquire in death a lustre that was scarcely discernible in life. It was not so in the early 1970s. There were no obituaries pages in Scottish newspapers then; obituaries, such as they were, popped up in any corner of the paper or none. Quite major figures, such as politicians and judges, who would nowadays be granted the privilege of a large photograph and 600 words, tended to be dismissed in a couple of dry paragraphs.

This made the job of compiling the book more difficult than it would be now. For example I spotted a few lines on a physician named Katherine Macphail. They said practically nothing about her, yet it was clear from the bare bones of the notice that here was a courageous Scotswoman who deserved to be rescued from obscurity. Almost as the book went to press we had discovered little more about her, despite persistent attempts. A last-minute breakthrough yielded rich rewards and a thrilling narrative by Macphail herself. We had begun to feel as a detective might feel in successful pursuit of an awkward case.

The giants of the book, though less rewarding from the point of view of original research, presented fewer problems. The pre-eminent personalities of 1971-75 were a broadcaster (John Reith), two writers (Eric Linklater and Neil Gunn), a surgeon (Norman Dott), a scientist (John Boyd Orr) and an artist (William Gillies). Some might add a film-maker (John Grierson), a politician (James Stuart, who presided over that amazing phenomenon, a Conservative majority in Scotland), and an architect (Robert Matthew). Each of these is the subject of an essay or personal memoir. Two of the most fascinating (and painfully candid) are by children of the subjects.

Yet, who remembers the trade unionist who revelled in his reputation as the ugliest man in Scotland? Or the soldiering lawyer who considered Lt. Col. Winston Churchill a poor disciplinarian? Or the Rangers footballer who turned up for training wearing a bowler hat? These lights are no less colourful for being lesser.

There are 250 biographies in the pages that follow: an average of about one a week for five years. We commissioned essays or memoirs on 29 of them. Many others are illustrated by contemporary anecdotes or extracts from books and papers. The rest are briefer lives, remembered with a passing nod, not invariably respectful. This eclectic approach gives each subject what the editor (if no one else) considers his or her due weight and importance. The choice and the treatment are of course subjective. I have included a professional criminal who endeared himself to the popular imagination, though worthier persons are excluded because, after an interval of quarter of a century, there did not seem anything of interest left to say about them.

Towards the end I came to appreciate that what I had been recording as I went along was the death of the first world war generation. One of the most telling phrases in the book is quoted by R.D. Kernohan of the Dundee evangelist D.P. Thomson, who served as an officer in France and Salonika and whose two brothers were killed in action. It left Thomson with "an awesome experience of some special purpose for which he had been spared" – words uncannily echoed by others, including and most famously John Reith. Time and again one is left with the impression of driven men and women, haunted by a sense of guilt at having survived when so many perished, a guilt which found expression in a Calvinistic appetite for work and an overwhelming desire to improve the lot of humanity. Few of the people in this book appear to have relished holidays or recreation. There is a sense of time running out, of every available hour having to be used for some worthwhile purpose. That is why, so many years after their deaths, we remember them here.

Kenneth Roy
Irvine
January 1999

EDITOR'S NOTE

Two minor points of style. I have an instinctive aversion to the over-use of higher case in the expression of titles. For this reason I have preferred director to Director, chief executive to Chief Executive, professor to Professor, and so on. But I acknowledge that the rule can be carried too far, so the occasional higher has been allowed when lower felt merely perverse.

In the alphabetical arrangement of individuals whose names suggested an alternative – does one introduce the former secretary of state for Scotland as plain James Stuart or more grandly as the 1st Viscount Stuart of Findhorn? – I have chosen either the name by which the subject was generally known or which otherwise seemed appropriate. – K.R.

Biographies by subject

Agriculture and fishing

Sir Frederick Bell
Dr James Durno

Aristocracy

3rd Marquess of Aberdeen and Temair (Dudley Gladstone Gordon)
4th Marquess of Aberdeen and Temair (David George Ian Alexander Gordon)
11th Duke of Argyll (Ian Douglas Campbell)
8th Duke of Buccleuch (Walter John Montagu-Douglas-Scott)
28th Earl of Crawford and 11th Earl of Balcarres (David Robert Alexander Lindsay)
13th Lord Elibank (James Alastair Frederick Campbell Erskine-Murray)
17th Baron Elphinstone (John Alexander Elphinstone)
14th Duke of Hamilton and 11th Duke of Brandon (Douglas Douglas-Hamilton)
12th Baron Kinnaird (Kenneth FitzGerald Kinnaird)
7th Earl of Mansfield and Mansfield (Mungo David Malcolm Murray)
30th Earl of Mar (James (Clifton) of Mar)
5th Earl of Minto (Victor Gilbert Lariston Garnet Elliot-Murray-Kynynmound)
19th Earl of Moray (Archibald John Morton Stuart)
6th Earl of Rosebery (Albert Edward Harry Meyer Archibald Primrose)
9th Duke of Roxburghe (George Victor Robert John Innes-Ker)
16th Earl of Strathmore and Kinghorne (Timothy Patrick Bowes-Lyon)

Arts

Eleanor Adler
Phyllis Mary Bone
Helena Brodie of Brodie
Sandy Brown
William Alexander Burns
Isobel Dunlop
Horace Fellowes
James Gibson
Sir William George Gillies
2nd Baron Glentanar (Thomas Coats)
Dr John Grierson
Dr Tom John Honeyman
Charles D'Orville Pilkington Jackson
James Lovell
David McCallum
Leslie Grahame MacDougall
Lex McLean (Alexander McLean Cameron)
William McMillan
Sir Robert Hogg Matthew
John Miller
Professor Sidney Thomas Mayow Newman
John Noble of Ardkinglas
Jeannie Robertson
James Norval Harold Robertson-Justice
Algernon Ross-Farrow
Eric Schilsky
Paul Shillabeer
David Macbeth Sutherland
J(ohn) Murray Thomson
Murray Macpherson Tod
Mary Eileen Ure
Sir David (Lumsden) Webster
Dave Willis (David Williams)
William Wilson
Fenton Wyness

Business

Sir Wilfrid Ayre
Lt. Col. Ian Glen Collins
Sir Charles Connell
Dr Charles Hepburn
Frederick Mair Johnston
Sir Alexander Boyne King
Georgina Russell Davidson MacKinnon
Sir Edward (James) Reid
Major Noel Graham Salvesen
Robert Paterson Smith
Hugh Cowan Stenhouse
Sir Alexander Murray Stephen
Sir (James) Douglas (Wishart) Thomson
John S. Thomson

Civil service

Sir William O'Brien Lindsay
Sir John Macpherson
Sir David Milne
Sir Robert Edwin Russell

Education

Kurt Hahn
Ian Donald McIntosh
A(lexander) S(utherland) Neill
Robert Robertson Rusk
Dr Arthur Lionel Forster Smith
Sir John Mackay Thomson

Gaelic culture

Rev. Archibald Beaton
Rev. Angus Duncan
James Thomson

Journalism and broadcasting

William Macdonald Ballantine
Ivor John Carnegie Brown
Dr Melville Dinwiddie
John Rutherford Gordon
Lex Hornsby
Jessie Miller House
Sir Francis Low
Hugh McMichael
Frank Moran
David Murray
John Charles Walsham Reith (Lord Reith of Stonehaven)
Robin Richardson
Jack Robson
Philip Stalker
A.C. (Sandy) Trotter

Law

Rt. Hon. Lord Clyde (James Latham McDiarmid Clyde)
Andrew Dewar Gibb
Rt. Hon. Lord Grant (William Grant)
Sir Thomas Innes of Learney
Rt. Hon. Lord Milligan (William Rankine Milligan)
Lord Morton of Henryton (Fergus Dunlop Morton)
Brigadier Sir John Spencer Muirhead
Charles de Bois Murray
Lord Reid of Drem (James Scott Cumberland Reid)
Hon. Lord Russell (Albert Russell)
Hon. Lord Walker (James Walker)

Literature

Honor Arundel
March Cost (Margaret Mackie Morrison)
Helen Burness Cruickshank
Marryat Ross Dobie
W. Murdoch Duncan
Sir James Fergusson of Kilkerran
George Friel
Neil Miller Gunn
Eric Linklater
Fionn Mac Colla (Thomas J. Douglas Macdonald)
Agnes M. Macdonald
Stuart MacGregor
Sir (Edward Montague) Compton Mackenzie
Moray David Shaw McLaren
Robert Duncan Macleod
Florence Marian McNeill
William Mathie Parker
Edith Anne Robertson
George Scott-Moncrieff
Sydney Goodsir Smith
Dorothy Emily Stevenson (Mrs J.R. Peploe)
Lesley Storm (Margaret Cowie)
Douglas Cuthbert Colquhoun Young

Medicine

Dr George Bell
Dr Margaret Brotherston
Sir John Bruce
Dr John Menzies Campbell
Professor William Stuart McRae Craig
Professor Robert Cruickshank
Norman McOmish Dott
Professor John Glaister
Dr Douglas James Guthrie
Arthur Jacobs
Dr Katherine Macphail
Dr Angus Macrae
Sir Walter Mercer
Dr Robert B. Robertson
Alister Burns Wallace
Sir John Weir
William Combe Wilson

Military

Brigadier Arthur Edward Cumming
Admiral Sir Frederick Hew George
    Dalrymple-Hamilton
Brigadier Dame Helen Shiels Gillespie
Maj.-Gen. Douglas Alexander Henry Graham
Brigadier Hector Robert Hume Greenfield
Vice-Admiral Sir (George) David (Archibald)
    Gregory
Brigadier Alasdair Gillean Lorne Maclean
Maj.-Gen. John Simson Stuart Martin
Maj.-Gen. Sir Aymer Maxwell
Admiral Sir (John) Peter (Lorne) Reid
General Sir Thomas Sheridan
    Riddell-Webster
Vice-Admiral Sir James Andrew Gardiner
    Troup

Miscellaneous

Robert Gray
Sir Ivison Macadam
Johnny Ramensky
Sir Robert Arthur Wilmot

Police

Sir William Booth Rennie Morren
Lt.-Col. Sir Hugh Stephenson Turnbull

Politics

Col. Sir Patrick James Blair
James Clunie
Sir John (Clarke) George
Tom H. Gibson
Sir John Henderson
John D. Kidd
Francis James Patrick Lilley
Sir John McWilliam
John Mains
Lt. Col. Sir Thomas Moore
Col. Sir Basil Hamilton Hebden
    Neven-Spence
Sir John Ure Primrose
John Rankin
James Gray Stuart (1st Viscount Stuart of
    Findhorn)
Sir Duncan Mackay Weatherstone
Sir Garnet Douglas Wilson

Religion

Father William James Anderson
Rev. Dr William J. Baxter
Rev. Leonard J.A. Bell
Rev. Duncan Campbell
Very Rev. Dr James Hutchison Cockburn
Rev. Karl S.G. Greenlaw
Cardinal William Theodore Heard
Rev. Dr Archibald Clive Irvine
Rev. Vera Kenmure
Very Rev. Dr James B. Longmuir
Rev. Kenneth MacKenzie
Rev. Dr William MacNicol
Rt. Rev. Dom Columban Mulcahy
Rev. Anderson Nicol
Mgr. Gerard Rogers
Very Rev. Dr Robert Forrester Victor Scott
Very Rev. Dr Robert Henry Wishart Shepherd
Rev. Dr William Aitken Smellie
Rev. Dr Oliver Springer
Rev. Dr Jack Stevenson
Rev. D.P. Thomson
Rev. Dr Forbes S. Tocher

Scholarship

Professor James Houston Baxter
Sir Denis (William) Brogan
Professor Andrew Browning
Professor Charles Arthur Campbell
Annie Isabella Dunlop
Professor Christian James Fordyce
Rev. Professor John Foster
Professor William Gauld Maclagan
Professor James Wilkie Nisbet
Professor David Talbot Rice
Sir David Ross
Professor James Alexander Roy
Professor John Waugh Scott
Professor William Marshall Smart
Dr Alexander Burt Taylor
Professor Andrew McLaren Young

Science

Dr Tom Leadbetter Cottrell
Professor (James) Norman Davidson
Professor Harald Drever
Sir Edmund (Langley) Hirst
Dr John M. Holm
John Boyd Orr (1st Baron Boyd Orr
    of Brechin)

George Adam Reay
D(avid) Alan Stevenson
Professor Conrad Hal Waddington
Professor John Walton
Sir Robert (Alexander) Watson-Watt

Sport

Gerry Birrell
Sir George Graham
Tom Haliburton
Helen Holm
Sir Robert Kelly
John Kerr
George W. Mackie
Alan Morton
David Murray
Lady Rowallan (Gwyn Mervyn Grimond)

W. Maxwell Simmers
Dr Arthur Robert Smith
Ian Smith
Andrew King ("A.K.") Stevenson
Sir Stewart Stewart-Clark
Dr William Halliday Welsh

Trade unionism

George Middleton
Abe Moffat
Mary Elizabeth Sutherland

Voluntary service

Lady Marjorie Louise Dalrymple
Countess of Minto (Marion Cook)

Notes on Contributors

Stewart Conn
Personal memoir of Neil Miller Gunn
Poet and playwright, born in Glasgow in 1936, brought up in Kilmarnock and educated at Glasgow University. As a BBC drama producer, he encouraged the work of many Scottish playwrights. His own work has been extensively produced on the professional stage and several collections of his poetry are in print.

Rt. Rev. Gerard Mark Dilworth, OSB
Essay on Father William James Anderson
Essay on Cardinal William Theodore Heard
Abbot of Fort Augustus Abbey since 1991, born in 1924 and educated at Fort Augustus Abbey School and the Universities of Oxford and Edinburgh. He is a former keeper of the Scottish Catholic Archives.

Walter R. H. Duncan
Essay on John Boyd Orr, 1st Baron Boyd Orr of Brechin
Former lipid chemist on the staff of the Rowett Research Institute. Since he retired in 1989 he has been honorary archivist there.

Bob Ferrier
Note on Sir George Graham
Essay on Alan Morton
Writer and sports journalist, born in Tarbert, Loch Fyne, in 1922, brought up in Dumbarton and educated at the Academy there. He began his career on the *Daily Record* in Glasgow, spent eight years with the *Daily Mirror* in London and 10 years with *The Observer*.

Tom Fleming, OBE
Essay on James Gibson
Actor and director, born in Edinburgh in 1927. He made his professional theatre debut in 1945, co-founded the Edinburgh Gateway Company, and was appointed director of the new Royal Lyceum Theatre Company in 1965. For many years he has been a television commentator on royal and state occasions.

Dr Miles Glendinning
Essay on Sir Robert Hogg Matthew
Writer and historian. At the Royal Commission on Ancient and Historical Monuments he heads the topographic and threatened buildings survey department. He has co-authored numerous books on modern housing and Scottish architecture.

Jim Gorie
Essay on William Macdonald Ballantine
International business consultant, born in Yorkshire in 1932 and educated at Glasgow High School and Buckie High School. He moved from Scottish Office public relations into industrial development and was a director of the former Scottish Development Agency.

James Halliday
Essay on Tom H. Gibson
Chairman of Scots Independent Newspapers, born in Wemyss Bay in 1927 and educated at Greenock High School and Glasgow University. He is a former teacher and lecturer in history and a former chairman of the Scottish National Party.

Ian Hamilton, QC
Personal memoir of Andrew Dewar Gibb
Personal memoir of Douglas Cuthbert Colquhoun Young
Queen's Counsel, born in Paisley in 1925 and educated at John Neilson School, Paisley, Allan Glen's School, Glasgow, and the Universities of Glasgow and Edinburgh. He was one of a group of young patriots who removed the Stone of Destiny from Westminster Abbey. Since 1954 he has been practising at the Scottish bar (with interludes).

Andrew Hargrave
Essay on George Middleton
Journalist, born in Budapest in 1910. He was Scottish correspondent, then Frankfurt correspondent, of the Financial Times.

William Hunter
Essay on Lex McLean (Alexander McLean Cameron)
Essay on Dave Willis (David Williams)
Journalist, born in Paisley in 1931 and educated at Paisley Grammar School and Glasgow University. He is a former staff journalist with the *Glasgow Herald*.

Victoria Kellar
Essay on Sir William George Gillies
Freelance art historian, employed by the Royal Scottish Academy. She is the co-author of books on William Gillies and Alberto Morrocco.

R.D. Kernohan, OBE
Essay on Very Rev. Dr James B. Longmuir
Essay on Very Rev. Dr Robert Forrester Victor Scott
Essay on James Gray Stuart (1st Viscount Stuart of Findhorn)
Essay on Rev. D.P. Thomson
Journalist, writer and broadcaster, born in Lanarkshire in 1931 and educated at Whitehill School, Glasgow, and the Universities of Glasgow and Oxford. He is a former staff journalist with the *Glasgow Herald* and a former director-general of Scottish Conservative Central Office. For 18 years he was editor of *Life and Work*, the Church of Scotland's magazine.

Marista Leishman
Personal memoir of John Charles Walsham Reith (Lord Reith of Stonehaven)
Daughter of Lord Reith. Senior partner in a management and training consultancy, born in 1932 and educated at St Andrews University. She was the first head of education at the National Trust for Scotland.

Andro Linklater
Personal memoir of Eric Linklater
Son of Eric Linklater. Writer and journalist, born in Edinburgh in 1944 and educated at Winchester College and Oxford University. He specialises in biography, travel and history.

Professor Ian Lockerbie
Essay on Dr John Grierson
Former professor of French and of educational development at Stirling University. He was born in Dumfries in 1930. Among his public appointments, he was chairman of the John Grierson Archive at Stirling University and of the Scottish Film Council, and founder chairman of the Scottish Film Production Fund.

Dr Margery Palmer McCulloch
Essay on Neil Miller Gunn
Teacher of Scottish literature at Glasgow University. She has written studies of Gunn and Edwin Muir.

Rt. Rev. Lord Abbot Donald McGlynn, OCSO, STL, SLJ
Essay on Rt. Rev. Dom Columban Mulcahy
Monk, born in Glasgow in 1934 and educated at the Gregorian University, Rome. He has been a monk in the Order of Cistercians of Strict Observance since 1952 and abbot of Nunraw since 1969.

Iain F. MacLaren, FRCSE, FRCS, FRCPE
Essay on Sir Walter Mercer
Surgeon, born in Edinburgh in 1927 and educated at Edinburgh Academy, Fettes College, and Edinburgh University. He was consultant surgeon at the Royal Infirmary, Edinburgh, for 18 years and is a former honorary secretary and vice-president of the Royal College of Surgeons of Edinburgh.

John MacRitchie
Essay on Eric Linklater
Librarian, born in Dumfries in 1958 and educated at Strathclyde University. He is a librarian with Angus Council Cultural Services.

Ronald Mavor, CBE
Essay on Dr Tom John Honeyman
Writer, born in Glasgow in 1925 and educated at Glasgow University. After being in medical practice, he became drama critic of *The Scotsman* and then director of the Scottish Arts Council. He is the author of several plays.

Gavin Miller
Essay on George Friel
Teaching assistant in the department of English literature at Edinburgh University. He is completing a critical study of the work of Friel and Alasdair Gray.

John Shaw, FRCSE, FRCS, FRCPE
Essay on Norman McOmish Dott
Retired consultant neurosurgeon, born in Calcutta (though "a Scotsman through and through") in 1922 and educated at Dulwich College and Guy's Hospital, London. He was a consultant in the department of surgical neurology at the Royal Infirmary and Western General Hospital, Edinburgh.

Professor Derick S. Thomson
Note on James Thomson
Gaelic scholar and writer, born in Stornoway in 1921 and educated at the Nicolson Institute, Stornoway, the Universities of Aberdeen and Cambridge, and the University of North Wales, Bangor. He was professor of Celtic at Glasgow University for 28 years and edits *Gairm*, the Gaelic literary magazine.

Acknowledgements

Many people have assisted us in the preparation of this book. To the authors of the essays, personal memoirs and notes, we express our special thanks for the authority and wisdom of their contributions. We are particularly grateful to Andrew Hargrave for his permission to use a previously unpublished manuscript on George Middleton and to Andro Linklater for permission to re-publish his introduction to Michael Parnell's book, Eric Linklater: a critical biography (Murray, 1984).

For advice and help, we single out: Simon Bennett of Glasgow University archives; Audrey Canning of the STUC archives; Dr Cairns Craig of the department of English literature at Edinburgh University; Sir James Dunbar-Nasmith; Professor John Izod of the department of film and media studies at Stirling University; Bruce Laidlaw of the Royal Scottish Academy; Magnus Linklater; Kevin McCarra; Alistair McNeill of the Scottish Information Office; the National Museum of Labour History; the Royal College of Surgeons of Edinburgh; the Save the Children Fund; William Wolfe of the Scottish National Party.

Finally, a word of thanks to the unsung staff of the Mitchell Library, Glasgow, who, during a prolonged industrial dispute which coincided with the preparation of the book, were unfailingly helpful in unearthing source material.

A

Aberdeen and Temair, 3rd Marquess of
Dudley Gladstone Gordon
(1883-1972)
Shipbuilder and engineer whose family, the Gordons of Haddo, trace their descent in an unbroken male line from their Norman founder, who came to Scotland in the reign of David I and received a grant of lands at Gordon, Berwickshire. The third marquess developed an interest in shipbuilding when crossing the Atlantic as a boy, which he did on many occasions while his father was Governor-General of Canada. After leaving Harrow he served an apprenticeship in Hall Russell's yard at Aberdeen and became the first person to swim from the River Dee to the River Don. During the first world war he commanded the 8/10th battalion of the Gordon Highlanders and won the DSO. He was chairman of an engineering company in the south of England.

Aberdeen and Temair, 4th Marquess of
David George Ian Alexander Gordon
(1908-74)
Landowner, educated at Harrow and Balliol College, Oxford, where he won representative honours at rugby. He qualified as a chartered land agent and managed the family estate of Haddo, Aberdeenshire, from 1944. During the second world war he served as a major with the Gordon Highlanders and the 2nd London Scottish and was mentioned in despatches. He became a county councillor and Lord Lieutenant of the county, and was convener of the Scottish Landowners' Federation for four years. In 1939 he married June Boissier, daughter of a former headmaster of Harrow, and helped her with the running of the Haddo House choral society which she founded in 1946. The cheerful laird not only took part in various productions at the house but could often be found washing up in the kitchen after supper for the performers. He succeeded his father to the title in 1972.

Adler, Eleanor
(c1940-74)
Opera singer, born Eleanor Ramsay, who was educated in her home town of Kirkcaldy. In 1962 she was awarded a scholarship to study singing in Berlin. While there she met and married the conductor Eberhard Adler. From 1967 she was under contract with the Berlin Opera House, where she sang soprano. In 1970 the couple moved to Keil, where they both worked at the Opera House. She died at the age of 34.

Anderson, Father William James
(1894-1972)
Roman Catholic historian, born in Arbroath and educated at George Watson's College, Edinburgh University, and Christ Church, Oxford. He was ordained as a priest in 1926 and became official archivist to the Scottish hierarchy.

Essay by
Mark Dilworth

William James Anderson – he always insisted on both forenames – had two outstanding characteristics: rugged independence and seriousness of purpose. The carnage he saw when serving in the Medical Corps made him reflect on the purpose of life, and he became a Catholic and later a priest. After gaining first class honours at Edinburgh and Oxford, he studied for the priesthood in the Westminster diocesan seminary. But as a man of property, he was very much a freelance and so he took up work for E.A. Lowe's Codices Latini Antiquiores, examining early manuscripts all over Europe. Pope Pius XI, a former librarian, encouraged him and thwarted Cardinal Bourne's efforts to recall him to London.

After seven years of this work, he was priest from 1934 to 1954 in a London parish. He then returned to Scotland and at once took charge of his church's national archives. His impact on the Scottish church history scene was enormous, for he wrote and lectured and criticised incisively. His gift was not for careful compilation but for brilliant analysis and demolition of pre-suppositions, his lethal criticisms made more effective by formidable erudition and a mordant humour. A particular bugbear for him was the assumption that the Roman Catholic Church in Scotland owed everything to Irish immigration. Once, when asked what that church would be like without the Irish, he answered "Small but respectable", and when a questioner wanted names of Irishmen making their mark in Scotland, he suggested Burke and Hare.

The impact of what he said was enhanced by his strong Angus accent, quite unimpaired after almost 40 years away from Scotland. In his later years he was having afternoon tea in an Edinburgh hotel, when some Angus farmers came in, jovial and celebrating a good day's trading. One called out: "Will you hae a drink, minister?" In exactly the same accent and just as loud he replied: "I'm nae a minister, I'm a priest, I'll hae a whisky."

Although he could be forthright to the point of rudeness, in his personal relations he was very kind. He was also extremely generous both to libraries and to individuals. A wealthy man, he spent little on himself and when he died, the last of his family, he left his whole estate for the archives he had worked for unpaid.

Argyll, 11th Duke of
Ian Douglas Campbell
(1903-73)
Landowner and chief of the Clan Campbell. Born in Paris, he was educated in the United States and at Christ Church, Oxford. As Captain Ian Douglas Campbell he served with the 8th Argyll and Sutherland Highlanders (TA) during the second world war and spent five years as a prisoner of war in Germany. Many years later he was a prominent opponent of a Labour government's decision to abolish his regiment. In 1949 he succeeded his cousin to the title of 11th duke, his grandfather, Lord Walter Campbell, having been younger brother of the 9th duke.

His marital history was complex. In 1927 he married the Hon. Janet Gladys Aitken, daughter of Lord Beaverbrook, who divorced him after seven years. By this marriage there was a daughter. In 1935, one year after the dissolution of his first marriage, he married the Hon. Mrs Louise Vanneck, who divorced him after 16 years. By this marriage there were two sons. Later in the year of his second divorce, 1951, he married Margaret Whigham, formerly Mrs Charles Sweeny, wife of an American golfer. This marriage was dissolved in 1963. Within weeks he married Mrs Mathilda Coster Mortimer, an American. A baby daughter of this marriage died in 1967.

Of his three divorces, the third proved sensational. A *cause célèbre* in its own right, it acquired a wider resonance when Harold Macmillan's Conservative government became engulfed in the Profumo scandal and standards of private morality in public life began to be seriously questioned.

The hearing of his action against the duchess lasted 11 days in the Court of Session and the judgment was one of the longest in the history of the court, taking the judge, Lord Wheatley, four hours to read. Wheatley, granting a decree on the grounds of the duchess's adultery, made a devastating attack on her character. "There is enough in her own admissions," he said, "to establish that she was a completely promiscuous woman whose sexual appetite could only be satisfied by a number of men, and whose attitude to the sanctity of marriage was what moderns would call enlightened, but in plain language could only be described as wholly immoral."

The duke attributed his unhappy marriage to his wife's insatiable desire for social life, while he preferred a quiet existence. The duchess's response was that his drinking habits and his dislike of social engagements left her dependent on the company of others. The court heard that the duke had returned from a holiday some days before the duchess, his suspicions of her adultery confirmed by an admission she had made during the holiday. He hired a locksmith to force open a cupboard in their London house. Inside he found letters from two men and a number of pornographic photographs. The following month – May 1959 – he had a bolt put on to his bedroom door to prevent the duchess getting into bed with him.

The photographs were considered exceptionally lurid, though perhaps only by the standards of the time. Lord Wheatley said they showed a woman – the duchess – and the body of a male nude, but not the head. The judge said he would spare the duchess the indignity of describing the photographs, which revealed persons indulging themselves in a "gross form of sexual relationship". The duke had admitted showing them to a mixed party in New York and seemed to think it was a joke. "I do not commend his standard of tastes and habits," said the judge.

Earlier the duke had been the subject of happier publicity for his "attempt to end all attempts" at finding the Spanish galleon in Tobermory Bay. In 1950, with the help of the Royal Navy, he launched a search lasting two months. The vessel was located and identified as a ship of the Spanish armada, but the treasure said to be on board remained elusive. Two ancient sword sheaths, part of a dagger blade, and two silver medallions were found, but this was the limit of the bounty.

At first he took an active interest in restoring the ancestral seat of Inveraray Castle, but in 1969 he and the fourth duchess decided to live abroad for tax reasons. He was cremated at a private, non-religious ceremony in Edinburgh attended by two members of his family and two friends, and was succeeded to the title by Ian, elder of the two sons of his second marriage.

Arundel, Honor
(d 1973)
Children's author, critic and dramatist, who was married to the actor Alex McCrindle. She wrote her first book, *Green Street*, to entertain her two young daughters. A number of her plays were broadcast on radio. She and McCrindle lived at Castle Wynd, Edinburgh, overlooking the esplanade, and she campaigned vigorously against the noise produced by the annual military tattoo. In 1966 she stood as a Communist candidate at Leith in the general election.

Ayre, Sir Wilfrid
(1890-1971)
Leading figure in British shipbuilding, born in South Shields. After studying naval architecture he served an apprenticeship at Newcastle upon Tyne. In 1918 he and his brother founded the Burntisland Shipbuilding Company, designing and developing the so-called Burntisland "economy" ship between the wars. A former president of the Institute of Engineers and Shipbuilders in Scotland, he was knighted in 1945.

B

Ballantine, William Macdonald
(c1907-74)
Journalist and civil servant, with family roots in the west Highlands, who grew up in a Glasgow tenement. He became a journalist in the city at the time of the Depression and the human misery he encountered in the course of his work made a lasting impression. As editor of the *Glasgow Weekly Herald*, he generated a flow of ideas for making Scotland a better country. In 1938 he joined the government information service in Edinburgh and was appointed director of the Scottish Information Office eight years later. During his 32-year career at St Andrew's House, he served under 11 secretaries of state and was actively associated with the work of the Scottish Tourist Board, Scottish Council (Development and Industry), and Films of Scotland Committee.

Essay by Jim Gorie

W.M. Ballantine was one of the founding fathers of the government information service and claimed to be the first established officer in this class, being appointed as the first press officer at the Scottish Office in 1938 when the present St Andrews House was opened. This was a formative time for a greatly strengthened Scottish Office and Willie in his 32 years as head of information saw the evolution of a devolved administration embracing health, home affairs, housing, agriculture, education, and latterly regional development.

He instituted high standards in providing press information, combining honest, unslanted releases with high stylistic quality.

Over the period he built up an excellent relationship both with the Scottish editors and specialist correspondents and with the parliamentary lobby and press gallery.

Willie originally had literary aspirations, reflected in the quality of his writing. He was editor of the influential *Glasgow Weekly Herald* before accepting the post of press officer to Niven McNicol, the senior civil servant charged with the responsibility of promoting the new Scottish administrative machine.

Within a year, with the outbreak of the second world war, Willie had the added responsibility of covering the Scottish activities of the Ministry of Information. Along with his deputy Alastair Dunnett, later editor of the *Daily Record* and of *The Scotsman*, he built up a reputation for authoritative communications with the general public and media without lowering standards – despite the pressures of wartime propaganda.

Willie, working with successive secretaries of state, was largely responsible, through his influence as a speech writer and public relations advisor, for the enhanced image of "Scotland's minister" as the devolved power of the Scottish Office developed. In addition to the growing influence of the Scottish Information Office with both the Scottish media and parliamentary correspondents, he had a profound influence on other Scottish institutions. He founded the Films of Scotland organisation, working with his friend and colleague John Grierson. Films of Scotland won many awards, including an Oscar for *Seawards the Great Ships*, and launched the Edinburgh Film Festival.

Another of his staff, Bill Nicholson, was the first director of the Scottish Tourist Board and Willie helped to create a pervasive Scottish image overseas through his own writing and by means of a Scottish newsletter which was distributed through the consular service world-wide. He accompanied secretaries of state on overseas tours as far afield as Los Angeles and Moscow and developed his ideas of a network of 20 million people of Scottish origin who formed themselves into a Scotland which was "a country of the mind".

Lesser known is his role in founding a Scottish media committee in London under the chairmanship of Sir Leonard Paton. Apart from ensuring better coverage of Scotland in the London media, the Paton group instigated the project which provided the secretary of state with an official residence in Charlotte Square, Edinburgh. This project was humorously encoded "Paton Place".

Willie was a believer in open government and honest standards of reporting, and deplored any tendency to news management. He established a close rapport with parliamentary correspondents as well as Scottish editors, and the annual parliamentary lobby tour of Scotland, which usually embraced the Highlands and Edinburgh Castle, was seen by journalists as a highlight of the year.

Baxter, Professor James Houston
(1894-1973)
Ecclesiastical historian, born in Glasgow and educated at Whitehill School, Glasgow University, and Aberdeen University, where he graduated in divinity. In 1922, after a brief period as parish minister at Ballantrae, Ayrshire, he was appointed regius professor of

ecclesiastical history at St Andrews University, a chair he held for 48 years. Between 1933 and 1939 he was in charge of excavations on the site of the Byzantine Imperial Palace, Istanbul, and made several important discoveries. He served as an instructor commander with the Royal Navy, 1943-45. His prolific output as author and editor included a dictionary of Later Latin, a bibliography of St Andrews, selected letters of St Augustine, a history of the Church from 312 until 800, and an account of the Reformation in Dundee.

From Baxter's *Dundee and the Reformation* [1960]

"After the defeat of Pinkie, in September, 1547, the whole border country lay exposed to plunder and destruction, the larger towns were occupied and a fleet was sent to control the Firths of Forth and Tay. Broughty Castle was seized and Dundee threatened. The English commander appears to have looked to a more subtle weapon than arms or force: he reported that 'the most part of the town favours the Word of God and loveth not the priests and bishops very well. They are much desirous here in the country of Angus and Fife to have a good preacher and Bibles and Testaments and other good English books of Tyndale's and Frith's translation, which I have promised them.' But even if this hunger existed, it did not lead to any weakening of the resistance or any slackening of the attack."

Baxter, Rev. Dr William J.
(c1885-1972)
Minister, one of the longest serving in the Church of Scotland, born in Glasgow and educated at Glasgow University. He was minister of Dowanhill Church, Glasgow, for 38 years, celebrating his 50th anniversary as a minister in 1962, and was a member of the committee which brought about the union of the Church of Scotland and the United Free Church. He served on Glasgow Corporation education committee for 41 years.

Beaton, Rev. Archibald
(c1908-71)
Church of Scotland minister and champion of the Gaelic cause, born in Glasgow, of parents from Skye and Uist, educated at Portree High School and Glasgow University, where he was president of the Ossianic Society. In his youth he was a keen hammer-thrower and shot-putter. After a period as assistant minister at the Highlanders' Memorial Church, Glasgow, he became parish minister of Lochgilphead. He served in France during the first world war as a chaplain to the 8th battalion, Argyll and Sutherland Highlanders. Invalided out of the army, he joined the Gaelic department of the BBC before returning to the parish ministry at Dundonald, Ayrshire. He was chaplain to the Argylls at Stirling Castle. In his third year as president of An Comunn Gaidhealach, he died suddenly in a hotel room in Stirling a few hours before he was to have performed the opening ceremony at the national Mod.

From Beaton's programme note, 1971 national Mod

"I do not think there could be found a more suitable spot to unfurl the Gaelic banner at this particular time...In this year of grace it is no alien foe from a foreign land that threatens us, but a much more subtle enemy – apathy, indifference and lack of unity among Gaels themselves."

Bell, Sir Frederick (Archibald)
(1891-1972)
Farmer, educated at Loretto School, Musselburgh. He served with the Royal Engineers during the first world war, was twice mentioned in despatches, and won the MC. In 1920 he took up farming in Peeblesshire and became one of the pioneers of clean milk production. His chairmanship of the Herring Industry Board, 1944-61, coincided with a growing scarcity of herring and the evolution of a smaller, more efficient fleet. He was knighted in 1947.

Bell, Dr George
(1900-71)
Psychiatrist, born in Galashiels and educated at the local academy and Edinburgh University. He held appointments at Stratheden (Cupar) and Ladysbridge (Banffshire). As physician superintendent at Dingleton Hospital, Melrose, 1945-1962, he introduced reforms in the conventional treatment of mentally deranged and nervously disordered patients, freeing them from the restrictions of a prison-like atmosphere. He was acknowledged as a pioneer of the "open door" policy of mental hospitals.

Bell, Rev. Leonard J. A.
(c1913-72)
Minister and editor, born in Kilsyth, ordained and inducted in 1937. He served with Church of Scotland huts and canteens in Orkney and in Italy, then as minister of Gardner Memorial, Brechin. In 1965 he became editor of *Life and Work*, the Church of Scotland's magazine, and introduced a lighter, more populist tone which incurred the displeasure of some influential Kirk figures. The first hint of trouble came at the 1969 General Assembly when he was urged to include more articles on the fundamentals of the Christian faith. Unrest with his work came to a head in December 1970 when he was informed by the department of publicity and publications that his editorship was being terminated. Two days later he suffered a heart attack. On Christmas Eve he received confirmation of his dismissal in a recorded delivery letter sent to his home, but he refused to accept the dismissal notice and maintained that the only body competent to deal with the matter was the General Assembly. The Assembly agreed, declaring his dismissal unlawful, and he continued as editor until his premature death nine months later.

From James Drawbell's *Scotland Bitter-Sweet* [1972]

"The silent Assembly heard his QC quietly state his [Bell's] case...It was a satisfaction to me that the implications of the case were clearly understood and that while various people introduced the question of the quality of the magazine under the editorship of Mr Bell, all understood that this was not the matter being debated. 'I don't care if he is the worst editor in the world,' said one, not necessarily subscribing to that view, 'this is a matter of simple justice.' A man who was an ordained minister of the Church, and had ministered to his own congregation for many years, had suffered, no justification had been given for his sacking, he had been allowed no say for himself. I cannot remember if anyone said that it was a disgrace to the Church, but the mounting judgment that the Church could have no part in such an injustice, was unmistakable."

Birrell, Gerry
(c1945-73)
Racing driver, from Milngavie, who died from injuries sustained in practice for a Formula 2 race. A competitor of outstanding promise, he was awarded the Jim Clark Trophy by the Royal Scottish Automobile Club for services to international motor racing. His sights were set on the Grand Prix circuit.

Blair, Col. Sir Patrick James
(1891-1972)
Soldier, advocate and political secretary, son of an Edinburgh chartered accountant, educated at Edinburgh Academy and Balliol College, Oxford. He served in France and Belgium with the 9th battalion of the Royal Scots during the first world war and continued in the regiment after the war, winning the DSO and the Croix de Guerre. He was admitted to the Faculty of Advocates in 1921. The following year he became political secretary to the chairman of the Unionist Party in Scotland, a post he held for 38 years.

Bone, Phyllis Mary
(1894-1972)
Animal sculptor, born in Lancashire and educated at St George's School for Girls, Edinburgh, who studied sculpture at the Edinburgh College of Art and in Paris and Italy. Aberdeen Art Gallery purchased two of her bronzes and Glasgow Corporation another. She executed all the animal sculpture on the Scottish National War Memorial and in the new zoology buildings at Edinburgh University. Some of the finest examples of her work are the large heraldic panels in St Andrew's House. A bronze group was bought by the Ministry of Works as part of a scheme for decorating British embassies throughout the world. In 1944 she became the first woman to be elected an academician of the Royal Scottish Academy.

Brodie of Brodie, Helena
(d 1972)
Actress, great-great-great grand-daughter of Sarah Siddons. She met Ninian Brodie of Brodie, of Brodie Castle, Forres, while they were playing in repertory together at Perth Theatre and they married in 1939. A year before her death she sold the Brodie pontifical to the British Museum for £14,000, having discovered the pontifical, dated pre-Norman conquest, and believed to be one of only eight of that period in the world, in a stable loft at the castle.

Brogan, Sir Denis (William)
(1900-74)
Political economist and writer, born in Glasgow, who was ill more or less constantly between the ages of 12 and 18 and spent a great deal of time reading on his own. When he was well enough he attended Rutherglen Academy. He went on to Glasgow University, Balliol College, Oxford, and Harvard. After lectureships at University College London and the London School of Economics and a fellowship of Corpus Christi College, Oxford, he was appointed professor of political economy at Cambridge University in 1939, a

post he held until he retired in 1968. A figure of outstanding political intelligence with a legendary memory for detail, he wrote a number of influential books on the American political system. It was said of him that he did more than anyone else to explain American life and institutions to a European audience. He was a congenial companion who enjoyed the pleasures of the table and the glass, and as one of the new breed of celebrity dons made regular appearances on *Round Britain Quiz* and other popular programmes. His habit of boarding the wrong train and going to meetings on the wrong day made him the very model of the absent-minded professor. He was knighted in 1963.

Times obituary

"Brogan was not an original thinker, and his books were not so much profound or methodical as entertaining and suggestive. His real skill was in presenting information rather than in analysing it or drawing conclusions."

Alastair Hetherington, who arrived at Corpus Christi College as an undergraduate in 1938, recollected Brogan's influence

"As to Corpus teaching, for me one name stands out: Denis Brogan, the politics tutor. I had put myself down to read English as my main subject, but first we had to pass through two other hoops. The one that was to matter most to me, though I did not realise it at first, was politics. It took up most of my first two terms.

Brogan drove me hard. At first he frightened me, but I soon got over that. He asked fast and difficult questions, and he expected a quick response. He, like me, came from a Glasgow background, but Brogan had no intention of allowing that to make life any easier for me.

Scott, my brother, had been under him for three years. He had won a class 1 on PPE, led by Brogan and others, and then, in one further year, just before I came, he had won another class 1 on modern history. Brogan had similar expectations of me, which I was never likely to achieve. But he did me great good, guiding me towards the political journalism that was to become my life. He egged me on, as my father also did, to work for the *Glasgow Herald* the following summer, and again in the summer of 1940. This led to a staff appointment on that newspaper on my return from the army in 1946."

Brogan on America

"Any well-established village in New England or the northern Middle West could afford a town drunkard, a town atheist, and a few Democrats."

From Brogan's *The American Political System* [1933]

"It has to be remembered that a presidential year [in the USA] is also a year full of other elections and if the public eye is concentrated on the main campaign, the many eminent politicians running for other offices are not all in a self-sacrificing mood, nor is the victory of the presidential candidate a complete substitute for local triumph. It is true that, as a rule, a successful presidential candidate can pull up the total vote and especially in the case of a Republican victory, drag into office many minor candidates whom the electors would never have chosen in cold blood. Yet a great presidential triumph may have little effect on local or Congressional victory...The union, in time, of a series of elections that have little else in common, produces more effect than it deserves, in the way of producing a nominal uniformity of political decision in the country at large, but the strength of American parties is, as a rule, too sectional, too much divorced from any current national controversies, for there to be anything like our 'swing of the pendulum'."

From Brogan's
The English People
[1943]

"What is extraordinary is the sudden rise in the nineteenth century of the idea that only a 'public school' could give an education fitting a boy for command in business, in politics, in the army, the civil service, even in the arts. Only in England – and there in modern times – did the idea grow up that the effects of education between the ages of thirteen or fourteen and seventeen or eighteen were decisive. All the most important lessons, intellectual, moral and social, had to be learned then or not at all. The old saying attributed to the Jesuits, 'give us a boy from seven to twelve and we can let anybody have him after that', was transformed into an English version of a more negative kind. 'If you don't give us a boy between fourteen and eighteen, nobody will ever make anything of him', or if not anything, at least enough to justify his being a leader of the nation. Nor was this all. It became an accepted dogma of English life that the male population was divided into two classes, public-school and others. The products of the public schools were assumed to have certain valuable moral and social qualities which, if not quite unattainable by the products of other schools, were at any rate rarely attained by them. The public-school boy started with a bias in his favour, the outsider with a bias against him. There was nothing like this in any European country or in the United States."

Brotherston, Dr Margaret
(c1877-1971)
Pioneer in maternal and child welfare, born Margaret Merry Smith, daughter of a Wigtownshire farmer, educated at George Watson's Ladies' College and the Medical College for Women, Edinburgh. (At that time – 1896 – women were not admitted to medical classes at Edinburgh University, though they were permitted to graduate from it – which she did.) After appointments in Belfast and Lancashire she returned to Edinburgh as resident medical officer to Craigleith poorhouse, where she was impressed by the need for preventive medicine. In 1905, as the first medical supervisor of midwives in Manchester public health department, she was largely responsible for the foundation of the city's maternity and child welfare service. While in Manchester, she became actively involved in the women's suffrage movement and helped to establish the British Federation of University Women, of which she was the first vice-president. She married William Brotherston, an Edinburgh lawyer. Returning to Edinburgh, she worked as organising secretary for the recently founded Voluntary Health Workers' Association, which assisted young mothers in their own homes. Later she helped to promote the toddlers' playground movement, based in Edinburgh.

Brown, Ivor John Carnegie
(1891-1974)
Critic and author of Buchan roots, whose grandfather, a minister of the Church of Scotland, followed Dr Chalmers into the Free Kirk. Born in Penang, he was educated at Cheltenham College and Balliol College, Oxford. In 1913 he entered the civil service, but his career at

the Home Office lasted precisely two days in which he "sat in a dark, forbidding chamber and was confronted with much drab and depressing correspondence". He claimed later to have been a shorter time in the civil service than any other successful entrant to the administrative grade. Literary work, which he then took up with immediate success, he found much more to his taste. He wrote a novel – "a work which I should blush to re-read" – and found a billet at an impecunious weekly review called *The New Age*. Later he worked briefly for the *Daily Herald* before being tried out as London dramatic critic of the *Manchester Guardian*, his only qualifications for the job being "enthusiasm and such experience as I had enjoyed since boyhood by going to theatre pits and galleries". This post he held for 16 years.

In 1929 he began a 25-year association with *The Observer* as dramatic critic, having earlier done bits and pieces for the paper, mainly as an occasional cricket reporter. For six years from 1942 he was also the paper's editor, though ill-cast for the role. He found the editorial discussions on foreign affairs particularly uncomfortable, felt uneasy in the company of the paper's exotic collection of émigré writers, and was criticised for his lack of weight and authority. Politically he was eclectic, having been converted from "boyish Tory into stripling Socialist and maturer Liberal", but his heart was simply not in political science. He preferred Shakespeare. When another newspaper referred to his having "left the editor's chair" in 1948, Brown responded bluntly: "I was sacked". He did, however, continue as dramatic critic until he was succeeded by the *enfant terrible*, Kenneth Tynan, in 1953.

Brown served the Council for Encouragement of Music and the Arts (a precursor of the Arts Council) as its director of drama and the British Drama League as its chairman. His output as a writer was as prolific as it was versatile, including novels, essays, a popular series of books on language, theatrical studies and collected criticism, a history of London, biographies of literary figures, and an affectionate evocation of summer in Scotland. Heavily built, he had a gruffness of speech which belied his generous and kindly nature. It was said of him that he worked on his editorial proofs while chewing on a handkerchief hanging out of his mouth.

Times obituary

"The exercise of composing seemed to be as effortless for him as it had been for Chesterton. He did not chuckle to himself as the words came, as Chesterton did, but his hand moved smoothly and steadily, almost as though it were automatic, and his countenance as he wrote was as relaxed as that of a man in a club armchair."

From Richard Cockett's *David Astor and The Observer* [1991]

"Warming to his [Tynan's] writing, Astor [the paper's proprietor] asked Ivor Brown to retire – the most difficult interview of his life. Ivor Brown accepted his fate with dignity, but was shocked to find that Tynan might succeed him. He regarded the young man as little more than a show-off..."

From Brown's *The Way of My World* [autobiography, 1954]

[1] "Many young people have asked me how one becomes a dramatic critic. The obvious answer is that one does it by obstinacy and luck. The important thing for a beginner is somehow to get his foot inside a good door. Luck may bring him to it and persistence (call it impudence, if you like) will do the rest...Many seem to think

that dramatic critics begin as such. Why should they? It is much better for them to have knocked about Fleet Street, seen a bit of life, and learned to write quickly, clearly, and to the point on other topics under a strict surveillance. I hold strongly that nobody should be only a dramatic critic and never have been anything else. The task does not demand 'all of a man' and the theatre is a mirror of life, not life itself."

[2] "...it is good that the right to be different should be maintained in our world of crushing and colossal assimilations. There is an infuriating complacence of the English, many of whom do really regard the two old and small kingdoms, which their ancestors conquered and ravaged, as still quaint and even barbarous provinces – but not bad landscape for a holiday. Having received the ordinary English education, which gave me no information about Scottish, Welsh, and Irish history beyond a few battle-names, I was myself completely ignorant about my own country of Scotland when fully informed as to the minor internal wars of Ancient Greece."

From Brown's *Chosen Words* [1955]

"One of the chief occupations of journalists in war-time is finding polite names for set-backs and disasters. How well accustomed readers everywhere must have grown to strategic retirements, movements to prepared positions, elasticity of defence, and tactical regroupings on more favourable ground. While reading the history of Bonnie Prince Charlie's fatal campaign in 1745 and 1746 I came across one of the most charming of these euphemisms. On the night of Culloden, Macleod, the Prince's *aide-de-camp*, wrote from Gortleg to Cluny MacPherson:

Dear Sir,

You have heard no doubt ere now of the ruffle we met this forenoon...Dispatch is the more necessary that His Highness has something in view which will make amends for this day's ruffle.

Well, there was no panic there. But ruffle! At least a thousand of the scanty Highlanders were dead and many were doomed to slaughter in the next few days. Of course there could be no 'amends for this day's ruffle'. The game was up and Charles Edward Stuart knew it: he could tell a ruffle from a rout. Brave in his own defeat and escapade, he never mustered the clans again."

From Brown's article on James Bridie in *Scottish Theatre* magazine [1970]

"I can see him now with the eyes glinting behind his spectacles, the cigarette ash dropping on his coat, his murmured, fanciful, whimsical thoughts tumbling out amid the smoke and over a glass. He was clever, he was kind, he was unpredictable. But this one could always foretell. He might be suddenly silent, but when he spoke one had to listen even though it strained one's ears to hear him. He was a master of the quiet and so often wasted word. He needed a Boswell."

Brown on Scottish literature

"Why is it that your literary pundits are so down on the Kailyarders? It wasn't their fault that some of them could write so well."

Brown, Sandy
(1929-75)
Jazz musician. Born in Edinburgh, he was educated there at the Royal High School, Edinburgh University, and the College of Art.

He left for London in 1954 and formed a highly effective partnership with Al Fairweather – Brown on clarinet, Fairweather on trumpet. Critics consistently voted him the best jazz clarinettist in Europe. For 16 years he was head of acoustics at the BBC and also ran his own architectural and acoustics firm in London. His versatility extended to writing and painting, and he was a fine singer of the blues.

Alastair Clark wrote in *The Scotsman*
"In the early 1950s he stepped triumphantly out of the stylistic rut with a gloriously idiosyncratic, uninhibited sound that served to demonstrate for perhaps the first time that British musicians need no longer be content to act as pallid and enervated stand-ins for their American idols."

Brown on himself
"I was self-taught from the age of 12 and heard few other clarinettists in person for the first 10 years of my career. When I did, it occurred to me that I didn't conform with what were usually considered to be normal clarinet techniques: it seemed a bit late to do much about it except to continue along the same course."

Browning, Professor Andrew
(1889-1972)
Historian, educated at Glasgow University and Balliol College, Oxford. He was professor of history at Glasgow University, 1931-57. His principal interest was the Restoration period, though he also wrote with authority on the Elizabethans.

Bruce, Sir John
(1905-75)
Surgeon, born in Dalkeith and educated at Edinburgh University, who began his career at the Royal Infirmary, Edinburgh, in 1935. He served throughout the second world war with the RAMC, was twice mentioned in despatches during the campaigns in Norway and Burma, and with the rank of brigadier became consulting surgeon to the 14th Army. After the war he lectured on surgery at Edinburgh University and practised at the Western General Hospital. He was regius professor of clinical surgery at Edinburgh University, 1956-70, and honorary surgeon to the Queen in Scotland from 1960 until his death. Regarded as an exceptionally sound if not particularly original surgeon, he was fond of lecturing and did so in all five continents. He was president of the Royal College of Surgeons of Edinburgh, 1957-62, but for some reason chose not to list in *Who's Who* his chairmanship of Hibernian F.C.

Times obituary
"He was a *bon viveur* who loved company, and was never happier than when arguing – whether with his colleagues or his juniors."

Andrew Wilkinson, a colleague, wrote
"He stoutly maintained and advanced the standards of surgical education in Scotland...an outstanding teacher and lecturer in the best Edinburgh surgical tradition."

Buccleuch, 8th Duke of
Walter John Montagu-Douglas-Scott
(1894-1973)
Landowner, farmer and soldier, educated at Eton and Oxford. As a young man he was master of the Buccleuch foxhounds and known

as "Dashing Dalkeith". He was commissioned in the 3rd Royal Scots on the outbreak of the first world war and transferred to the Guards division with whom he served for four years. After a year as ADC to the governor-general of Canada, he retired from the army in 1921. Two years later, as Lord Dalkeith, he was elected Unionist MP for Roxburgh and Selkirk and retained the seat until 1935, playing a useful bat for the House of Commons cricket XI. He retired to devote more time to agriculture and followed his father both as governor of the Royal Bank of Scotland and as honorary president of the Scottish Agricultural Organisation Society. His public work included, as well as the county convenership of Roxburgh, membership of several committees connected with agriculture and forestry. In 1956 he became Lord Clerk Register of Scotland and Keeper of the Signet and later he was made Chancellor of the Order of the Thistle. He possessed an intimate knowledge of his own vast estates. The story is told of how one of his factors received an application for a country policeman's cottage and station to be built on Buccleuch land. When the duke saw the plan he said immediately that it would not do: the policeman would be looking at the side of a hill and would have no outlook. He pointed instead to a site nearby where the policeman would be able to see what was going on.

Times obituary "In everything he did his physical energy seemed to be astonishing. He moved from one house and estate to another, and even after two hip operations at the age of 70, thought nothing of dancing into the small hours."

Burns, William Alexander
(1921-72)
Artist, educated at Hyndland School, Glasgow, who served in the RAF as a pilot, 1939-42, and afterwards studied at Glasgow School of Art and Hospitalfield Art College, Arbroath. He taught in schools in Glasgow, Argyll, and East Lothian before being appointed lecturer, later principal lecturer, in art at Aberdeen College of Education. He was elected an academician of the Royal Scottish Academy in 1970. His paintings are included in the Arts Council collection, in several British embassies, and in Glasgow Art Gallery.

C

Campbell, Professor Charles Arthur
(1897-1974)
Philosopher, educated at Glasgow Academy, Glasgow University, and Balliol College, Oxford. He served in the first world war as a 2nd lieutenant in the 10th Border Regiment, at home and in Egypt, before being invalided out. In 1924 he became assistant in moral philosophy at Glasgow University, and apart from several years as professor of philosophy at the University College of North Wales he was associated with Glasgow University throughout his career. He was professor of logic and rhetoric, 1938-61.

From Campbell's *Philosophical Lecture-Notes* [1945]	"The motive to philosophy may be just sheer intellectual curiosity about the nature of the universe around us. The philosopher may pursue his enquiries with zest without giving a thought to any bearings which such enquiries have upon his interests as a human being. In principle philosophy can be as disinterested as pure mathematics."
From Campbell's *On Selfhood and Godhood* [Gifford Lecture, 1957]	"It comes to this, then. If we agree that God has endowed man with a power to resist temptation by a moral effort which he is absolutely free to exert or refrain from exerting, then man is, in general, justified in a claim to personal achievement when he resists temptation, and he is guilty of spiritual pride in making the claim only where that claim ignores or fails to take due account of empirical evidence of an *ad hoc* intervention of divine grace...There is surely nothing irreligious about taking pride in ourselves for using the freedom given us by God in the way that we know God wants us to use it, any more than there is in despising ourselves when we use that freedom in a way we know that God would disapprove. And this pride of achievement, be it noted, is completely compatible with humbly and reverently acknowledging that the power which makes our resistance possible itself comes from God."

Campbell, Rev. Duncan
(c1898-1972)
Evangelist, born in North Connel, Argyll. He entered the ministry of the United Free Church after serving in the first world war. In 1949 he became principal of the Faith Mission Training College, Edinburgh, an international ministry with members in the United States, India, South Africa and Europe as well as many parts of Britain. Under his influence many young men entered the ministry.

Campbell, Dr John Menzies
(1887-1974)
Dental historian, born in Paisley, educated at George Watson's College, Edinburgh, and the University of Toronto, where he became the first British graduate from a Canadian dental college. He achieved a number of other "firsts": he was the first dental surgeon to be honoured with a degree by the Royal College of Surgeons, gave the first radio talk in Britain on oral hygiene, and delivered the first British university lecture devoted exclusively to the history of dentistry. He edited *A Dental Bibliography, 1682-1880*.

Clunie, James
(1889-1974)
Politician and trade union leader. He was brought up in Lower Largo, Fife, where his father, a fisherman, died when he was very young. In the village of his boyhood, "the children took music and singing lessons, went to the academy and were trained as nurses and teachers or simply became children of prosperity". When, excited by the ideals of the Russian revolution, he escaped from this conventional rural environment and became a socialist, his behaviour was considered peculiar – not least by his mother. He worked as a house painter and decorator, and developed into an

effective trade union agitator. In 1926 he was prosecuted for making a seditious speech in Dunfermline during the general strike. He was chairman of his craft union, the Scottish Painters' Society, three times and a member of Dunfermline Town Council for 17 years before being elected MP for Dunfermline, which he represented from 1950 until 1969.

John Maclean wrote of Clunie in 1920

"Comrade Clunie is only known to a few outside Fife because modesty is his failing grace."

Report in Dunfermline Press, 19 June 1926

"At the outset [of the speech for which he was prosecuted], Clunie said he was not going to keep the crowd very long, as it was a very bad day. He went on to say he wanted to give them some advice, and the first thing witness heard him say after that was to boycott the public houses and keep away from them as much as possible during the crisis, and if they saw, as he had seen that morning, a waggon of beer at a public-house door, to let it go stale on their hands. Then he came on to something about keeping a diary in their heads or in their pockets of all the men who were acting as special constables, or working against them, and they would settle with them at a later date. 'I thought it was too hot for me, being a special constable and a publican,' witness added, 'and I made my presence scarce and got away.'"

From Clunie's The Voice of Labour – the autobiography of a house painter [1958]

[1] "Of the few Biblical texts that were provided us in my childhood one that stands out was the exhortation to behold the lilies of the field in the fullness of richness and dignity and beauty, and how they behaved and prospered, and yet they 'toil not nor spin'. Even as a child I had implicit belief in this exhortation, for the whole plan of the Biblical ideology, within my extremely limited knowledge, always reached out to the inherent communism in the teaching of Jesus. Why should not man serve his fellows? Why should man exploit his fellows? It was primitive man, classless and without knowledge and class distinction, who made the first tool, and the modern machine came from the first tool. 'It is so,' my teacher said."

[2] "...my first indiscretion [in Moscow for an international congress] took place on asking for a spoon to eat my egg at breakfast. An Austrian lady doctor leaned over to me and said: 'Comrade, if you ever hope to take part in the Revolution you'll have to learn to eat your egg without a spoon.' I confess the doctor cut me to the bone."

Clyde, Rt. Hon. Lord
James Latham McDiarmid Clyde
(1898-1975)
Lord Justice-General and Lord President of the Court of Session, whose autocratic reign as Scotland's senior judge frequently invited controversy. "Hamish", as he was known to some, was dux of Edinburgh Academy, just as his father had been. Both were elected members of Parliament for the same constituency (Edinburgh North, though the younger Clyde found the rough and tumble of the Commons not at all to his taste), both were appointed Lord Advocate, and to complete the cycle, both became Lord President. He went on to Trinity College, Oxford, and Edinburgh University, and was called to the Scottish bar in 1925. For many years a leading

counsel in civil and criminal cases, he represented Oscar Slater in his appeal against his wrongful conviction for murder.

Slight of stature and deceptively mild-mannered, he was elevated to the bench in 1954. Lord Clyde was fond of saying that people preferred the rule of law to the whim of a dictator, but his own actions often had a cavalier streak. In 1960, in a landmark ruling, he fined a newspaper £5,000 and its editor £500 for contempt of court for publishing interviews with witnesses on the morning after a man's arrest for murder in Edinburgh – a judgment which had the long-term effect of severely prohibiting the investigation of crime by the media. Clyde was no friend of newspapers, deploring any tendency to use them as a means of peddling scandal.

Two years later he caused ructions in Edinburgh society, not to say a certain amount of amusement, when he insisted that the Very Rev. Dr Charles Warr, Dean of the Chapel Royal, a former minister of St Giles, should take the annual service to mark the re-opening of the law courts after the summer recess. His view was that, as he and his colleagues were the Queen's judges, it ought to be the Queen's chaplain who took the service. This broke with the tradition that it was the minister of St Giles, present not past, who took the service – and Dr Harry Whitley, the incumbent, reacted furiously, maintaining that a real issue of principle was involved. Neither side was prepared to compromise in an increasingly bitter and public row, and it took two years for the rift to be healed.

In 1968 Lord Clyde appeared to treat the judiciary as little more than an extension of the Conservative Party when, on his nomination, a fellow judge, Lord Avonside, was appointed to a committee set up by the Tories to look into a proposal for a Scottish Assembly. The Lord Advocate of the day, Henry Wilson, attacked the appointment as constitutionally inappropriate and maintained that the judiciary should not be involved in the forming of policy by a political party. Clyde denied that it was a party political appointment, though Avonside did eventually resign in the face of much public criticism.

Clyde was also known for severe sentencing, particularly on appeal. So often did he increase the sentence if he considered the grounds for appeal frivolous that many convicted prisoners abandoned their case when they heard that it was to be heard by Clyde. He warned repeatedly that appeals must not be brought merely to secure a break from the monotony of prison. When he died *The Scotsman* complimented him on his passionate belief in the Scottish legal system.

From Harry Whitley's *Thorns and Thistles* [1976]

"In spite of placatory suggestions, the Lord President decided that unless the service was conducted by Dr Warr alone – the royal dean instead of the parish minister – the judges would not attend. Edinburgh buzzed like a bee-hive...I stood my ground for it seemed to me if I gave way, I would be selling the past, and future ministers of St Giles' might find themselves in an awkward position, with the status of the parish ministry severely undermined."

Poem in letters page of *The Scotsman* by "Raven"

Our pious Senators abhor
The thought of worshipping unfitly
And rather face a holy War
Than bend the knee with Dr Whitley

The lesser breeds avert their eyes
Regarding it as rather odd:
The object of the exercise
Being (they thought) to worship God.

Cockburn, Very Rev. Dr James Hutchison
(1882-1973)
Church of Scotland minister, son of a schoolmaster, educated at Paisley Grammar School and Glasgow University. After his early charges of Mearns and Battlefield (Glasgow), he was minister of Dunblane Cathedral, 1918-45. During the first world war he served in France with the YMCA and as a chaplain in Egypt and East Africa. He became one of the Kirk's outstanding leaders, playing an important role in the negotiations which led to the 1929 union and going on to be convener of the church and nation committee, clerk to the committee on restatement of the church's faith, and convener of the committee on inter-church relations. In 1941-42, during his year as moderator of the General Assembly, he visited Canada and the United States, speaking on spiritual issues of the war. He was vice-chairman of the British Council of Churches, 1942-44. After the war he went to Geneva as director of the department of reconstruction and inter-church aid at the World Council of Churches, a post he held until he retired in 1948. Budapest University appointed him an honorary professor in recognition of the help he gave Hungary during the war. He was chaplain to King George VI for eight years.

From Cockburn's The Celtic Church in Dunblane [1954]

[1] "He [Saint Columba] has been made the founder of monasteries and churches all over Scotland and been sent to places near which he never was. Such reputation has been thrust upon him that it has swallowed the work of earlier, and of contemporary, and of later, figures of noble proportions. And this very human saint, of mighty intellect, yet of a certain ferocity of temper, as well as of lovable ways, is reduced to a plaster-saint of everlasting sweetness and docile piety."
[2] "Within the enclosed area, then, each monk had his own cell or dwelling. In Ireland and in Iona, these dwellings were at first built of wood or of wattle and daub, as Adamnan tells us, but later they were often built of stone in the shape of a bee-hive. They were only sufficient in size to house one individual, with one door generally three and a half to four feet high, and no windows. Inside there was room to stand up and a little more; there was a stone ledge to sleep on, and in some cases unenclosed recesses in the circular walls, which might be more than a foot thick, for books, utensils, and clothing. These bee-hive dwellings were built of stones, generally not thick and fairly flat, and had no mortar to bind them together, though it is possible that an outer covering of clay kept out the wind and the rain."

Collins, Lt. Col. Ian Glen
(c1903-75)
Publisher, soldier and sportsman, born in Glasgow and educated at Harrow and Magdalen College, Oxford. He joined the family firm of William Collins Sons & Co. Ltd., in 1925, and retired in 1972. His

distinguished military career, for which he was awarded the OBE, the Legion of Honour, Croix de Guerre and Belgian Croix Militaire, included service during the second world war with the Coldstream Guards, Royal Marine Commandos and the Special Air Service, in the Middle East, North Africa and Europe. A versatile sportsman, he won a number of Scottish tennis championships, represented Britain in the Davis Cup, and was a regular competitor at Wimbledon between 1925 and 1939, losing two men's doubles finals and one mixed doubles final. He also played cricket at international level. Three years before his death, he married.

Connell, Sir Charles
(1900-72)
Shipbuilder, born in Glasgow, educated at Fettes College and Clare College, Cambridge. He joined the family firm, Charles Connell & Co., in 1921 became a director nine years later, and was knighted in 1956. In the turmoil over the collapse of Upper Clyde Shipbuilders, the company's Scotstoun yard was absorbed into Govan Shipbuilders in 1971.

Cost, March
Margaret Mackie Morrison
(d 1973)
Novelist, born in Glasgow and educated at Park School and Glasgow School of Art. She joined Sir Frank Benson's Shakespearean touring company, but left the stage to write her first novel, *A Man Named Luke*. Another of her books, *Rachel*, was a biographical novel about a French actress. Her novels were particularly popular in the United States, France and Germany, as well as in Britain. She came from a family which produced five well-known novelists, including Mary Morrison and N. Brysson Morrison.

Cottrell, Dr Tom Leadbetter
(1923-73)
Research chemist, born in Edinburgh and educated at George Watson's College and Edinburgh University. He joined the research department of ICI Explosives and was seconded to the physical chemistry laboratory at Oxford. Later he conducted research on physical chemistry and blasting explosives with the Nobel division of ICI. The Royal Institute of Chemistry awarded him the Meldola medal given to the chemist under the age of 30 showing most promise. In 1959 he was appointed to the chair of chemistry at Edinburgh University. From there, six years later, he gave up his distinguished career as a scientist to become the first principal and vice-chancellor of Stirling University. He was only 42, one of the youngest men to have held such a senior appointment in British academia. When the Queen was jostled by students during a visit to the campus, the incident did grave damage to the new university's reputation and Cottrell became a target of personal criticism which troubled him deeply.

Alastair Hetherington wrote "Tom Cottrell created Stirling University, and it killed him. In spite of its troubles last autumn, it is a good university which has established its academic merit within its first six years. Its difficulties have been greater than those of new universities in England, because already Scotland had proportionately more university places and because innovation and change come more slowly in Scotland than in England. Tom Cottrell had the imagination to see what could be done with a university which included new subjects, new ways of teaching them, and a modification of the established system of examinations. It also allowed some freedom to students to cross normal academic boundaries. He created a campus which is architecturally outstanding and whose buildings contain more good pictures than most universities enjoy.

It is a fatal irony, though, that a man who sought to his utmost to build understanding between staff and students should have died as he has done. From the start he made sure that students could mix freely with the staff and he was more accessible than most heads of universities. He made a particular effort also to build good relations between the new university and its neighbouring community. But the events of last autumn, at and after the disturbances during the Queen's visit, placed an intolerable strain upon him. In retrospect, what happened that day may come to seem insignificant; but it did not seem so to many people outside the university at the time. It gravely harmed what he had worked for. Although he showed little sign of the extreme pressures he has endured in the past six months, it was too much for him. The British universities have lost a valuable and imaginative man."

Craig, Professor William Stuart McRae
(1903-75)
Paediatrician and medical historian, son of a general practitioner in Yorkshire. He came by an unusual path to the chair of paediatrics and child health at Leeds University, which he held between 1946 and 1968. After graduating in naval architecture at Glasgow University he worked for a time in a Clydeside shipyard. He then turned to medicine and graduated at Edinburgh University, where he later worked as an assistant paediatrician. In 1936 he joined the Ministry of Health and spent 10 years there, chiefly as a hospital medical officer. When he was appointed to the chair at Leeds he was given a tiny room in the infirmary, but no department in the formal sense, yet from these beginnings established an enviable reputation for the quality of his teaching. He wrote a standard textbook on the care of the newborn, a biography of John Thomson (father of Scottish paediatrics), and a history of the Royal College of Physicians of Edinburgh. He retired to East Lothian.

Lancet obituary

"What a prodigious capacity for work he had! He did not seem to want to go on holiday, and was not very enthusiastic when others did. His ward-rounds were hard on lunch-lovers, and stomachs could rumble... He enjoyed teaching, and with the students he loved to encourage and probe and castigate and preach the virtues of the family doctor...he put children and their mothers above all."

Dr D.M. Morgan, colleague, wrote

"Professor Craig concentrated [at Leeds] on teaching medical students with a view to becoming family doctors. Although criticised for not building up a department dedicated to research, he was unrepentant in his view that his main task was to prepare medical students for family practice. He loved teaching.

He taught that the mother was always right and it was the doctor's duty to listen patiently. Towards the end of his career he found it incredibly hard to accept and was saddened to realise that mothers could indeed harm their children."

From Craig's *Nursing Care of the Newly Born Infant* [1955]

"In health the face is seldom completely motionless. Even when asleep slight changes of expression can be recognised. There may be occasional flickering movements of an eyelid or of a corner of the mouth, but the appearance of repose is not disturbed. A frown may be seen but lasts only a second. Fleeting 'smiles' can be recognised within a week or two of birth. They are not attributable to 'wind' as is commonly believed. By the age of six weeks, pleasure and satisfaction are revealed by an unmistakably beaming smile."

From Craig's *History of the Royal College of Physicians of Edinburgh* [1976]

"At a recent informal gathering outside the College, the altogether surprising view was expressed that in the past Edinburgh medicine had lacked initiative. As already stated, the College is an integral part of Edinburgh medicine and there can be no denying that its accomplishments give the direct lie to such an irresponsible generalisation. The origin of the College was itself solely attributable to visionary initiative. Many of its Fellows have since been recognised internationally as pioneers in clinical medicine."

Crawford, 28th Earl of, and Balcarres, 11th Earl of
David Robert Alexander Lindsay
(1900-75)
Premier earl of Scotland and head of the House of Lindsay, educated at Eton and Magdalen College, Oxford, who succeeded his father to the title in 1940. Referring to his family connection with Wigan, he claimed to be the original Wigan peer. He was Conservative MP for a Lancashire seat for 16 years, but devoted most of his life to the promotion of culture and the safeguarding of heritage. He inherited a love of art (as well as an enviable family collection of paintings) and worked vigorously for the cause through his associations with the British Museum, National Gallery, Tate Gallery, National Galleries of Scotland, and Royal Fine Art Commission. When he retired from the chairmanship of the National Trust for Scotland in 1965, he could look back at almost 20 years of vigorous expansion, both of membership and land owned.

Wilfred Taylor wrote

"A great and modest Scotsman who worked hard for the protection of those things which give life quality, who grew tired in the unselfish pursuit of civilised values, and who gave far more than he gained."

Times obituary

"He was a most valuable committee man and an excellent chairman, businesslike without being aggressively so, and even-tempered, betraying his rare impatiences by signs seldom perceptible except to close friends."

Cruickshank, Helen Burness
(1886-1975)
Poet, born in Angus, who learned her particular brand of Scots largely at her mother's knee. Educated at Montrose Academy, she left school at the age of 15 and joined the civil service. She worked

at first in London, but in 1912 came to Edinburgh where she was active in the suffragette cause and in Scottish nationalism. For many years she was an executive officer in the Department of Health for Scotland, concerned with child welfare. Her main contribution to the cultural life of Scotland was through her association with Scottish PEN, of which she was a founder member, succeeding Hugh MacDiarmid as secretary. She encouraged the work of MacDiarmid and of Lewis Grassic Gibbon, edited the poetry of Marion Angus, and was selfless in looking after the interests of her fellow writers. On her 70th birthday she entertained a number of poets to her home in Edinburgh, stipulating that there should be "no presents, no dirks, and no hatchets". In 1971, at the age of 86, she published her life's work in one volume of *Collected Poems*. She wrote best in Lallans, though more self-revealingly in English.

Marion Lochhead wrote

"Deeply rooted in her own country of Angus, though never parochial or provincial, she was, by virtue of that heritage as well as by her individual quality, in the true line of Scottish poets, having written nothing that is negligible, very much that is memorable and enduring...She had nobility, humour (stringent and sometimes bawdy), warmth of heart, generosity in giving and in hospitality."

Louis Simpson, American poet, wrote in *Memoirs of a Modern Scotland* [1970]

"On the fifth of July I went out to her house and was received warmly by a handsome woman in her seventies. We talked about my plan to write a book. As we were talking I saw on a shelf behind her a line of first editions of MacDiarmid. I began shaking with buck fever, the nervousness felt by hunters who sight a deer and are afraid that some precipitate movement on their part will cause it to dash off. I asked Helen Cruickshank if she would sell me any of the books, for I needed them desperately for my work. She said yes and lifted down the volumes I named. She looked at the price marked on a book-jacket and asked if I were willing to pay that much. I pointed out that the book in her hand, *Lucky Poet*, for which she was asking $3.50, was worth at least $25, and I could not pay less. She said that she was not interested in making money, that when she died her possessions would be dispersed and, besides, she liked me. Then we sat in the garden and had tea and the birds came."

From Cruickshank's *octobiography* [autobiography, 1978]

[1] "I told my astonished parents that I proposed to resign my Civil Service post when I returned to London. This time mother was struck dumb. My father said quietly, 'And how do you propose to earn a living?' I had thought this out and replied that I wanted to tackle several different jobs – factory life, going to sea as a stewardess, open-air life in some branch of agriculture – but first of all I thought it important to get a thorough grounding in domestic work, including cooking...So, I said confidently, 'I'll find a good mistress, skilled in all domestic work including cooking, and I'll work for her as a general servant until I feel I've mastered all that she can teach me.' My father looked scornfully at me and in broad Scots said: 'Naebody wad hae ye. Ye wad aye be speakin' back!' I had always felt that a deep unspoken sympathy and understanding existed between my father and myself, and now it didn't seem to be functioning. I was bitterly disappointed and, feeling curiously deflated, went tamely back to my desk in London when that holiday was over."

[2] "On this first occasion we all found him [Leslie Mitchell, aka Lewis Grassic Gibbon] modest and easy to get on with. My mother recited her party pieces – 'The Laird o' Cockpen' and 'Kate Dalrymple'...What we talked about I really don't remember, for I was the one who had to make the tea or coffee and send the sandwiches and conversation circulating. The hostess, as chief cook and bottle-washer, often misses the wittiest quips that make a party memorable. But after the guests had left, Leslie said: 'Come on, I'll help you with the dishes.'"

Cruickshank, Professor Robert
(1899-1974)
Bacteriologist, a graduate of Aberdeen University, who received his clinical training at the Royal Hospital for Sick Children and Belvedere Hospital for Infectious Diseases in Glasgow. In 1928 he was appointed lecturer in bacteriology at Glasgow University and bacteriologist at the Royal Infirmary. Later he became one of London County Council's group pathologists and director of the Central Public Health Laboratory. In 1949 he succeeded Sir Alexander Fleming as professor of bacteriology at St Mary's Hospital, London, and in 1958 he returned to Scotland as professor of bacteriology at Edinburgh University, retiring in 1966. He was an important figure in developing links between academia and public health bacteriology.

Cumming, Brigadier Arthur Edward
(1896-1971)
Soldier, privately educated, who attended the Cadet College, Quetta. At the age of 19 he obtained a commission and was posted to the Indian army, serving in Mesopotamia and Palestine with the 53rd Sikhs, Frontier Force. He won the MC in Palestine and was promoted to captain. Having served with the Frontier Force Regiment in the NW frontier, India, 1921-22, he returned in 1936. He became commandant of the 2nd battalion and served in Malaya, 1941-42. During the battle of Malaya, when the Japanese penetrated a position during a withdrawal, he decided to counter-attack. In so doing he enabled most men and vehicles to be withdrawn. He received two bayonet wounds in the stomach, but nevertheless drove in a carrier for more than an hour under heavy fire, collecting isolated detachments, until he lost consciousness. When he recovered he insisted on remaining where he was until he discovered that he and his driver were the sole survivors in that locality. For his bravery he won the VC – the second to be awarded in the battle of Malaya. After retiring from the army in 1947 he became superintendent of police in Kyrenia, Cyprus.

D

Dalrymple, Lady Marjorie Louise
(c1888-1971)
Traveller and voluntary worker, daughter of the 11th Earl of Stair.

She was awarded the OBE for her work tending the wounded during the first world war. After the war she travelled extensively, setting up a Guide company in British North Borneo. In 1931 she opened a girls' school at Oxenfoord Castle, where she continued to live with her sister, Beatrice, Countess of Eglinton. She was appointed WVS transport organiser for Scotland at the outbreak of the second world war.

From Dalrymple's *Memory's Voyage* [autobiography, 1963]

"When the idea of Guides was mooted [in North Borneo] a certain amount of difficulty arose. Chinese girls of the better class are very strictly brought up, and parents did not much relish the thought of 'mixing', which would be essential. Also the uniform was 'so immodest' – a *skirt* instead of the usual seemly black trousers. It all depends on one's point of view in life!

Gradually and patiently these little points were dealt with, and I held the first meetings with all the Chinese parents sitting in rows around the walls to watch over the girls and see they came to no harm. Games were a bit of a difficulty in the face of so much prim disapproval, but the children's keenness wore it all down, and finally we all joined happily in a good romp....

We had a bit of trouble over the Promise, as we could hardly ask a Confucian to swear loyalty to our God, and a Chinese subject to our King. With the aid of the Governor, the Bishop and the Scoutmaster we altered the Oath to run: 'I promise to be faithful to the best that I know, and to my country.' This seemed to us to fit the case and, I hope, exonerated us from any charge of innovation."

Dalrymple-Hamilton, Admiral Sir Frederick Hew George
(1890-1974)

Naval commander, from an Ayrshire landed family and a descendant of Viscount Duncan who commanded the British fleet at the battle of Camperdown. He was trained for the Royal Navy on the cadet ship Britannia and entered the service at the age of 15, serving throughout the first world war. For three years until the outbreak of the second world war he commanded the Royal Naval College, Dartmouth. When war broke out he was transferred to a sea command. On HMS Rodney, in 1941, he was instrumental in carrying out the final gun action which led to the destruction of the German battleship the Bismarck. Dalrymple-Hamilton, denied wireless contact by the exigencies of the situation, made a series of masterly deductions about the intentions of the German captain and contrived to bring the Rodney into battle at precisely the right place and moment, knowing that his only son was already engaged in the fight as a junior officer on another ship. In the last surface action of the war he commanded the British force when the Diadem and Mauritius engaged three German Narvik class destroyers and set two of them on fire. After the war he was flag officer commanding Scotland and North Ireland, becoming an admiral in 1948. Before his retirement he spent two years in Washington with the British Joint Services Mission. He retired to the family seat at Bargany, Ayrshire.

Davidson, Professor (James) Norman
(1911-72)

Biochemist and pioneer of molecular biochemistry, son of a fellow of the Royal Society of Edinburgh. He was educated at George Watson's College and Edinburgh University. After graduating in medicine, he worked in Berlin as a Carnegie research fellow in biochemistry. He was appointed Gardiner professor of biochemistry at Glasgow University in 1947, a post he continued to hold until his death. In 1969 he led a team of scientists and technicians at Glasgow in an important study of cell structure. He was twice president of the Royal Society of Edinburgh and took an active interest in Scottish cultural life as vice-president of the Saltire Society.

Dinwiddie, Dr Melville
(1892-1975)
Minister of the Church of Scotland and broadcasting administrator. A son of the manse, he was a divinity student in Edinburgh when the first world war broke out. He joined the Gordon Highlanders, was commissioned in 1914, and won several decorations. When he left the army in 1920 with the rank of major he was deputy assistant adjutant-general. On his return to Edinburgh he resumed his divinity studies on a shortened course and became assistant at South Leith Parish Church before being called as minister of St Machar's Cathedral, Aberdeen, 1925-33. He then succeeded David Cleghorn Thomson as Scottish regional director (later controller) of the BBC, a post he held until he retired in 1957. When he took up the appointment, broadcasting in Scotland was not so popular as in other parts of the country, and Dinwiddie had the task of increasing the number of licence-holders. In 1952 he supervised the introduction of the BBC's television service in Scotland.

Memo from Dinwiddie to John Reith, director-general of the BBC

"The task in Scotland is one of providing programmes for listeners, many of whom cannot afford proper receiving sets, and of breaking down the national reserve which is very apparent in many country districts. What is required, therefore, is a campaign of intensive propaganda and increased programme efficiency."

From Dinwiddie's article in Radio Times when television came to Scotland

"At the start, viewing will take up much time because of its novelty, but discrimination is essential so that not every evening is spent in a darkened room, the chores of the house and other occupations neglected. We can get too much even of a good thing. Television is one of those luxuries that will soon become a necessity of modern life, but we need to treat it with discretion."

Dobie, Marryat Ross
(1888-1973)
Librarian, born in India, son of an army surgeon, educated at Fettes College and Oxford. He became an assistant in the department of printed books at the British Museum. On the outbreak of the first world war he joined the London Scottish and was later commissioned in the Intelligence Corps, serving in Northern France. During the second world war he again worked in intelligence. He joined the National Library of Scotland in 1929 and became its librarian in 1946, retiring in 1953.

Dott, Norman McOmish
(1897-1973)
Neurosurgeon, a pioneer in his field, who earned an international

reputation for his research and teaching. Educated at George Heriot's School, Edinburgh, he intended to become an engineer but his experience as a hospital patient changed the course of his life and he graduated in medicine at Edinburgh University. He became neurological surgeon at the Royal Infirmary, Edinburgh, and created an important new department at the Western General Hospital, Edinburgh. He was professor of neurological surgery at Edinburgh University, 1947-62.

Essay by
John Shaw

A figure, slight in build, detached himself from the more eminent participants who had grouped together during one of the intervals of the congress. His suit was of a dark grey tweed and a watch chain straddled his waistcoat. Moving towards us, he walked with a slight but noticeable limp.

"I enjoyed your paper!" he said.

The person to whom I was talking had just described an ingenious and gentle forceps to the assembled neurosurgeons. This was for the temporary occlusion of small but vital arteries of the brain during surgery.

There was the merest hint of a Scotticism in his next phrase:

"We tried something like that a wee while ago."

There was no vaunting competition nor criticism, merely an intense interest in the technical discussion which followed. Eventually he took his leave, with courtesy, and moved away.

"That," said my friend, "was the famous Professor Dott!"

In that brief encounter I had perceived a benign, elderly gentleman but had missed the immutable determination in those eyes of his. So I pondered the idea of seeking my next training appointment in Edinburgh, if such became available. This, under his aegis, I felt, should not be too arduous a commitment to set against the pleasures of Scotland and her historic capital. Arrived in Edinburgh a few months later, it was not long before I discovered, tucked away in a cupboard at the Royal Infirmary but as if in modest proof, a precise and detailed drawing of forceps, similar to the one which had been under discussion. It had not been published but certainly dated from more than "a wee while ago".

This was my first, but by no means last, encounter with that persisting legacy of Dott's early apprenticeship in precision engineering. He had a continuing involvement in the design and maintenance of surgical equipment, both large and small, from whole departments of neurosurgery and their operating theatres to the finest instruments of brain surgery – an unusual blend of the humanities with the severely technical. And it reached into most aspects of his life, including his beautiful Alvis cars, his fishing reels, even the repair of his cigarette lighter.

It was not long either before I found that my initial assessment had been wildly astray and disciplines were rigid. I was not alone in such an introduction. We were a motley crowd from all quarters of the globe who were gathered there in Dott's famous ward 20 of the Royal Infirmary, to assist and be trained by this modest genius. From east and west, from far and near, we had come to submit ourselves to his disciplines. For he had much to impart in patient care, not only in major operative techniques for the brain and spinal cord but also in meticulous pre–operative assessment.

To take one example, we used to gather around him at the stereoscopic X–ray viewing screen. With an occasional "Uh huh!" or "What have we here?" he took us through the fine tracery of cerebral vessels and defined the best approach to the threatening lesion, as visualised by the angiogram. For had he not, in 1929, been the first in the United Kingdom to demonstrate such a malformation by cerebral angiography? And, as for after-care, today's "rediscovery" of holistic medicine grates on the ears of those who saw him daily insist upon its practice. An authority on the central nervous system he certainly was, but no patient left his care and supervision until he was restored, as fully as possible, to all aspects of the life which he had pursued prior to his illness. In this he enlisted the aid and encouraged the work of nursing and rehabilitation services. He participated actively in their organisation and training, accepting high office in their various associations.

I have said we came from far and wide, drawn by the reputation of this man, who needed none of today's advertising. American drawl mingled in outpatients with a Greek trying to interpret the accents of a Fifer's complaints. Tartan ribbons floated from the turban of a Sikh, and a South American paid us the compliment of wearing a kilt, unfortunately with the sporran slung at the back! And yet our consultations were accepted for it was known that Dott "could make a silk purse out of a sow's ear" and, in any case, would inform himself of all the details. Thus from his disciplined regimes stemmed more than one professor of neurological sciences and several departments of neurosurgery, in various countries, which were run on similar lines to that of Edinburgh.

If work was hard it was equally rewarding. An anthology of tales about serving Dott in ward 20 grew up over the years. Most were true, some a little doubtful. One soon learned that the duty list merely indicated who was to be in readiness to deal with emergencies: no one was actually off duty. And the duty registrar had to sleep in the ward. Telephone calls would come at all hours from Dott, seeking up-to-the-minute information about his patients. It was true that once a weary registrar was found slumped asleep in the ward telephone booth, the morning after Dott had initiated an evening call, but hardly true that he had persuaded a registrar to postpone his honeymoon because there was an unusual aneurysm to be operated upon, and "this would be excellent experience." It was only the first day of his summer holiday that was sacrificed! Dott's kindly loan of his superb Zeiss binoculars, presented to him by his South African trainees, was well meant compensation, "to study the wild life of the Highlands". But what a grave responsibility he had imposed. Knowing of Dott's insistence on the care and fine tuning of all his instruments, the choice of hotel for each night's stay in the Highlands was made more with the safety of the binoculars in mind than the pleasure of the holiday-making couple.

All was attuned to the care of patients, and none worked harder than Dott himself, from the moment sister reported the Alvis nosing its way through the infirmary gates in the morning to that last ward round in the evening. He would then retire to his room in the turret, beneath the infirmary's clock-tower and overlooking Heriot's, Greyfriars Kirk, and the Castle. There he would work at administrative tasks before returning home. And home was that unostentatious, grey-stone establishment in Chalmers Crescent, chosen because of its closeness to his places of work, the Royal Infirmary, Royal Hospital for Sick Children, and Edinburgh University. It was labelled with the single word "Dott" on a small brass plate. A neighbouring journalist reported that his study light burnt far into the night.

We saw him treat peers of the realm, and others so wealthy that, in convalescence, meals were ordered from a well-known restaurant and champagne discarded down the ward sink. Denizens of the Grassmarket and frightened citizens referred from countries of the Third World came with anxious hope, and his care and courtesy varied not a whit.

Just before retiral, he was invited to yet further prestigious visits and lectures abroad. But he declined, saying that he could not neglect his emergency duties in Edinburgh, for that would deny the younger men the opportunities for educational travel.

These day-to-day activities reflect the fibre of the man and the foundation of his fame. Inventories of his degrees, appointments, publications, fellowships, presidencies, honours, may be consulted for the hallmark of that fame, stamped by world opinion.

Thus I have described the man. For his appearance I will go no further. You must go to the Royal College of Surgeons in Edinburgh and seek that wonderful portrait by Sir William Hutchison, the Queen's limner. Dott, somewhat contemplative, gazes down. He seems to be cautioning that you maintain his standards. His expression is caught mid-way between those two well known utterances of his, "That will never do doctor!" and "Uh huh!" The latter was praise indeed. He is garbed as I have already described. I was going to say that I never saw him dressed otherwise. But this is manifestly untrue after assisting him during long hours on many days, in those specially chosen blue theatre caps and gowns. And yet again in ward 20, I see that characteristic figure, not disdaining to comply with disciplines that he has imposed upon others, making his way from the changing room at one end of the old ward to the operating theatre at the other end. He has discarded his suit and wears a drab-coloured ward dressing gown as he limps down the corridor, to perform some major operation. He is without ostentation so that, as he mingles with patients or their waiting relatives, they, unrecognising, wonder where this other patient is going.

Norman McOmish Dott was born in 1897 in Colinton, then a village on the outskirts of Edinburgh.

He was educated at Heriot's and left to take up an engineering apprenticeship, intending to make that his career. However, at the age of 16, riding a newly acquired motorcycle up Lothian Road, he swerved to avoid a horse-drawn dray and was struck by a taxi. He was admitted to the Royal Infirmary with compound fractures of his left leg. These were eventually healed but left him with a life-long limp and recurrent pain. His time in hospital made him resolve on a surgical rather than an engineering career and gave him a continuing sympathy with those who were disabled or in intractable pain. He entered Edinburgh University and qualified as a doctor in 1919. After qualification and holding surgical appointments in

Edinburgh, some original work on the pituitary gland led to a Rockefeller scholarship in the United States. There, from 1923 to 1924, he was a junior associate in surgery under Doctor Harvey Cushing, the famous American neurosurgeon, at the Peter Bent Brigham Hospital in Boston. He formed an almost filial admiration for Doctor Cushing and returned to Edinburgh determined to set up his own unit of surgical neurology and training centre, based on the techniques and disciplines which he had learned in Boston. "Surgical neurology" was the title Dott always preferred to "Neurosurgery". He considered that it indicated a competent neurologist, employing the surgical arm of therapy, as opposed to a technician operating at the behest of a neurologist, which was the state of affairs holding sway in some quarters.

This was a formidable undertaking for a young man, not yet in his thirties and in those days when neurosurgery was by no means an accepted specialty. Indeed a well-known one time resident of Dott reminds us that it used to be dubbed "the art of the impossible pursued by the irrepressible". However it is evident that, by dint of unrelenting effort and by declining invitations to the easier path of an appointment in London, he achieved his aims in his native city.

He started by operating in nursing homes, sometimes contributing to the patient's costs himself. Then, with foresight, he persuaded the authorities that, after the unfortunate ladies stricken by the maladies of Venus had picked up their skirts and left, ward 20 could be converted into a first-class neurosurgical unit. This was completed despite the necessity of changing the contours of the Royal Infirmary and thus altering Edinburgh's skyline. And lastly they built for him, in tribute, an "up-to-the-minute" department, a separate building, dedicated to his specialty and largely planned by himself. This is in the grounds of the Western General Hospital. Its opening, in 1960, by the secretary of state for Scotland was also the occasion of an international, almost laudatory, congress of surgical neurology. Dott was able to say, with well-modulated pride, "I consider that this is the best unit for in-patient care in elective surgical neurology at the present time. It will not be for long. Others will soon emulate and surpass, but it is a step forward."

In the short intervals of relaxation that Dott allowed himself from these courses, he went north to Sutherland and fished at Brora. As a younger man too, he had enjoyed family holidays at that Trossachs village of Brig o' Turk where, at least until recently, he was remembered with affection.

Perhaps it was his recollection of those Highland days which prompted him, when addressing an erudite, scientific audience far from Scotland, to illustrate the diagnosis of a certain cerebrovascular lesion by a homely comparison. He described how the buzzing noise which developed in the head of one of his patients with this condition, a crofter's wife, had caused her to go searching over the hills for the swarming bees!

How would Dott himself, a man of parts and master of much of neurosurgery, have wanted to be remembered? The bricks and mortar, the continuing excellence of his department? The inheritance of his teachings world-wide? His study and practice of pituitary surgery, which has played its part in the development of modern-day microsurgery of that gland? That famous operation in

1931, when first he conceived the idea, then successfully pioneered an intracranial operation for an aneurysm which had bled? It was a dangerous procedure in those days but, following his courageous example, soon became the accepted routine. That operation, against which colleagues had warned him, both because of the hazards entailed and the eminence of the first patient to present himself. "You won't succeed and it will ruin your reputation," they said. "My reputation has nothing to do with it," he replied. "He will die if I don't operate, he may live if I do." He operated and the patient lived for many years. The award of the CBE in 1948 for his wartime work as consultant to the army in Scotland and director of the brain injuries unit? Vice president of the Royal College of Surgeons in Edinburgh? I think not, and so one could continue scanning that long list of achievements, somewhat futiley.

No! I believe that his most treasured accolade came when, on 6 July, 1962, the mighty Usher Hall, only yards from the site of that original motorcycle accident, was filled to capacity by citizens of Edinburgh of all ranks. The lord provost's speech stated the purpose of their gathering:

"... and now the city of your birth gathers you to herself and in her own simple yet distinctive manner offers you the greatest honour it is in her power to bestow – the freedom of the city."

This was an award which, joining warmth with honour, placed Dott on that roll of fame which included Lister and Simpson. In his reply he left no doubt of his appreciation:

"I shall never be too old or too tired to carry it proudly – the greatest gift I could have ever dreamed of."

But his rider was so characteristic:

" – but we pay insufficient homage to the great, courageous, pioneer patients who, with implicit faith and unfaltering courage, have ventured with me into the unknown."

Of course that was "the greatest gift beyond any dreams", but he never saw the hundreds of letters which poured on to the desks of his biographers after his death. They came from all round the world extolling his skills but, above all, his acts of sympathy and kindness.

"That was the famous Professor Dott!" My fellow surgeon had been quite correct, but he hadn't told me half the tale: Dott was a Scot – of the best.

Drever, Professor Harald
(d 1975)

Geologist, son and brother of university professors, who himself held a personal chair at St Andrews University. He was educated at the Royal High School, Edinburgh, and at the Universities of Edinburgh and Cambridge. After he joined the geology department at St Andrews he led several explorations to Greenland and served on a national commission on Arctic affairs. In 1971 he was one of the principal investigators of lunar samples brought back from the moon by American astronauts.

Duncan, Rev. Angus
(c1888-1971)

Celtic scholar and Church of Scotland minister, born in Harris, who graduated in divinity at Aberdeen University in 1925. His first charge was at Sorbie, Wigtownshire. Later he ministered on Islay, where he established a reputation for eloquent preaching in Gaelic, at Ladybank and finally at Duns. In retirement he devoted himself to the Celtic Congress, drawing attention to the cultural problems of ethnic minorities, and helped to establish Scotland's first university folklore institute.

Duncan, W. Murdoch
(c1910-75)
Crime writer of prolific output, whose pseudonyms included John Cassells, Neill Graham, Peter Malloch, and Lovat Marshall. Born in Glasgow, he emigrated to Canada as a child and returned in 1930 to Glasgow University, where he graduated. Until the outbreak of the second world war he worked as a freelance journalist, but on being invalided out of the army in 1941 turned to full-length fiction. He published 150 novels and his work was translated into several European languages.

Dunlop, Annie Isabella
(1897-1973)
Historian and authority on medieval Scotland, whose father, a civil engineer, built the Glasgow underground railway system. She was educated at Glasgow High School for Girls and Glasgow University, trained as a teacher at Jordanhill College, and taught briefly in Sunderland and Edinburgh before deciding that she wished to devote her life to historical research.

At Edinburgh University, where she studied for a doctorate, she developed a lifelong interest in 15th-century Scotland. The ultimate result of her work, many years of painstaking research later, was her masterpiece, *The Life and Times of James Kennedy: bishop of St Andrews*, published in 1950. In the intervening years she lived and worked in Rome for an extended period, initially with the help of a Carnegie fellowship, latterly at her own expense. Initially she found the all-male preserve of the Vatican archives intimidating: "Many a time at first I could have fain run away, but being a dour Scot and a Cameron Highlander to boot, I held my ground." Unlike the male scholars, the signorina was noted for seldom speaking.

Although not a Roman Catholic (indeed, while in Rome she established links with the Scots Presbyterian kirk), her exploration of hitherto unexplored records earned her the admiration of the Vatican authorities. When her book on Kennedy was published, the Vatican asked her to present a copy personally to Pope Pius XII. St Andrews University, awarding her an honorary doctorate in 1950, described as the greatest living authority on relations between Scotland and the Vatican in the 15th century.

Until 1938 she worked in the Scottish Record Office. Her marriage in that year to George B. Dunlop, proprietor of the *Kilmarnock Standard*, enabled her to concentrate on her own historical interests. During the war she taught in the department of Scottish history at Edinburgh University, commuting weekly from her home in Ayrshire. In 1947 she succeeded with some difficulty in acquiring a visa to return to war-devastated Italy, likening herself to a medieval cleric who had made the journey five centuries previously "with perils and dangers by sea and road and the inconveniences caused by the waging of wars and internecine strifes". Stranded late at night in Turin, she found refuge in a convent. When, a day late, she finally arrived in the Vatican to resume her studies, it is said that a Swiss guard embraced her in the precincts. Her seat under the prefect's desk had been kept for the *nonna* (grandmother) of the *Archivo Vaticano*.

After her husband's death she attended many historical meetings at home and abroad, undertook a lecture tour of the United States, and made private visits to many parts of the world. In addition to the biography of Kennedy, she edited a three-volume work, *Calendar of Scottish Supplications to Rome*. She was a member of the Royal Commission on the Ancient and Historical Monuments of Scotland from 1955 until shortly before her death and was honorary president of the Scottish Church History Society. To the end Annie Dunlop remained an unassuming scholar.

Dr Ian B. Cowan wrote

[1] "A sojourn [to Rome] inevitably meant residence in the friendly atmosphere of the British School...To staff and students alike Mrs Dunlop soon became a well known figure. Solicitous care was always shown for her welfare and even her dislike of pasta was accommodated by the special provision of a more frugal lunch of cheese, fruit and the inevitable pot of tea."

[2] "This lifetime in the Vatican archives and the propagation of the value of Scottish material which it contains was fittingly recognised on 13th April 1972 when Pope Paul VI conferred upon her for her services to scholarship in the Vatican archives the papal *Benemernti* medal. Over forty years had passed since she had first entered these archives and nothing could have been more appropriate as her life drew to a close that recognition of her achievements should not only be recorded in her native Scotland but in the city which she had come to love."

From Dunlop's *A Cry from Europe* [anthology from the *Kilmarnock Standard*, 1939]

"With the Pope himself, of course, we had no direct contact, but on one memorable occasion the scholars of the Vatican School (la Scuola del Vaticano) were presented to him. It was a dull February afternoon when he came, clad in white, to unveil a memorial tablet in the Vatican Library. Upon news of his arrival we were posted at the outside door, where the papal car was waiting to take him for a drive through the Vatican Gardens. The reverend Fathers and Brothers, my classmates, clustered round the chauffeur and showed a lively interest in the motor horn, while I stood apart in an angle of the wall, hugging my portfolio.

Suddenly the 'reverendi' fell upon one knee, clapping their hands and exclaiming 'Viva il Papa! Viva il Papa!' Then, rising to their feet, they opened a lane in their ranks and thrust me also forward, books and all, to salute the Holy Father. The words which impressed themselves upon my astonished ears were these: 'Anche una signorina. Va bene!' ('Also a young lady. Splendid!')."

From Dunlop's *Life and Times of James Kennedy, Bishop of St Andrews* [1950]

"James Kennedy was born into a world of baronial horizons, and by his calling he was transplanted into a cosmopolitan fellowship. As kinsman of the King of Scots he owed allegiance to the Crown as head of the State; as a prelate in the Roman communion he rendered obedience to the Pope as head of the Church. By nature he was both a fervent patriot and a good citizen of the world; and by his power to harmonise these two loyalties, to blend the universal with the local, he was able to rise to the height of his opportunities as a 'public Father'. His fellow-countrymen in their different degrees had the same ability to prove themselves at once good cosmopolitans and provincial partisans. They had a European reputation both for vagabondage and for clannishness.

When it suited their purpose, the Scots were not slow to emphasise the remote isolation of their country among the kingdoms of Latin Christendom; but there is no indication that they felt any inferiority complex or were in any way remarkable for diffidence and humility. In spite of the 'great length and distance of the way from the parts of Scotland' to the continent of Europe 'and especially to the Roman Court', adventurous and needy men were always willing to risk the perils of land and sea when their interests were at stake. When William, Earl of Douglas, went to the Jubilee at Rome in 1450, we are told that he was accompanied by a great and honourable retinue, and that he bore himself nobly everywhere in clothing, expenditure and in all his actions, 'wherefore he was commended by the Sovereign Pontiff above all pilgrims'. Even if, as his detractors said, he went to parade his magnificence before foreign eyes – or for more sinister reasons – the picture is one of a haughty and self-confident young nobleman moving as an equal among the potentates of Christendom."

Dunlop, Isobel
(c1901-75)
Composer. She was concert organiser for the Arts Council in Scotland, 1943-48, and became music secretary of the Saltire Society in 1949. With Hans Oppenheim she founded the Saltire Music Group and the Saltire Singers, a vocal quartet for whom she wrote a number of works. Her children's opera, *The Scarecrow*, was performed at Malvern in 1955. A song cycle, *Prayers in the Ark*, received a lunchtime performance at the National Gallery in 1968, and a one-act opera, *The Silhouette*, was broadcast in 1969. A string quartet depicting the four seasons, commissioned by Glasgow University, was performed in 1972. In recognition of her work on behalf of the arts in Scotland, the Saltire Society elected her honorary president.

Durno, Dr James
(c1888-71)
Cattle breeder, a practical Buchan farmer with an active interest in the wider issues facing agriculture. In his early eighties he won the supreme championship of the shorthorn breed at Perth. He was the first honorary president of the Royal Highland and Agricultural Society of Scotland.

E

Elibank, 13th Lord
James Alastair Frederick Campbell Erskine-Murray
(1902-73)

Soldier and baronet, educated at Harrow and Sandhurst, commissioned in the 2nd HLI in 1922. During the second world war he served in France, North Africa, and the Middle East. Afterwards he became a mature student at Glasgow University. He helped to found the Murray Clan Association and to extend its membership internationally, and took an active part in the Scout movement as Scottish HQ commissioner for Rover Scouts. He was a keen piper and artist.

Elphinstone, 17th Baron
John Alexander Elphinstone
(1914-75)
Landowner and soldier, a first cousin of the Queen, whose mother was a sister of the Queen Mother. He was educated at Eton and Christ Church, Oxford, and served in the Black Watch as a captain during the second world war. After being taken prisoner he spent five years in captivity in Germany, part of it in Colditz, and was one of a group of leading PoWs whom the Germans intended to retain as hostages, but who were released by the advancing Allied armies. He succeeded to the title on the death of his father in 1955 and took an active interest in the management of his estates in the Highlands, though only a few months before he died he offered 7,600 acres in Inverness-shire for sale, claiming that times were hard. Among his public offices he was president of the Scottish Association of Boys' Clubs and of the Royal Zoological Society of Scotland, honorary president of the Scottish Football Association, and Scottish chairman of the British Red Cross Society. He never married.

F

Fellowes, Horace
(1875-1975)
Violinist, born into a musical family in Wolverhampton, who began studying the instrument when he was a boy, at about the time the family moved to Scotland. He gave his first public performance at the age of 10 and two years later was touring the country. From the Carl Rosa Opera Company, where he was principal second violin, he joined the Scottish Orchestra. After advancing to principal violin he became leader of the orchestra at the age of 34. He taught at the Scottish Academy of Music.

From Fellowes' *Music in my Heart* [autobiography, 1958]

"As a people we [Scots] like music, and we have produced many first-class musicians and some fine composers, but our contribution to the arts falls short of the standard set by many other countries. To appreciate the deeper aspects of music requires a devotion and study which few are prepared to give. It is only within the last thirty years or so that real encouragement to the art has been given by generous donors, among them Sir Daniel Stevenson. Of later years one aspect has given me serious thought, and that is the tendency for music in any form to disappear from family life. In my boyhood days it was the ambition of most parents to possess a piano and to encourage music-making within the home."

Fergusson of Kilkerran, Sir James
(1904-73)

Historian, journalist and eighth baronet, eldest son of General Sir Charles Fergusson, edited at Eton and Balliol College, Oxford. He began work as a bookseller and publisher. In 1934 he joined the BBC in Edinburgh as a talks producer, later working with the overseas service in London. He broadcast as a commentator on Nazi propaganda during the second world war. After the war he was a leader writer with the *Glasgow Herald* until he became Keeper of the Records of Scotland in 1949. He served on the board of trustees of the National Galleries of Scotland and was Lord Lieutenant of Ayrshire. His books included *Lowland Lairds* and *The Man Behind Macbeth*. Of him George Scott-Moncrieff observed: "I think he has some affinity with the 18th century that he so much admires."

From Fergusson's contribution to Scottish Country *[1935] about a valley in Ayrshire*

"It is a green and seductive country, this valley. It has neither the bleakness of the north nor the luxury of the south. It is the loveliest place in Scotland, which is to say, in the world. But to me a large part of its fascination derives from the strong impression it produces on my mind of continuity with the past. I can hardly walk a mile through it in any direction without coming on some scene or some object that revives that impression. It may be one of the pretty little stone bridges made by that eighteenth-century laird over the burn which goes singing down the glen of the Lady Chapel. Or it may be no more than the old half-decayed pump to which, according to tradition, he used to walk every day to drink a cup of its water, and from which water was brought to him as he lay on his death-bed at the age of eighty-one."

From Fergusson's Lowland Lairds *[1949]*

"The popular view of history tends to regard it in terms of the biography of monarchs and nobles. Occasional critics of today prefer to treat it in terms of economics or of nationalism, as the movement of vast impersonal forces. But in Scotland there is an increasing tendency to speak and write of the history of the Scottish *people*, as though their comparatively modern integration had existed much earlier than extant records suggest. It would be no more misleading, and might even be a useful counter-balance, to write the story of our country as that of the landed families of Lowland Scotland. For their influence on Scotland's growth and development has been steadier and more enduring than that of kings and regents, and far more direct than that of popular movements."

Fordyce, Professor Christian James
(1901-74)

Classicist and university administrator, born in Fraserburgh, only son of the schoolmaster of Banchory. His mother passed on her love of classical languages to her son who, as a precocious child, used to read Latin while lying on the hearth-rug. He entered Glasgow University at the age of 15, graduated in 1920, and went on a scholarship to Balliol College, Oxford, where he again performed brilliantly. He then taught Greek at St Andrews University and Latin at Edinburgh University, for a short time at each, before returning to Oxford in 1927 as a fellow, classical tutor and librarian of Jesus College, Oxford. It was a source of sorrow to Fordyce that his mother did not live to see him become an Oxford don. In 1934 he came back to Glasgow as professor of humanity with a determination to improve academic standards. On enrolment day, he told students that elementary errors in grammar and syntax would be heavily penalised. He delighted in finding English words to convey the exact shade of meaning of the Latin text, although his insistence on the use of the correct word in any situation was often taken to extremes. At a university lunch he once explained to a guest why the word used for bounty in the ancient Latin grace was *largitas* rather than *largitio*. But the stickler for accuracy was also an exemplary teacher and a formidable scholar. Although, as a conservative in outlook, he had reservations about some of the modern subjects which were brought into the faculty of arts during his long career, he had no qualms about the introduction of drama. He was fond of playing the part of a Roman Jeeves in Wodehousian comedies written by his wife. Another of his recreations was the study of railway timetables, particularly Bradshaw. In 1971 he retired both as professor of humanity, after 37 years in the chair, and as clerk of senate.

Foster, Rev. Professor John
(1898-1973)
Ecclesiastical historian, born in Yorkshire and educated at Bradford Grammar School and Birmingham University. After serving with the RNVR during the first world war he was ordained to the ministry of the Methodist Church, went to South China as a missionary, and became professor of church history at the Union Theological College, Canton. He was professor of ecclesiastical history at Glasgow University, 1949-68.

From Foster's *They Converted Our Ancestors* [1965]

"Let me begin with one discovery, not because it is important, but because it is one in which I shared. In 1957 I heard that a farmer above Ballantrae, repairing the dry-stone wall of one of his fields, had found among the topstones one which bore a roughly incised cross. This kind of detective work is the spice of an historian's life, so I went down to see. I judged it to be part of the headstone of an ancient grave. From what consecrated ground could it have come? The map showed a small loch named Kilantringan one mile to the east, and 'Ringan' is a common corruption of 'Ninian' in place-names. The loch proved to be artificial, made by damning a burn, little more than a century ago, so where did the name come from? The archaeological division of Ordnance Survey produced evidence for a hamlet of that name beside the burn, on what is now just a grassy knoll. Aerial photographs have not so far produced traces of a chapel, but such there must have been. 'Kil-ant-ringan' stands for *cella sancti Niniani*, 'chapel of St Ninian'. Crude work like this gravestone is hard to date. It may be a thousand years old. It is one more place where [Saint] Ninian was revered."

Friel, George
(1910-75)
Novelist, born in Glasgow and educated at St Mungo's Academy and Glasgow University, who trained as a teacher at Jordanhill College of Education and served in the RAOC during the second

world war. After the war he returned to teaching, but became steadily more disillusioned by the profession.

Essay by
Gavin Miller

At first sight, the work of George Friel seems cynical and pessimistic. The reader will encounter such topics as prostitution (*You Can See It For Yourself*), attempted child-murder (*Grace and Miss Partridge*) and paedophilia (*Mr Alfred, M.A.*). Friel's subject-matter and his dry, laconic prose often leave readers with the impression that he is essentially misanthropic. This is mistaken: his concern with the sordid and degrading reveals his fundamental faith in the value of human relations.

His earliest short story, *You Can See It For Yourself*, can be found in the collection, *A Friend of Humanity*. This story is, to an extent, a piece of slum journalism disguised as fiction. Friel, while at Glasgow University, was in love with a young canteen worker whose mother was a prostitute and keen to have her daughter pursue the same profession. The short story is based on a visit Friel paid to their family home – a visit interrupted by the arrival of a "client". The young woman – known in the story as Anna – has been forced by economic circumstances into a fraudulent family life. She is not her mother's daughter in any emotionally meaningful sense; rather, she is an employee in the service industry run from her household. This illusion of family is, for Friel, the real tragedy of the story: Anna is as anonymous and expendable as any other wage labourer.

The mores of the 1930s mean that Friel cannot describe the activities of Anna's mother and her client. However, the symbolism he does employ is vital to an appreciation of his work. The facade of Anna's family life is interrupted just as she, her boyfriend, and her mother are about to sit down and have a meal together. The importance to Friel of this commonplace ritual – the daily communion of a community – is hard to overestimate. It plays a vital role in *Grace and Miss Partridge*. In this novel, Annie Partridge, an ageing divorcee, attempts to murder Grace Christie, the young daughter of a neighbour. This might seem merely to be a step on from the tenement rapes and razor attacks found in the *No Mean City* approach to Glasgow life. Yet, behind this apparent sensationalism is Friel's continued concern with the everyday way in which family life is made and maintained. Miss Partridge has no child, or substitute, with whom to sit down at a common meal: the neighbouring children spurn her gifts of sweets and biscuits, and refuse her invitations to dinner. Her murder weapon is, then, especially symbolic: it is a poisoned sweet – a kind of lethal communion. Miss Partridge's murderous inclinations are merely the distorted and pathetic expression of her desire to have a family of her own. If Grace dies then, so it seems to Miss Partridge, she will be reborn into the community of Heavenly souls – and this is the best any mother could do for a child.

The central character of *Mr Alfred, M.A.* is driven by this same need to be part of a family. Mr Alfred is, like Miss Partridge, without spouse or children. Accordingly, he develops a bizarre obsession with one of his teenage pupils, Rose Weipers. She is at once a substitute daughter and, in his fantasies, a potential sexual partner. Sex with Rose would offer to Mr Alfred the possibility of a sexual partnership. This is why he refuses to have sex with the Glaswegian prostitutes who solicit his attentions. That kind of sexual intercourse would be as meaningless to finding companionship as drinking alone in a pub – itself one of Mr Alfred's favourite activities. Mr Alfred, the alcoholic paedophile, is beset by the distorted and destructive expression of his need to be part of a community.

Friel, we see, is obsessed with all that seems degraded and criminal precisely because within these things he finds the traces of genuine humanity. In this, he has had an important effect on other Scottish writers. Robin Jenkins in, for example, *The Changeling*, shows a similar compassion for those whose wrongdoing expresses their need for an authentic family life. Perhaps the author most influenced by Friel is his fellow Glaswegian, Alasdair Gray. Jock McLeish, the alcoholic sado-masochist from *1982: Janine*, and Duncan Thaw, the murderous schizophrenic in *Lanark*, owe a lot to George Friel – both are driven to these conditions by an inability to share their lives with others. This insistence that human life is essentially social is George Friel's enduring contribution to Scottish literature.

G

George, Sir John (Clarke)
(1901-72)
Politician and industrialist. Having left the village school in Ballingry, Fife, at the age of 14 to work underground at the local pit, he rose to become managing director of the New Cumnock colliery in Ayrshire before and during the second world war. After the war he was managing director of the Alloa Glassworks Company. At one time he served on both Alloa Town Council and Clackmannan County Council (as convener of the latter). He was Unionist MP for Glasgow Pollok, 1955-64, and chairman of the Unionist Party in Scotland, 1963-65, and was knighted in 1963.

Gibb, Andrew Dewar
(1888-1974)
Lawyer, educated at Glenalmond and Glasgow University. He was called to the Scottish bar in 1914 and to the English bar three years later, practising at the latter from 1919. Between 1929 and 1934 he enjoyed the unusual distinction of lecturing on the law of England at Edinburgh University and on the law of Scotland at Cambridge University, before succeeding his old master, Professor Gloag, in the regius chair of law at Glasgow University, a post he retained until 1958. In 1947 he took silk. He published papers on subjects as diverse as collisions at sea, bills of exchange, and negligence. During the first world war he saw active service in France with the Royal Scots Fusiliers, and was for a time adjutant to Lt. Col. Winston Churchill. In his book, *With Winston Churchill at the Front*, he confessed himself appalled by Churchill's unmilitary attitude towards discipline. Politically he began as a Unionist and contested Hamilton, 1924, and Greenock, 1929, under that label. Switching

allegiance to the Scottish nationalists, he fought the Scottish Universities seat three times (1935, 1936, 1938) and was chairman of the SNP, 1936-40.

Personal memoir by Ian Hamilton

The Scots law class started at eight o'clock in the morning. I lived in Maclay Hall across Kelvingrove Park from the University. They tolled a bell starting at 10 to eight, and I could just dress, and sprint across the park, to reach the classroom on the last clang. Professor Gibb was always there before me. He glared at me over his glasses, his great domed head shining in the 40-watt bulb above the podium. I don't know what he would have done if I had been late. Nobody tried.

Yet his classes were popular and so was he. "In a recent case," he would say, and quote something from 1883. We all stamped our feet as he went on with his lecture, ignoring us as the canaille we were. It was my first introduction to legal jokes, more illuminating than a term's lectures. We were all convinced that he was an old Tory, the very worst thing you could be in the late '40s. Gradually I learned that he was something quite different. He was one of those fabulous creatures, an early champion of the Scottish National Party. Before the war the Wallace sword had been stolen from the memorial at Stirling, and I know that Dewar Gibb was a trusted intermediary in its return. He was the first person, other than the conspirators themselves, to learn how the Stone of Destiny was taken from Westminster in 1950. We youngsters trusted him implicitly. Our trust was never misplaced.

While still a student I got to know him well. He lived at No. 1 The University, an address which defined him. I was often a visitor to his house. He had a son and two lovely daughters, both slightly younger than me. I looked at them, but dared not touch. He was the first true eccentric I had met and he fascinated me. He was unbelievably generous in large things and mean in all things tiny. He poured drams that dirtied the glass. "Put the stopper back on the decanter, Alison," I heard him say to his daughter. "Whisky's a spirit and it will evaporate." There is a magnificence in keeping whisky long enough for it to evaporate. It left me awestruck. Later we became close friends. We formed a team and I drove him to public meetings about Scotland. He liked me as a driver. "Others drink," he said darkly.

He had been Churchill's adjutant in the trenches, and had the reputation of a martinet. Here's a story to belie that. Along with others I published a tabloid newspaper called *Gilmorehill Girn*. It fell foul of the university padre who preached at us from his pulpit. We replied with a headline "Charlie: The University Chaplin". In those days university discipline was a serious matter and I was summoned to appear before the senate and dean's committee. I was later informed what happened. As I waited in an ante-room, the university principal, never a friend of mine, fulminated about discipline, heresy, how the floodgates had been opened, religion had been mocked, and so on. At this point Dewar Gibb was seen to be visibly shaking. Then he gave a wild cry. The professor of Scots law had broken into uncontrollable laughter. It was from then that our friendship really began.

I think of him often. Our ways parted. He lived to a great age, and with the selfishness of youth I never sought him out. Yet his hand is on my shoulder as I write these words. In this journey I have met few people I could laugh with and trust utterly. Andrew Dewar Gibb was one of them.

From Gibb's
With Winston Churchill
at the Front

[1] "It is difficult to see how his [Churchill's] ideas on this matter could receive sanction without serious detriment to the one essential of discipline, viz, prompt obedience to orders. It used to happen that a soldier when ordered, say, by a corporal, to perform some duty, did, through laziness or dislike of the corporal or distaste for the order given, refuse to obey that order, at the same time usually inviting the corporal to perform certain notoriously impossible physical feats or proceed to a certain non-existent destination, all in order to show his utter contempt of the corporal and emphasise his determination on no account to do as he was told. Now this is indiscipline in the highest degree, and a man is always 'run in' at once for it, and on the facts being proved against him he is usually heavily punished."

[2] "He [Churchill] considered that no man would wittingly incur the serious penalties inevitable in such a case [refusal to obey an order], did he know that his conduct was in fact precisely such conduct as would render him liable to them. In any event, the Colonel used to say, whether or not the man knew, it was only fair to explain the position to him there and then, and there and then to give him a chance to depart from his insubordinate attitude...I am afraid the men began to realise that they might at least once indulge themselves in the luxury of telling their sergeants to go to hell!"

From Gibb's
Law From Over
The Border:
a short account of a
strange jurisdiction
[1950]

"It may be said that after 1707 the law was affected by English influence in three ways. First, by direct legislation. In all legislative effort which was the outcome of some change great or small in the social outlook, Scotland simply moved at the same pace as England. Instances could be drawn from legislation as to land, the franchise, municipal affairs, commerce, shipping, the emancipation of women and many other important spheres. Secondly, text-writers, under the lead of Hume and Bell, were rapidly anglicising instead of romanising their treatment of Scots law and especially those portions of it which had been left inadequately illustrated by Scottish precedent. And thirdly, the possession by Scotland and England of a common court of ultimate appeal in the House of Lords had, as it was bound to have, an influence upon the laws of the country which possessed in this tribunal not a single representative. That country was Scotland."

Gibson, James
(c1894-1973)
Actor, born in Ayrshire and affectionately known as "Gibbie", who was fascinated by the art of acting from an early age. In 1924 he joined the semi-professional Scottish National Players, turning fully professional five years later. After the National Players disbanded, he joined Bertha Waddell's Children's Theatre. Later he worked extensively in London, appearing with the Old Vic and toured America as John Brown in *Victoria Regina*. In 1943 he joined the Glasgow Citizens' Theatre founded by James Bridie, who had earlier written a play specially for Gibson, and stayed with the company

for 10 years. He was founder producer of the Gateway Theatre in Edinburgh.

Essay by
Tom Fleming

The lifetime of James Gibson encompassed the transformation of the theatre in Scotland into a recognisable organism called the "Scottish theatre". In the evolution of a distinctly national style of acting his name has a special place of honour.

From his earliest days he loved theatre and was fascinated by the art of acting. His father, the postmaster at New Cumnock, was a gifted amateur actor, and James inherited from him the essential attribute of a "character" actor, love for and interest in people. Because there were few opportunities for professional and character actors in the Scotland of his youth he worked in the Post Office and then in a well-known stationery shop in Glasgow. The theatre companies with which he was later associated all benefited from the meticulous attention to detail and the flare for economy learned in his business years.

His professional career began as one of the three full-time officials of the Scottish National Players (who were amateur in status but not in skill) and, through his appointment as their advance booking and publicity manager, he became known from John O'Groats to the Borders. The esteem in which "Gibbie" was held by his colleagues in Scotland throughout his long career was shared by all the great names in theatre with whom he worked across the years: W.T. Guthrie, appointed third resident producer of the Scottish National Players in 1926 (later Sir Tyrone Guthrie); Sybil Thorndike and Lewis Casson, with whom he toured in the Old Vic Company during the early years of the second world war; Helen Hayes, whom he played opposite on Broadway; James Bridie, who wrote *The Golden Legend of Shults* for him in 1939; and Ingrid Bergman, with whom he made his last West End appearance in London, two years before his death.

Audiences all over Scotland, and particularly in Glasgow (at the Citizens' Theatre) and Edinburgh (at the Gateway Theatre where he became the first resident producer in 1953 and stayed on as an actor for most of the following 11 seasons) warmed to the realism of the eccentric character studies he presented. As a tramp, one critic claimed, "you could smell him at the back of the stalls"! As old Ekdal in Ibsen's *The Wild Duck* he moved the audience to tears nightly as he slowly made his way to bed (muttering *sotto voce* to his fellow actors "pee-pee, toothiepegs, and bye-byes"...) His "Falsehood" in *The Thrie Estaites* was a classic foil to Duncan Macrae's "Flatterie".

As a director he left behind a quaint theatrical language cherished by generations of Scottish actors. "Speak up, you're not on the stage now!"; "There's no need to get up her nose" (You're standing too near that actress); "The brew of the bean of Brazil" (Coffee break!); "Gurgle gurgle down the tubes" (Coffee break over!); "Eleven o'clock on the eleventh of November in Whitehall" (Will someone please give a prompt!). When a young actor was struggling with the Scots tongue at the Citizens' and rushed on to the stage in rehearsal saying "Capet'n! Capet'n! he's oot o' the Tolbooth!", Gibbie's voice echoed from the empty auditorium "Caapt'n! Caapt'n! Capet'n's in S'th Aafrica!"

If a fellow thespian was being careless with a burning cigarette in the dressing-room, Gibbie's cracked voice would quietly intone the following ditty (to the tune of John Brown's Body):

> Somebody's going to set fire to the t-h-e-a-t-r-e,
> Somebody's going to set fire to the t-h-e-a-t-r-e,
> Somebody's going to set fire to the t-h-e-a-t-r-e,
> And we'll all be OUT OF WORK!

Gibbie was, above all, a "company" man, and a caring and selfless actor. For years at the Gateway he ran a "menodge", or savings bank, collecting from young actors on pay-day any sum that was a multiple of half-a-crown. He kept immaculate individual accounts, banked the money in the Post Office up the road, and at Christmas-time or the end of the season paid out what in the '50s was a small fortune. (Two members of the company went on their honeymoon to Yugoslavia on their savings.) And Gibbie's reward for all the time and the trouble which he took was seeing another youngster in the theatre learning that thrift is not to be despised. A lesson many a mature director has had to learn more painfully.

In his sixties he took over the "juvenile lead" in one of his own productions at a few hours' notice when the young actor playing the part was admitted to hospital. In his seventies he still had to whiten his hair for "old" character roles. In his eightieth year he was rehearsing for a television play in London when his last illness struck him down.

His epitaph might be the words he spoke at Stratford in the summer of 1963. He was watching a production of *Julius Caesar* from a central seat in the front stalls (he was already getting pretty deaf) and a well-known actor was "milking" the end of part one with an interminable pause before the lights slowly faded. Gibbie's unmistakable stage whisper echoed from the tannoys in all the dressing-rooms: "Well...that would appear to be that!..."

Gibson, Tom H.
(1894-1975)

Scottish nationalist agitator, born in Glasgow, a lawyers' clerk who became secretary of the British Steel Federation. A life-long supporter of home rule, he was the proposer of the resolution which gave birth to the National Party of Scotland (which subsequently became the SNP) in 1928. He was the new party's first vice-chairman and its president from 1950 until 1956, and for a time one of the joint editors of the *Scots Independent*.

Essay by James Halliday

Tom Gibson represented the Scots National League at the meeting which saw the formation of the National Party of Scotland in April 1928. The meeting had seemed about to end in failure until Gibson suggested that the attempt to merge three different organisations should be abandoned and that those present should instead agree, as individuals, to form the new party. He so moved, and the others agreed.

Within the new party Gibson's influence was considerable, because the NPS soon came to be guided by the principles and programme of the League, rather than by those of the Home Rule Association or the Scots National Movement. These had a tradition of working, as nationalists, within existing parties and pressure groups, hoping by their activities to guide their parties in directions favourable to Scottish political aspirations. The League instead insisted that to be effective the new party must be independent of all others and free to determine its own priorities. Existing parties were not potential allies to be wooed but obstructive opponents to be challenged and, if possible, defeated, in parliamentary elections. The League's journal (of which Gibson was a co-founder), the *Scots Independent*, had argued for this strategy, and the NPS in its early years followed suit.

At times members of the NPS (and its successor the SNP), disheartened by frequent electoral failure, were persuaded instead to adopt the alternative strategy, derived from the Home Rule Association, of seeking to influence and work through existing parties. On such occasions, as in 1934, 1942 and 1948, Gibson stood with those who rejected any such strategic change. He played a leading role in drafting the constitution and rules which emphasised independence from all other parties, and in producing policy statements whose very existence proved the separate identity of the NPS/SNP. The wisdom of his convictions was borne out by events as, gradually, all nationalist activity came to be concentrated within the SNP and committed to its methods.

As president of the SNP between 1950 and 1956, and thereafter as a member of the national executive committee, Gibson gave stalwart support to the various chairmen and national officials who were all well aware that he would be quick to resist any abandonment of the basic ideas for which he had stood throughout the years. Supporting him, and sharing his convictions, was another founder member of the party, Elma Campbell, who became his wife, and herself a deeply valued and respected figure in the party.

Tom was never far from controversy and he never sought to avoid it, as he was always aware that the party was vulnerable to damage arising from any errors of political judgment in political or in campaigning tactics. In debate he could give and take hard knocks, but his arguments were always about issues and options, never about personalities or ambitions.

In his professional life he had had to deal with people at the highest levels in industry, especially in the Iron and Steel Federation, and in government, especially in the wartime Ministry of Supply. Perhaps as a result he was always, in the best sense, business-like, ready and able to stand up to any critic or opponent regardless of power and influence.

He lived to see the party reaching degrees of strength and public support beyond his expectations. Because his most active years of service came so early in the party's history he was not so well known to the generations which came to know success as he deserves to be. Those of us who did know him know that the party's debt to him is historic.

Gillespie, Brigadier Dame Helen Shiels
(1898-1974)
Nurse, born in Edinburgh and educated at George Watson's Ladies' College. She trained at the Western Infirmary, Glasgow, and joined Queen Alexandra's imperial military nursing service in 1926, serving in India between the wars and in the Middle East and South

East Asia during the second world war. Between 1952 and 1956 she was matron-in-chief and director of army nursing services at the War Office.

Gillies, Sir William George
(1898-1973)
Artist, one of the outstanding students in the first decade of the College of Art in Edinburgh. He became an academician of the Royal Scottish Academy in 1947 and principal of the College of Art in 1961. He was knighted for services to art.

Essay by Victoria Kellar

William Gillies is perhaps Scotland's best-loved landscape painter of the 20th century. He was born in Haddington, where his father ran the local tobacconist's shop. Gillies received early encouragement in his artistic interests from R.A. Dakers, editor of the *Haddingtonshire Courier* and a keen amateur painter, and his maternal uncle, William Ryle Smith (1862-1945), a professionally-trained artist and art master at Grove Academy in Broughty Ferry. His uncle spent part of his own summer holidays with the Gillies family and the two of them would paint watercolours together either in the neighbourhoods of Haddington or the local countryside.

In 1916 Gillies entered the Edinburgh College of Art, where he studied for two terms before being called up for duty in the trenches of France during the first world war as a member of the Scottish Rifles. He was fortunate to survive and was invalided out, in 1918, spending the better part of the year in the Barshaw auxiliary hospital near Paisley. He always considered his military service as two years of wasted time and never spoke about it. In 1919 he resumed his studies at the College of Art where he received a traditional art college training in the painting of still life and portraiture. Landscape painting was not a part of the curriculum, but an activity that Gillies pursued in his spare time and in holidays.

When Gillies's father died in 1921, his sisters ran the family business while he continued his studies, which he finished in 1922. With a fellow student, William Geissler (1896-1963), he was awarded a travelling scholarship for study in Paris and Italy. In the late autumn of 1923 and early 1924 he and Geissler studied in Paris with Andre Lhote (1885-1962), who taught them much about Cubism, and they copied paintings in the Louvre and visited the commercial galleries. In the spring of 1924 they travelled on to Italy, visiting Venice, Padua, and Ravenna. They spent the longest period in Florence, where they visited the Uffizi, copied frescoes in churches such as S. Maria Novella, and painted the view from their *pensione* window of the Arno and the Ponte alle Grazie.

On his return to Edinburgh in the summer of 1924, Gillies took up a teaching post at Inverness Royal Academy for the academic year 1924-25. In the autumn of 1925 he was given a part-time teaching post at the Edinburgh College of Art. He was to remain on the staff until 1966, when he retired as principal.

From the time of his appointment, Gillies developed a working pattern that was to serve him well for many years to come. In the long summer breaks from teaching at the college, he would travel Scotland with family or colleagues and friends from the art college. They travelled the length and breadth of Scotland, usually camping in tents and they painted ceaselessly. Gillies had such a skilful watercolour technique, based strongly on the landscape he had before him, that he could produce a prodigious number of watercolours a day. From these watercolours, done on site, he would work up oil paintings in the studio when he returned home. It was in this way that his early landscapes, still influenced by the Cubism of Andre Lhote, even as late as 1928, gave way to the violent expressionism of his landscapes influenced by the exhibition in 1931 at the Society of Scottish Artists' annual exhibition of the landscapes of Edvard Munch. The watercolours and oils of the 1930s come as close as his work ever did come to abstraction, but it is the abstraction of pattern making, turning landscapes of fields and houses or fishing ports and boats into patchworks of colour.

Gillies was not, however, just a painter of landscapes, though that is how he is best known. He was trained at college to paint still lifes and portraits. His portrait painting was initially influenced by his teachers at college and his early attempts were in a traditional mould. But after he returned from France and Italy in 1924, Cubism and the Italian early quattrocento influenced his art, both in landscape and portraiture. By the 1930s his portraiture, like his landscape painting, was characterised by an expressionist use of paint and colour, with bold and deliberately childlike figures. His own self-portrait (Scottish National Portrait Gallery), painted in 1940, was the last of these extremely self-confident paintings. He returned in it to a more traditional mode of expression but the bravura handling of the paint make it one of his most important paintings.

Landscape painting was part of Gillies's lifeblood, an almost intuitive activity for him, where spontaneity, especially in the early stages of a drawing or watercolour, was all important. The painting of still life was, for Gillies, an extremely intellectual activity. From the late 1920s, when his still life painting was influenced by Braque, throughout the 1930s when Bonnard was his great hero, through to the mid-1960s when he discovered the work of Julius Bissier, Gillies sifted through all these influences and it showed in his still life painting. Still life painting was a proving ground for ideas about composition that can later be seen in his landscapes in a much more refined way. The landscapes of the Scottish countryside are what people most associate with Gillies's painting, but he also painted urban scenes.

The Gillies family lived in Edinburgh for 10 years, from 1929 until 1939, after they moved there from Haddington. His elder sister, Janet, worked in a solicitor's office and his younger sister, Emma, enrolled as a pottery student at the art college. Tragedy hit the Gillies family when Emma died, of a thyroid condition, in 1936, when she was 36. The family was devastated by her death. Already closely-knit, it turned in on itself even more, and Gillies, his sister Janet, and their mother moved back to the country, to the village of Temple in the Borders. Gillies felt that returning to, as he put it, "the fine, bare, Moorfoot hills", and being surrounded by the countryside that he wanted to paint, was just what he needed. It was not a bad commuting distance from the college and he could either take the bus or drive. Motors were a great passion with him and he owned a number of cars as well as a motorcycle.

Throughout the 1940s and 1950s Gillies's exhibition career and teaching career grew apace. By 1947 he had been made head of the school of drawing and painting at the College of Art and in 1951 he was one of the artists invited to participate in the Arts Council of Great Britain's exhibition to celebrate the Festival of Britain. In 1960 he became principal of the college. That same year his sister Janet died and in 1963 his mother died, just short of her 100th birthday.

From the late 1950s to the mid-1960s Gillies did not have the time or energy to produce very many major paintings, though there are a handful (notably *Dusk* in Aberdeen Art Gallery and *Garden, Temple, Winter Moon* in Paisley Art Gallery). However, after his retiral in 1966 his work began to blossom again and he explored new avenues of expression, which were particularly strong in paintings of still-lifes and interiors, where he could place an arrangement on a window ledge, and include parts of a room with views out to the street or garden beyond.

People liked Gillies enormously. To many he was a man of puckish humour, ever willing to offer cigarettes or sweets and to lend a helping hand to his students and friends. But he also survived, and accomplished much, in 40 years of working in an art college, with all the administrative duties, politicking, and strife that goes with working in any large institution. And he produced an enormous body of work, on paper and in oils: portraits, still-lifes and, above all, landscapes. He died in Temple, quietly sitting at his kitchen table, on 15 April, 1973. It may be trite, but it is true, that many people cannot look at the landscape of Scotland without seeing it through the eyes of William Gillies.

From George Scott-Moncrieff's contribution to *Memoirs of a Modern Scotland* [1970]

"In painting, Gillies was to me what MacDiarmid was in poetry: re-interpreting some part of the Scottish scene for me, making me more aware of, and so enriching, the life around me...Gillies brought an innocent eye – quickened but not betrayed by French influence – to both the Highland and Lowland scenes...In the Lowlands Gillies recaptured the small mystery of winding by-roads flanked by sensuously stretching beech limbs or austerely plumed pines. He revealed the innate beauty of the mess of mud and tangled sodden herbage of a winter field. Gillies and his more abstract contemporary, Johnnie Maxwell, were painters of a stature to give us a new look at our country's face."

Glaister, Professor John
(1892-1971)
Forensic scientist and medico-legal specialist, educated at the High School of Glasgow and at Glasgow University, where he succeeded his father in the chair of forensic medicine, a post he held for a similar period (31 years). Glaister's wife, Isobel, was the only daughter of the late Sir John Lindsay, a former town clerk of Glasgow. He served with the RAMC in the first world war before joining the university as assistant and then lecturer in his father's department. In 1925 he qualified as a barrister of the Inner Temple. Three years later he was appointed professor of forensic medicine at the University of Egypt in Cairo. He returned to Glasgow on his father's death and was regius professor of forensic medicine, 1931-62. In his most famous case, in 1936, he identified dismembered

human remains found in the Borders as those of the wife and housemaid of Dr Buck Ruxton, who was subsequently convicted of their murders.

From John Glaister's *Medico-Legal Aspects of the Ruxton Case* [1937]

"The injured right hand might have been responsible for the blood stains on the banisters, provided Dr Ruxton, on coming downstairs, had held his unprotected hand, from which there was a brisk haemorrhage, above the level of the top rail and had swung the hand about. But it is hardly to be expected that a doctor with such an injury, the bleeding from which could have been controlled, would have refrained from adopting some preliminary measure to staunch the flow of blood. In any case this injury would not account for the condition of the carpets, the pads, the bath, and the front of the built-in seat in the bathroom. Against the suggestion that the blood on the carpets and pads had been there since 1932 was the contradictory fact that no stains on the carpets had been seen by the domestic servants employed at Dalton Square before the disappearance of Mrs Ruxton and Mary Rogerson."

Glentanar, 2nd Baron
Thomas Coats
(1894-1971)

Artist, architect, actor, playwright, singer and philanthropist, reputed to be one of Britain's richest men, only son of George Coats, of the Paisley cotton-thread manufacturing family. He was educated at Eton and Oxford and served in France during the first world war as a lieutenant with the 2/6th Black Watch and Signal Service RE, earning a mention in despatches. In 1918 he succeeded to the title. He was chairman of the British Legion Scotland and Scout commissioner for Scotland. In his youth he was a splendid baritone in Gilbert and Sullivan operas, as well as an accomplished organist and pianist, and when he took his seat in the Lords he became known as "the singing peer". He lived in Aboyne and was a familiar figure throughout Deeside. He left no heir.

Gordon, John Rutherford
(1890-1974)

Journalist, born in Dundee and educated at Morgan Academy. Having left school at the age of 14, he began his newspaper career on the *Dundee Advertiser* before moving to London. He was appointed chief sub-editor of the *London Evening News*, leaving to join the Beaverbrook organisation as chief sub-editor of the *Daily Express*. In 1928, at the age of 38, he became editor of the failing *Sunday Express* and succeeded in increasing its circulation from 450,000 to 3,200,000 by the end of his 24-year reign. He introduced the first crossword puzzle and the first astrology column in a British newspaper, and contributed an acerbic, tub-thumping weekly column, Current Events, which he continued until his death.

From his successor John Junor's *Listening for a Midnight Tram* [1990]

[1] "He had an enormous capacity for sensing what ordinary people were thinking. He himself came from a humble background in Dundee. He remained throughout his life a Scots Presbyterian but it was extraordinarily difficult to like him. He had a huge conceit of himself and an absolute unwillingness ever to admit to having been wrong. Once when in his column he had made a dreadful error and

was forced the following week to apologise, he put all the blame on 'my trusted researcher'."

[2] "In the weeks before Gordon's death I went to see him at his house in Croydon. I had never been there before, and because he had talked about it so grandly, I had expected a mansion. Instead I found an ordinary suburban house in a street with a bus route running through it. Inside the house was freezing and if there was central heating it most certainly wasn't turned on. It occurred to me that there were not too many trappings of wealth around a man who had had such a long and distinguished career."

Graham, Maj.-Gen. Douglas Alexander Henry
(1893-1971)

Soldier, commissioned at Sandhurst in 1913. He was wounded during the first world war and awarded the MC and Croix de Guerre. Between 1936 and 1939 he served in Palestine. He led the "fearless fiftieth" (Northumbrian) division as part of the Allied spearhead in the D-Day invasion of Normandy. From 1940, he was a much-honoured brigade and divisional commander in the Mediterranean and NW Europe, retiring from the Army in 1947. He was colonel of the regiment, 1954-58.

Graham, Sir George
(1892-1974)

Football administrator, educated at Allan Glen's School, Glasgow. In 1912, at the age of 20, he joined the staff of the Scottish Football Association. He served with the Ayrshire Yeomanry during the first world war, but otherwise worked for the SFA until 1957, for the last 29 years as its secretary and dominating influence. In 1958 he would have been on the Manchester United plane which crashed at Munich had it not been for a meeting of the Grand Lodge of Scotland which he chose to attend instead. He was for a time deputy grand master of the lodge.

Note by Bob Ferrier

George Graham was brisk, sometimes brusque, always domineering in his dealings with SFA councillors and was apt to be abrasive with Sir Stanley Rous, his opposite number at the Football Association, the governing body in England.

One bewildering illustration of his intransigence came with the World Cup of 1950, scheduled in Brazil. FIFA, the world governing body, had allocated final places for the top two countries in the British championship, effectively England and Scotland. Graham decreed, and somehow his decree was accepted, that Scotland would compete only if they finished British champions. That required a victory over England in the late-season international at Hampden. England won 1-0 with a goal from Roy Bentley of Chelsea, and went to Brazil. Scotland stayed at home.

It should be said that Graham sustained the game in Scotland throughout the second world war, and was an advocate of the spread of European club competition after it.

Grant, Rt. Hon. Lord
William Grant
(1909-72)

Judge of the Court of Session, born at Clarkston, Renfrewshire, and educated at Fettes College and the Universities of Oxford and Edinburgh. He was admitted to the Faculty of Advocates in 1934. During the second world war he served in the army and was appointed deputy adjutant-general at the War Office in 1944. Four years after taking silk, he became Solicitor-General for Scotland in 1955 and was one of the few holders of that office to be made a Privy Counsellor while Solicitor-General. In 1955 he won Glasgow Woodside for the Unionists and was appointed Lord Advocate in 1960. Two years later he left the Commons on his elevation to the bench as Lord Justice-Clerk. He enjoyed music, serving on the board of Scottish Opera, but in court could seem a daunting figure. Notorious for his fast driving, he was killed in a crash on the Perth-Inverness road, near Kingussie.

Gray, Robert
(c1896-1975)
Monumental sculptor. After the removal of the Stone of Destiny from Westminster Abbey in 1950, he repaired the stone before it was returned to Arbroath. Later he appeared to cast doubt on its authenticity by declaring that he had confused it with one of two replicas he had made. Shortly before his death, his interest in the stone having become somewhat obsessive, he was reported as having said that the genuine one contained a message, written on parchment, which was concealed inside it when the repair was made.

Greenfield, Brigadier Hector Robert Hume
(1893-1975)
Soldier, from Ardrishaig, educated at Eton and Sandhurst. He served for a year in the Merchant Navy as an apprentice in a sailing ship to Australia and round Cape Horn. In 1912 he became a 2nd lieutenant in the Argyll and Sutherland Highlanders and was severely wounded during the first world war. Between the wars he held various appointments in France, Gibraltar and India. When the second world war broke out he was commanding the 2nd battalion, Argyll and Sutherland Highlanders. Promoted to brigadier, he commanded the 15th Infantry Brigade and the Middle East Staff College, Haifa. After he retired from the army in 1946 he was appointed deputy secretary of the Government hospitality fund and ceremonial officer of the Festival of Britain. He returned to his native Argyll and was appointed chairman of Lochgilphead Hospitals Board.

Greenlaw, Rev. Karl S.G.
(c1907-75)
Minister of the Church of Scotland. A son of the manse, he came from a family with ministerial connections going back seven generations. He was born in Orkney and educated at Buckie High School and Aberdeen University. His first charge was Kinloss and Findhorn. In 1938 he moved to Old St Paul's and St David's, Dundee, where he remained for 20 years with a break for war service as a chaplain to the forces. In 1958 he left the parish ministry to become assistant secretary of the church and ministry department in Edinburgh. He was appointed secretary of the department in 1966

and established himself as one of the best-known administrators in the Kirk. He died five months before he was to have retired.

Gregory, Vice-Admiral Sir (George) David (Archibald)
(1909-75)
Naval commander, with family roots in Perth. He was educated at the Royal Naval College, Dartmouth. In 1931 he joined the submarine service and served at home and on China station. During the second world war he commanded HMS submarines. Later he was commodore of Hong Kong and admiral superintendent of HM Dockyard, Devonport. He was knighted in 1964. Between 1964 and 1966 he held his last service appointment as flag officer, Scotland and Northern Ireland.

Grierson, Dr John
(1898-1972)
Film producer, father of the British documentary movement and creator of the National Film Board of Canada. He thought fondly of his native Stirling as a battle-site which had shaped the history of Scotland, and as a gateway to the Highlands. His father was headmaster at Cambusbarron, his mother was also a teacher, and Grierson had four brothers and three sisters. By lying about his age – he added a year – he joined the RNVR at the age of 17 and served in minesweepers during the first world war. Later, studying at Glasgow University, he was much influenced by contact with the Red Clydesiders. He might indeed have entered politics, but said later that he chose to make his contribution to the socialist movement by producing films about the working man.

After graduating he spent three years in the United States on a Rockefeller research fellowship, studying the press and cinema. Returning to Britain, he founded the Empire Marketing Board's film unit in 1928. This was later attached to the GPO and re-named the Crown Film Unit on the outbreak of war. After a period as controller (films) at the Central Office of Information in London, he was director of Group 3, producing *The Brave Don't Cry* (1952), a feature film based on an Ayrshire mining rescue and inspired by his own kinship with the mining communities. He claimed that it was his favourite film, but his critical reputation rests chiefly on his documentary work, including *Drifters* (1929), a portrait of the herring industry, and *Night Mail* (1936), a lyrical evocation of the post crossing the border into Scotland overnight. For Films of Scotland he wrote the treatment of *Seawards the Great Ships*, on Clyde shipbuilding, which won a Hollywood Oscar in 1961. His face became known to a wider public when he launched *This Wonderful World* on Scottish Television.

Essay by
Ian Lockerbie

John Grierson is one of the two or three most important figures in the history of documentary film and mass communications. Although not the first to make or produce documentary films, it was he who gave documentary its crucial theoretical foundations and who put this film form on the world map by his pioneering establishment of film institutions specialising in the production of documentaries. If documentary is now rarely seen in cinemas, it has secured an even more important niche in television as a type of programme which is seen almost daily on the small screen. If one looks for a benchmark by which to judge such TV factual programmes, Grierson is, from every point of view, an inescapable figure.

His achievement was three-fold. Firstly, as a philosopher by training who was passionately interested in the role of democracy in a mass society, he forged a theory of documentary which was both social and aesthetic. He saw film as a new medium with an unparalleled power to educate the public about the important social issues of the day and thus to create in viewers a sense of involvement in the workings of their society. Film could do this by its striking visual power, its ability to show social phenomena with startling immediacy, but also by its ability to create pattern and stylised movement. Grierson's aesthetic is not simply one of "showing" – he owed as much to the complex cinematic style of silent Russian cinema as he did to the notion of immediate transparency.

Secondly, he pulled off the astonishing coup of persuading first the British government and then industrial sponsors (Shell and the gas industry among others) to fund the production of documentaries as part of their public relations activities. He was well aware of the various limitations and dangers of such partnerships and was never wholly satisfied with them. His biggest single creation, the National Film Board of Canada, was much nearer to his ideal form of institution, being a BBC-style of public corporation with greater creative freedom. Nevertheless, these working arrangements gave him an enviable production basis which allowed a solid and socially important body of films to be produced which would not otherwise have seen the light of day. Films like *Housing Problems*, *The Smoke Menace*, *Enough to Eat*, *Children at School*, were forceful exercises in public education, while others like *Drifters* and *Night Mail* raised awareness of the contribution of ordinary workers to the well-being of society. Among its other strengths, the documentary movement put working people on the screen in a way which British feature films of the period rarely managed to do.

Thirdly, he was not only a social philosopher, a remarkable organiser and seminal theorist, but also a hands-on film-maker of great skill. Although his name as director appears on only two films (*Drifters*, 1929, and *Granton Trawler*, 1934), his vision permeated the whole movement and he had a creative input, not least in sound and image editing, to the vast majority of the films made under his aegis. While the common habit of referring to the films of the movement as "Grierson films" does not do proper justice to the other creative talents involved, it is an understandable form of shorthand, in the light of the all-encompassing role he played.

Despite his central importance in the documentary tradition, Grierson has not escaped criticism from more recent commentators, particularly from those schooled in the semiological and ideological approach to film of the 1970s and 1980s. The charges made against him sometimes touch on his theory but at bottom are based on what is alleged to be his political position. Essentially, he is held to have been too close to the establishment and in cahoots with the state and big business. Far from advancing democratic consciousness, therefore, his films are judged to be propaganda exercises which reinforced the social and political status quo. *Song of Ceylon*, it is alleged, showed the beauty of that island and its culture, but it ignored the question of colonial exploitation; *Industrial Britain* mythologised working people and simply made beautiful images out of factories and workers' houses instead of showing them for the harsh environment that they were; *Housing Problems* reassured the spectator that poor living conditions were a purely temporary problem that would be smoothly rectified by benevolent forces in the existing social order.

Such criticisms raise questions that can be usefully explored, but in their crudest form they rest on a serious failure to look properly at the historical context in which Grierson was working and to understand both his social and aesthetic ideas.

Undoubtedly, if Grierson worked so readily with government departments, it was because he saw himself essentially as a public servant and had a strong belief in the ability of the public service to work for social progress. A properly contextualised examination of his political ideas and of his concept of documentary will show that his aim was beyond doubt to work for what he called "a more sufficient democracy". This can readily be conceded to be a gradualist philosophy of social reform, but that is a far cry from the reactionary practice that has been attributed to him.

Similarly, any serious look at the films he produced will show the best of them to be artistically striking, rather than examples of "naive realism". Although he vigorously denounced "art for art's sake", Grierson believed passionately in art with a social purpose and was among those in the 1930s who wanted to "make it new". It is worth remembering that he recruited writers, musicians and painters of the calibre of W.H. Auden, Benjamin Britten and William Coldstream to work on his films, as well as innovative film-makers like Alberto Cavalcanti and, later, unconventional animators like Len Lye and his fellow Scot from Stirling, Norman McLaren. He had connections with most of the progressive thinkers, writers and artists of his time, including Graham Greene, Julian Huxley, Aldous Huxley and T.S. Eliot. The whole context from which his films sprang was more *avant-garde* and artistically modernist than complacent and conservative.

Although the general public has not as many chances nowadays to see his films and to judge for themselves, at least one of them, *Night Mail*, continues to be shown with great regularity on television. It is as fine an example as any of what Grierson called the "creative treatment of actuality", with both elements being held in a very effective balance.

Times obituary	"He was regarded by film-makers as a hard taskmaster, but he rewarded hard work with a complete loyalty. As a producer he was brilliant. He never imposed his own ideas, but compelled each director to extract from his own inner resources the solutions to his problems."
From *Grierson on Documentary* [1946]	"First principles. (1) We believe that the cinema's capacity for getting around, for observing and selecting from life itself, can be exploited in a new and vital art form. The studio films largely ignore this possibility of opening up the screen on the real world. They

photograph acted stories against artificial backgrounds. Documentary would photograph the living scene and the living story. (2) We believe that the original (or native) actor, and the original (or native) scene, are better guides to a screen interpretation of the modern world. They give cinema a greater fund of material. They give it power over a million and one images. They give it power of interpretation over more complex and astonishing happenings in the real world than the studio mind can conjure up or the studio mechanician recreate. (3) We believe that the materials and the stories thus taken from the raw can be finer (more real in the philosophic sense) than the acted article. Spontaneous gesture has a special value on the screen. Cinema has a sensational capacity for enhancing the movement which tradition has formed or time worn smooth. Its arbitrary rectangle specially reveals movement; it gives it maximum pattern in space and time. Add to this that documentary can achieve an intimacy of knowledge and effect impossible to the shim-sham mechanics of the studio, and the lily-fingered interpretations of the metropolitan actor."

Grierson on Scotland

[1] "I will swear that I have found in the pubs of Scotland a larger passport to what the Scots spirit is about than I ever got from church or academy."
[2] "Glasgow I regret to say is too big, immigrant and sprawling a city to have belonged to Will Fyffe or anyone else."

Gunn, Neil Miller
(1891-1973)
Novelist, born at Dunbeath, Caithness, one of nine children of a fishing skipper and a domestic servant. At the age of 13 he was sent away from Caithness to live with his married sister in Kirkcudbrightshire. Two years later he passed his civil service exams and began work as a clerk in London. He became a Customs and Excise officer in 1910 and held a series of temporary posts, many of them at whisky distilleries in the Highlands. Two of his brothers were killed during the first world war and another died later of war-related injuries, Gunn himself having been exempted from call-up because of the nature of his work. In 1921 he married the daughter of an Inverness jeweller. They lived in Inverness when he established himself in a permanent job at the Glen Mhor distillery. Their only child was still-born. His duties as an excise officer in Inverness, 1923-37, left him time for writing, mainly short stories at first, and for an increasing involvement in Scottish nationalist politics. He served on a committee examining post war hospitals and on a commission of inquiry into crofting conditions. The first of his novels, *Grey Coast*, appeared in 1926. The critical success of *Highland River* in 1937 encouraged him to quit his job and become a full-time writer. After his wife's death in 1963 he lived alone on the Black Isle. The Neil Gunn International Fellowship was established in his memory.

Essay by
Margery Palmer
McCulloch

Neil M. Gunn is one of the principal writers associated with the 20th century Scottish literary revival of the inter-war period known popularly as the "Scottish renaissance" and associated to a significant extent with the Scots-language poetry of Hugh MacDiarmid (C.M. Grieve). Gunn and MacDiarmid were close friends and collaborators, Gunn describing MacDiarmid as "the finest Scots poet since Burns" and in turn being himself acclaimed by MacDiarmid as "the only Scottish prose-writer of promise...in relation to that which is distinctively Scottish rather than tributary to the 'vast engulfing sea' of English literature". Both writers shared the belief that a nation's literature and art could not be divorced from its social, economic and political life and that lasting cultural regeneration in Scotland must go hand-in-hand with the revitalisation of the life of the nation as a whole.

Unlike the Borderer MacDiarmid, Gunn came from the far north. He was born in Caithness and brought up in the small fishing and crofting village of Dunbeath on the "Grey Coast" that was to become the setting of many of his narratives. He was one of nine children and the fifth of seven sons. His father was a fisherman, much respected for his skill and bravery, but like the mothers in his later novels, his own mother did not wish her sons to follow their father's dangerous occupation, and at the age of 13 Neil was sent south to Galloway to live with his sister and her doctor husband. From there he sat examinations for the civil service and was posted to London in 1907. He returned to Scotland in 1909, first of all to Edinburgh and then to the Highlands where he took up a permanent civil service position as a Customs and Excise officer.

Gunn's childhood in the straths and sea-coasts of Caithness had made a powerful impression on his imagination. His novels are alive with the boy's sense of the richness of his physical environment, with the excitement of poaching expeditions, with the daring and skill of the seamen who brought their fishing boats through formidable seas to the safety of harbour. Now, in adulthood, his work as excise officer gave him the opportunity to travel widely in the Highlands and thus to build up the store of information about Highland life and its communities and relationships which would serve him well as novelist of the Highlands.

A recurring theme in Gunn's fiction is that of the exile who returns to the Highlands and he himself was indeed "the man who came back" – the title he gave to a short story and a play on this theme. Unlike the characters in these narratives of the returned Highlander, however, where return was equated with failure by the indigenous community, Gunn's own return was motivated by the regenerative impulse which characterised the later cultural revival of the 1920s and 1930s. Early books such as *The Grey Coast* (1926), *Morning Tide* (1931), and *The Lost Glen* (1932) depict in an objective and unromanticised way the impoverishment and decline he saw around him as he travelled about the country, while *Sun Circle* (1933) and *Butcher's Broom* (1934) attempt to uncover the historical reasons for present degeneration. In this approach to history and the relationship between past and present, Gunn was therefore different from his most famous predecessor in the historical novel, Sir Walter Scott, whose objectives were to a large extent antiquarian, "tracing the evanescent manners of his own country", as Scott described it in *Waverley*. For Gunn, Scott's history was "story-telling or romance set in a void [which] had interpretative bearing neither upon a present nor a future". Gunn, on the other hand, believed that a secure future could be built only through the recovery and revitalisation of the relationship between past and present, what he called in the essay "Highland Games" a "growing and blossoming from our own roots".

Tradition and "the essence of nationalism" therefore lay at the heart of Gunn's work as novelist, just as in his everyday life he supported the movement for Scottish self-determination and in the post-1945 period was an active member of the Highland Panel set up to initiate improvements in the social and economic situation of the region. In the many articles he wrote for the *Scots Magazine* in the 1930s and 1940s he investigated the contemporary social, economic and cultural situation of the Highlands while at the same time in novels such as *Highland River* (1937), *The Silver Darlings* (1941), *Young Art and Old Hector* (1942), and *The Green Isle of the Great Deep* (1944), he depicted what he saw as the positive qualities of the Highland way of life, its "essential social tradition". He saw *The Silver Darlings* as paying tribute to the seafaring skills of seamen such as his father and also as a sequel to the tragic story of the Clearances given fictional form in the earlier *Butcher's Broom*, a novel which told of the people's triumph over the disaster of the Clearances and one in which the Highland traditions were evoked through story-telling, myth, song and dance as well as through the more recent tradition of seafaring. *Young Art and Old Hector* depicts the togetherness of the crofting tradition and the importance of keeping faith with the past by passing on one's knowledge of it, so that it will not be "nameless". Its sequel, *The Green Isle of the Great Deep*, is a fable which takes its place with Orwell's distopian *1984* in its investigation of a totalitarian state and it shows how the sense of togetherness given form in the *Young Art* narrative can stand against the attacks – both insidious and overt – of such a regime.

Although Gunn is known primarily as a novelist of the Highlands, he also explored city life in significant sections of novels such as *Wild Geese Overhead* (1939), *The Serpent* (1943), *The Drinking Well* (1946), and *The Lost Chart* (1949). Philosophical themes are implicitly present in most of his narratives and in his later work this philosophical preoccupation becomes more explicit. Throughout all his work, however, one finds his belief in the importance of tradition and nationalism and his concern that literature should be related to life. Writing about nationalism in the 1930s and 1940s, Gunn fully realised that this had become a discredited term for what many considered to be a dangerous and discredited philosophy; yet, for him, nationalism was neither the jingoism of the warmongers nor a parochial preoccupation with one's own kailyard. He wrote in the 1931 article "Nationalism and Internationalism" that nationalism "is founded in tradition, and we can no more get away from tradition than from ourselves...a nation's traditions are the natural inspirations of its people...and it is only when a man is moved by the traditions and music and poetry of his own land that he is in a position to comprehend those of any other land, for already he has the eyes of sympathy and the ears of understanding". For Gunn, then, nationalism and internationalism are not opposing positions, but are irrevocably linked and both accept diversity and the importance of the individual's contribution.

Although the themes and principal settings of Gunn's fiction derive from the Scottish Highlands, his significance as a writer goes beyond purely Highlands and Scottish concerns. In addition to the fine qualities present in his writing, his 1930s analyses of the economic situation of the Highlands and his discussions about national identity and internationalism have much relevance to the situation of post-colonial nations in our own time and to our preoccupations in western Europe with national sovereignty in relation to European unity and the effects of the "global village". His philosophical interests and in particular his interest in later life in Zen Buddhism which he saw as having a relationship with Celtic culture speak in a relevant way to those searching for spirituality in our contemporary secular world. In all these ways, Neil Gunn has an assured place in 20th century Scottish writing as a novelist of national and international significance.

Personal memoir by Stewart Conn

I'd a deep affection for Neil Gunn's novels. We corresponded. I first met him at Kessock, to record a radio talk; then in Edinburgh through a mutual friend, playwright Alexander Reid. Alex dramatised and I directed *The Well at the World's End*. I remember learning the source of the novel; Neil describing how he and his wife Daisy, on holiday, had found a well – its crystal water made invisible by fern-fronds intercepting the light.

We didn't meet often. Despite or maybe because of this, each occasion remains crystal-clear. I found him unfailingly gracious and tolerant; and constantly encouraging. Once when, with the angst of youth, I said I'd finished writing something and had nothing else gnawing at me, he gave a knowing nod: "Enjoy it while you can". I suppose he became something of a guru (almost a father) figure. He was impassioned, but never browbeating, in argument. His atoms of delight (and the accompanying dram) could have me going round in circles.

I respected the *inter*nationalism in his nationalism: itself a key to why the SAC fellowship in his honour meant so much to him. I sensed it also countered a deep hurt that his novels were out of fashion (and print) at the time. I still find it difficult to dissociate the man from his work: each the embodiment of the other, in moral and vocal tone. And in letting in the light.

Our first son, born 10 days before Neil's death in January 1973, was called Arthur – mainly after Young Art: something Neil knew we had in mind. I would have liked them to meet. As for me, there's still no-one I more wish I could have been taken fishing by than Neil Gunn – with a salmon-rod, or a bent pin.

J.B. Caird wrote

"Many people have remarked that after spending an hour or two in his company, they felt elated, uplifted; the best in themselves had been brought out...Gunn was one of the least egotistical of men. He did not seek to dominate, but rather to influence quietly. In conversation he tended to bring you with him, to involve you in his observations and experiences, and he was seriously interested in *your* experiences."

From Gunn's *The Atom of Delight* [autobiography, 1956]

It [the civil service exam] was a disillusioning experience in one way for he realised that he did not possess the kind of temperament that produced the best under the surveillance of an examiner and a clock. Things went wrong. He was cast down. The examination was spread over several days and he knew no one. There may have been a hundred boys in the hall and of these only six or seven would pass...As a first real encounter on his own with the outside world it was such a levelling experience that on his return from Edinburgh he merely said he had not done very well. The amount of unconscious pride a boy carries around he realises only when he has been floored; and even then he can still carry a little."

From Gunn's contribution to *Scottish Country* [1935] about Caithness

"From that background [Ben Laoghal], or as it were from that door, you walk out upon Caithness, and at once experience an austerity in the flat clean wind-swept lands that affects the mind almost with a sense of shock. There is something more in it than contrast. It is a movement of the spirit that finds in the austerity, because strength is there also, a final serenity. I know of no other landscape in Scotland that achieves this harmony, that, in the very moment of purging the mind of its dramatic grandeur, leaves it free and ennobled."

Guthrie, Dr Douglas James
(1885-1975)

Ear, nose and throat surgeon and historian of medicine, son of a United Free Church minister in Dysart, Fife. He was educated at Kirkcaldy High School and the Royal High School, Edinburgh, and graduated in medicine at Edinburgh University. A post-graduate travelling fellowship enabled him to study in Hamburg, Jena, Berlin, and Vienna. Afterwards he was in general practice in Lanark for six years. He served for two years with the Royal Army Medical Corps and later with the RAF as commandant of a hospital for officers wounded during the first world war. In 1919 he was appointed ear and throat surgeon at the Royal Hospital for Sick Children, Edinburgh, and over the years made many contributions to knowledge of the ear and throat. He also did original work on disorders of speech. But it is as a medical historian that Guthrie is principally remembered. In 1948 he founded the Scottish Society of the History of Medicine and became its first president. Shortly before he retired from practice, he published *A History of Medicine*, a standard work which was reviewed by George Bernard Shaw and translated into several European languages.

H

Hahn, Kurt
(1886-1974)

Teacher, founder of Gordonstoun School where several members of the royal family, including Prince Charles, were educated. Born in Berlin, he was educated at Christ Church, Oxford, and at the Universities of Berlin, Heidelberg, Freiburg, and Göttingen. During the first world war he was lector of English newspapers, first for the German foreign office, then for supreme command. In 1919 he became private secretary to Prince Max von Baden, the last imperial chancellor, and the following year helped him to found Salem co-educational school. Arrested by the Nazis in 1933 and imprisoned for his public opposition to Hitler, he was released through the intervention of Ramsay MacDonald, then prime minister, and emigrated to Britain, becoming a British citizen in 1938. After opening a small school at Rothiemurchus with three pupils, he moved to Elgin and founded Gordonstoun in 1934. With its coastguard service as well as mountain and sea rescue teams, a fire fighting unit and a Red Cross group, the school gained a reputation for spartan living and outdoor adventure. Hahn was one of the pioneers of the Outward Bound Trust.

Haliburton, Tom
(c1915-75)

Golfer, Scottish-born, who was resident professional at the Wentworth club in Surrey. Playing over the east course one Saturday afternoon with his fellow Scottish professional, Bernard Gallacher, he collapsed and died on the first green. After coming to prominence as a boys' international, he turned professional in 1933, and won a number of tournaments including the Daily Mail in 1949 and the Yorkshire Evening News in 1969. Among his representative honours, he played for Scotland in the 1954 Canada Cup and for the UK in the Ryder Cup matches against the United States in 1961 and 1963. But it is for his hot streaks of scoring that he is chiefly remembered. In the 1963 Open championship at Lytham he went out in 29 strokes, and his 36-hole aggregate of 126 (61-65) in the 1952 Spalding tournament set a record. He was regarded by his peers as the complete professional, a man who loved the game and who, having been trained as a club-maker in his youth, was later simultaneously a model club professional and respected international competitor. "A golfer is an individual," Haliburton said, "and must be coached as such." But sometimes individuality could be carried too far. After they had won the Sunningdale Foursomes in 1951, his partner Jean Donald expressed a natural desire to partner him again. He replied bluntly: "Only if you change that hooker's grip of yours."

Bernard Gallacher said after his death "Mr Haliburton helped me more than any other professional. I joined him at Wentworth in 1969 and shortly afterwards, when I was at my lowest ebb, even thinking of packing up the game, it was Mr Haliburton who talked me out of any such notion. He was a particular help when I was improving my grip, but apart from anything he did for my game, he was a great influence in the sphere of how a professional ought to behave, on one's general lifestyle. He himself always did the right thing, never gave offence if he could help it, and was very proud of his own profession and concerned for its image."

John Panton said "Tom was not long but very straight, a safe putter with a beautiful touch in his chipping and the little running shots around the green."

Jean Donald said "To me he had a classical swing – one of those players you want to watch on every tee."

Hamilton, 14th Duke of, and Brandon, 11th Duke of
Douglas Douglas-Hamilton
(1903-73)

Premier peer of Scotland, aviator and boxer, educated at Eton and Balliol College, Oxford, who succeeded his father to the titles in

1940. While at Oxford he represented the university in boxing and became known as "the fighting marquess". He was also a skilled aviator and as chief pilot of the Houston expedition took part in the first flight over Mount Everest in 1933, for which he was awarded the Air Force Cross. He and his co-pilot, David McIntyre, were given the freedom of Prestwick for their pioneering service in the development of aviation in Scotland. Together they wrote an account of their achievement, *The Pilots' Book of Everest* (1936). He served in 602 City of Glasgow RAAF squadron, which he commanded, and in the RAF, 1939-45, being mentioned in despatches.

During the second world war he was involved in a sensational incident – the flight to Scotland of Rudolf Hess, Germany's deputy Führer. In May 1941 Hess baled out over Lanarkshire on a "peace mission" and surrendered to the Home Guard and the police. He told them that he wanted to see the Duke of Hamilton and had intended to land near Dungavel, the duke's residence. As a result the prime minister sent for the duke and later Hess was identified by a representative of the Foreign Office.

Before succeeding to the dukedom on his father's death, he was Unionist MP for East Renfrewshire, 1930-40. Later he was Deputy Lieutenant of Lanarkshire, Lord High Commissioner to the General Assembly of the Church of Scotland on four occasions, chancellor of St Andrews University, and Hereditary Keeper of the Palace of Holyroodhouse. He took an active role in the building society movement. In 1962 he was president of the sixth international congress of genealogy, held in Edinburgh. He acquired the historic house of Lennoxlove, near Haddington, the ancestral home of Hamilton Palace having been demolished.

From Douglas-Hamilton's *The Pilots' Book of Everest* [1936]

"Everything was working excellently in both machines, with the exception of my telephones. These telephones had worked well on both test flights, but as soon as Blacker and I tested them in the air, they started buzzing, and this we could not stop. It was annoying enough at the start, but the noise seemed to get worse as the aeroplane climbed, and became more and more irritating. Neither of us could hear a single word the other spoke. This may have been just as well, because our language deteriorated with the continuance of this incessant noise every time we tried to communicate with each other. The telephones became useless, and all communications had to be made by notes written on slips of paper."

From James Douglas-Hamilton's *Motive for a Mission – The Story Behind Rudolf Hess's Flight to Britain* [1979]

"Hamilton had the impression that Churchill was looking at him sympathetically, as though he were suffering from war strain and hallucinations...Churchill then asked Hamilton very slowly and with great emphasis: 'Do you mean to tell me that the Deputy Führer of Germany is in our hands?' Hamilton replied that the man had certainly declared himself to be Hess. He then produced the photographs of the unidentified prisoner. Churchill looked at them and said, 'Well, Hess or no Hess, I am going to see the Marx Brothers.'"

Heard, Cardinal William Theodore
(1884-1973)
Priest, educated at Fettes College, Edinburgh, where his father, the

Rev. Dr W.A. Heard had been headmaster, and at Balliol College, Oxford. When he received the red hat from Pope John in 1959, he became the first Scots convert to be made a cardinal and the first Scots-born priest to achieve the honour for 400 years. He visited Edinburgh in 1960, the first visit by a cardinal to Scotland for 400 years.

Essay by Mark Dilworth

William Theodore Heard, it seems, did not have a happy childhood. His mother died when he was four and he lived, and later was a pupil, in a boarding school where his father was headmaster. Probably contact with the life of Edinburgh was minimal. When he left school and went to Oxford, he enjoyed life, often dancing through the night and gaining his blue in the boat race of 1907. This is perhaps the key to his totally English career.

He became a solicitor in London in 1910, which proved to be a turning point in his life, for his work took him into the east end, where he was appalled by the deprivation and neglect. He bought a football and began to spend evenings with the youngsters and after a while lived in the district with Catholic clergy. Having become a Catholic, he entered the English College in Rome, returning to London eight years later as a priest and with doctorates in philosophy, theology and canon law. For six years he then worked in the east end, until in 1927 he was called to Rome to be a judge in the Rota, dealing with matrimonial cases. He remained in Rome until his death 46 years later.

He was clearly a caring and compassionate person but with a serious, not to say stern, exterior. A fellow student in the English College described Heard's breakfast as "black coffee and a frown". As a Rota judge and later a cardinal, he continued to have close relations with his old college and acted as confessor to the students. Rather to their surprise, it would appear, they found him gentle and kind as well as wise. One student kept a record of his humorous asides.

Aged 74 and in poor health, he had given orders to admit no visitors. One man refused to go away, until at last Heard decided to give him a piece of his mind. The visitor was a special messenger from the Pope to tell him he was being made a cardinal. The old man broke down and wept. As a cardinal, he seems to have had more contacts with things Scottish. In the last 18 years of his life, he spent part of each summer in Scotland, staying with Archbishop Scanlan of Glasgow, a fellow canon lawyer. His grandfather Heard, one learns, was from Forres.

Henderson, Sir John
(1888-1975)
Politician, educated at Martyrs School, Glasgow. He was a member of Glasgow Corporation, 1926-46, and entered Parliament in 1946 as Conservative MP for Glasgow Cathcart, a seat he held for 18 years. A member of the Salvation Army, he worked tirelessly for religious charities and was president of the International Council for Christian Leadership.

Hepburn, Dr Charles
(c1891-1971)
Whisky millionaire and philanthropist, educated at Hillhead High

School, Glasgow. He founded the Red Hackle whisky firm shortly after the first world war, reportedly from a few hundred pounds of war gratuity. In 1959 he sold his business interests for £2 million. A notable patron of the arts, he owned one of the best private collections of paintings in the country, including works by Rembrandt, Reynolds, Raeburn and Ramsay. Among his gifts to Glasgow Cathedral was a 15th-century Persian rug which had been used in Westminster Abbey at the coronations of Edward VII and George V. He was an equally generous benefactor of Glasgow University and of Scottish rugby, financing the protection of the Murrayfield pitch against frost.

Hirst, Sir Edmund (Langley)
(1898-1975)
Organic chemist, educated at Madras College, St Andrews, and at St Andrews University, where he began his career as an assistant in the chemistry department in 1920. From there he went to Manchester, Durham, Birmingham, and Bristol Universities, until he was appointed Forbes professor of organic chemistry at Edinburgh University, 1947-68. A pioneer researcher on the chemistry of carbohydrate and vitamin C, he was awarded the Royal Society's Davy medal in 1948 and was president of the Royal Society of Edinburgh, 1959-64.

Holm, Helen
(c1907-71)
Golfer, born Helen Gray, the daughter of a university professor. She was Scottish ladies' champion five times between 1930 and 1950, was selected to play for Scotland in 14 home international series, and represented Great Britain three times in the Curtis Cup match against the United States. A women's stroke-play tournament named in her honour is played annually at Troon, where she lived.

Holm, Dr John M.
(c1908-72)
Explosives expert, a graduate of Glasgow University. He joined ICI in 1934. Shortly after the outbreak of the second world war, he was seconded to the Ministry of Supply, becoming director of explosives responsible for the co-ordination of supplies of all propellants and high explosives to the British armed forces. After the war he rejoined the explosives group of ICI, which was re-named the Nobel division. He was chairman of that division, 1961-66.

Honeyman, Dr Tom John
(1891-1971)
Promoter of the arts, educated at Queen's Park School, Glasgow, and Glasgow University, from which he graduated in medicine. Like his friend O.H. Mavor (James Bridie) he abandoned medicine in favour of the arts. Between 1939 and 1954 he was an innovative director of the Glasgow Art Galleries and Museums where he was responsible for 50 special exhibitions.

Essay by
Ronald Mavor

Tom (or Tommy) Honeyman was born on 10 June, 1891, in Stevenson Street in the Calton district of Glasgow, the sixth son of a railwayman from Fife who was a devout, and became a full-time evangelistical, temperance worker. Tom's grandparents had been rather too enthusiastically of the other persuasion. The teetotal discipline was to survive through at least three generations.

The family moved to Langside and Tom, after Queen's Park School, was prepared for university and the ministry, but after the death of his much-loved elder brother lost any mild sense of vocation and opted for medicine. He qualified, though taking two years off trying to make a living in Bradford, in 1916 and was rapidly posted in the RAMC to a hospital in Salonika.

Already clearly a restless spirit, he had developed a passion for the arts and, although after his return from the war a successful general practitioner, with connections with the Royal Infirmary, he deserted his safe profession and became an art dealer in 1929.

He joined the Glasgow firm started by Alexander Reid (whose portrait by Van Gogh is in the Glasgow collection) in partnership with McNeil Reid and Duncan Macdonald (an old school friend) and, when the firm moved to London, as Reid and Lefevre, Tom kept the Glasgow shop until the lease ran out and then moved to London. The Lefevre Gallery as it was known had inherited from old Alex a close interest and many connections with the post-Impressionists but did not neglect Scottish painters like Peploe, Cadell, Hunter and Fergusson.

As a dealer Tom travelled widely and made some remarkable purchases. He was sufficiently successful to say that his, to many surprising, appointment to run the Glasgow Art Galleries and Museums in 1939 meant a cut of three quarters in his earnings. But he loved Glasgow and he had a passionate desire to bring his fellow citizens towards his own love of, not just painting, but all the arts.

He didn't find the Kelvingrove Galleries in very good shape. A bomb shortly blasted half the building, but Tom said it hadn't destroyed the right bits. He took the Victorian plaster goddesses out of the main hall and put them in the Kibble Palace in the Botanic Gardens. He mounted two staggeringly successful exhibitions of Picasso/Matisse and Van Gogh, and scores more, sometimes less art than publicity. But he brought queues round the block; and every exhibition had lectures and sometimes music to bring people in. He started work with schools. He started the Glasgow Art Gallery and Museums Association and its magazine, the *Glasgow* (later *Scottish*) *Art Review*. He brought in Henry Farmer to revolutionise the museum's Asian collection and Helmut Ruhemann to restore paintings. He took the considerable risk, not everywhere applauded, of having Glasgow's greatest painting, Giorgione's Woman Taken in Adultery, restored. And he bought Dali's Christ of St John of the Cross (for what many thought an extravagant price, although he also bought the copyright which has brought the gallery many times that sum through the years).

Many important collectors, believing in Honeyman, gave or left major works or collections to the galleries, notably William McInnes and David Cargill – though Cargill's brother decided not to leave his collection when Tom Honeyman resigned.

His major coup, however, was his acquiring the Burrell Collection for Glasgow. Only he could have done it.

When he finally fell out with the Town Council and resigned, he was far from idle. He was one of the founders of the Citizens' Theatre where, characteristically, he formed and chaired the Citizens' Theatre Society, to build a base of interested supporters. He was asked by Tom Johnston to draw up a plan for a Scottish Tourist Board, of which he was, later, a founder member. He became rector of Glasgow University (and, later, assessor for Chief Luthuli who was not allowed to leave South Africa). He was one of the first members of the Scottish Committee of the Council for the Encouragement of Music and the Arts (CEMA), later the Scottish Arts Council; and he lectured world-wide to St Andrew societies and arts groups.

Tommy Honeyman, although a teetotaller, always seemed a couple of whiskies over par. With a build and a carriage reminiscent of the film actor James Cagney, he was lively company always. He carried his considerable learning lightly, but was always happy to pass it on to serious students. After all, he had known most of the master painters and sculptors of his day and, no doubt, charmed and amused them as he charmed and amused everyone who met him.

Through his life he had the love and support of his wife Cathie, a quiet but spirited consort and a fine pianist. He had three children and, surely, a happy life if always in the front of the battle. He died on 5 July, 1971, not long after a very large and companionable 80th birthday party. Cathie, as in the poem, "for a little tried/To live without him./Liked it not, and died."

From Honeyman's Art and Audacity [1971]

"Twenty-two people applied [for the job]. Glasgow's advertisement, with the unusual 'must be prepared as one of the duties of the position to deliver lectures on various branches of art as the Corporation may require' had attracted some excellent candidates. They could not have been thinking of the emoluments...Some had Museum or Art Gallery experience. Others, like myself, thought we could fill the post through reliance on other qualifications. C.M. Grieve (Hugh MacDiarmid) had a shot at it. We had been together on the staff of the 42nd General Hospital in Salonika in World War I. I often wondered how he would have tackled the job. Poetry in Scotland would have suffered, but as a dynamic personality he might have stirred things up. I remember on a special occasion attending a conference aimed at starting an Academy of Scottish Art and Letters. My contribution was 'What's the use of having Christopher Grieve in anything like this? He always resigns.' 'It is a lie' came back the defiance. 'I get expelled'."

Honeyman on art and artists

[1] "I was moved by it [the Dali], and I still am. I can be moved by a hymn, but it may be bad poetry."
[2] "I have always believed that a gallery should put on a performance – that art should be as alive as music and drama. Galleries should be open in the evenings and there should be lectures with every exhibition."

Hornsby, Lex
(c1901-75)

Public relations executive, born in Glasgow. A pioneer of public relations, he worked for the Ministry of Labour and National Service for 13 years during and after the second world war. He coined several slogans which caught on, among them "Coughs and sneezes spread diseases".

House, Jessie Miller
(c1910-74)
Journalist, a graduate of Glasgow University, who wrote under the name Jessie Miller. She was women's page editor of the *Glasgow Evening News* before joining the *Scottish Daily Express*. Later she freelanced. She was the wife of Jack House, journalistic authority on Glasgow.

I

Innes of Learney, Sir Thomas
(1893-1971)
Genealogist, educated at Edinburgh Academy and Edinburgh University. Called to the Scottish bar in 1922, he was known to appear in Parliament House wearing his wig and gown over cycling breeches. According to one, perhaps not wholly reliable, account he once secured the acquittal of an accused by assuring the jury: "My client must be innocent. He tells me so himself." A member of the Lyon Court for more than 40 years, he served as Carrick Pursuivant and Albany Herald before succeeding Sir Francis Grant as Lord Lyon King of Arms, 1945-69. He was responsible for arranging and supervising the ceremonial connected with the Queen's state visit to Edinburgh after her coronation in 1953. He re-introduced several historic names into the Lyon register, including the clan chiefships of Macmillan and Macnab, and was zealous in exhorting burghs to register more appropriate symbols. In his tabard of red and gold, or in the flowing green mantle of the Order of the Thistle, of which he was secretary, Innes's unkempt hair, high-pitched voice and notoriously poor eyesight made him an unmistakable figure in Edinburgh society. Assuming a stiff gait on formal occasions, he delighted in marshalling peers and commoners in a precise order of precedence. "Lyon speaking," he declared crisply when answering the telephone.

From Innes's *Scots Heraldry* [1934]

[1] "Heraldry is a simple and practical science, invented and used for the convenience of everybody, in days when few could write, and education was of an elementary standard."

[2] "The term 'coat of arms' is derived from the armorial jacket or 'tabard' worn by knights over their armour. This coat still survives in the heraldic tabard, the significance of which originated in the theory that the herald, when arrayed in his master's coat, actually represented him."

Irvine, Rev. Dr Archibald Clive
(d 1974)
Church of Scotland medical missionary, educated at Aberdeen University and ordained as a minister in 1933. He carried out most of his missionary work at Chogoria in the Meru district of Kenya,

where he founded a hospital, pioneered evangelism and education, and brought new prosperity to the district through the introduction of coffee-growing. Two of his sons followed him as Church of Scotland missionaries in Africa.

J

Jackson, Charles D'Orville Pilkington
(1887-1973)
Sculptor, born in Cornwall and educated at Loretto School, Musselburgh. He served in both world wars and was mentioned in despatches during the first. His best-known work was the larger-than-life equestrian statue of King Robert the Bruce at the site of Bannockburn, which the Queen unveiled on 24 June, 1964, the 650th anniversary of the battle. While he was creating the three and a half ton statue, he had a studio attached to his house. When funds ran low he opened the studio at weekends and allowed the public to see the plaster cast of the work in progress, for which he levied a small admission charge. He took considerable satisfaction in making the weapons and trappings incorporated in the design as accurate as possible. Although he made his name with the Bruce statue, he said that the work which gave him most pleasure was the group of 83 statuettes made in the 1930s for the United Services Museum at Edinburgh Castle. He was also responsible for a small carving depicting David Livingstone's last journey, which is displayed at the missionary's birthplace at Blantyre. Other examples of his work can be seen in Paisley Abbey, the Imperial War Museum and the Scottish National War Memorial. He was a past president of the Society of Scottish Artists.

Jacobs, Arthur
(c1899-74)
Urologist, educated at the Universities of Glasgow and Edinburgh, who later studied urology in London and on the continent. He returned to Glasgow to take charge of a specialist urology unit at the Royal Infirmary. His textbooks on the subject earned him international respect and in 1965 he was awarded the St Peter's Medal of the British Association of Urological Surgeons.

Johnston, Frederick Mair
(1903-73)
Newspaper proprietor, born in Leith and educated at Daniel Stewart's College, Edinburgh. After training in accountancy he entered journalism and joined the reporting staff of *The Scotsman*. He left to join his uncle in the long-established family newspaper business in Falkirk. From its roots owning two weekly papers in the Falkirk area, the company expanded under Johnston's direction into one of the largest privately owned group of papers in Scotland. He was a founder member of the Press Council.

K

Kelly, Sir Robert
(1902-71)
Football administrator, educated at St Aloysius College, Glasgow, and St Joseph's College, Dumfries, whose long association with Glasgow's Roman Catholic club earned him the epithet "Mr Celtic". He came from a prominent West of Scotland footballing family, his father, James, having been one of the players around whom the original Celtic team was established. Kelly himself played at junior level, but was prevailed upon to give up the game because his withered right arm, the result of a childhood accident, was having an unsettling effect on opponents. In 1932, following his father's death, he joined the board of Celtic. He was appointed chairman of the club in 1947, a position he occupied until shortly before his death 24 years later. He was president of the Scottish Football League for six years and of the Scottish Football Association for four years. In 1952 he caused outrage in the SFA by defending Celtic's policy of flying the Irish flag at Parkhead, but nevertheless won the argument. His domineering influence made him unpopular with the club's own supporters, for he insisted on interfering with the team selections of the manager Jimmy McGrory – occasionally with disastrous results. He was tolerant in the fielding of players of different religions, and in 1965 demolished arguments that the top jobs at the club were always filled by Catholics when he appointed Jock Stein as manager. With Stein's arrival as the complete professional, the benevolent despot took a back seat for the first time. In 1969 he was knighted for services to the game.

From Tom Campbell and Pat Woods's *The Glory and the Dream: the history of Celtic FC 1887-1987* [1987]

[1] "White-haired and stern in appearance, he inspired respect rather than affection; his occupation as stockbroker and sometime JP confirmed his air of rectitude. Blunt and outspoken, he rarely seemed relaxed at social gatherings and scorned small talk."

[2] "Robert Kelly had an idealistic vision of the sport, a Corinthian approach inherited from his father whom he venerated. It was a simple outlook, uncluttered with artifice or sophistication: to play the game hard and fair, to respect but not fear opponents, to offer handshakes at the end regardless of the result. It was a philosophy that he never abandoned."

John S. Thomson, chairman of Morton F.C., on Kelly's physical disability

"Whenever I met him at Celtic Park or Greenock, I just stuck out my left hand instead of the right. The first time I had to explain that I used to be in the Scouts. Once he accepted that he wasn't being initiated into the masons, we got on really well."

Kelly on football

[1] "We have a field here and a ball; there's a referee and two teams waiting. We don't need anything else." [His response to a suggestion that the European Cup final between Celtic and Feyenoord in 1970 should be postponed because of a transport strike and other problems.]

[2] "If I have heard correctly, you claim that you learned the game from us early this century. Let me assure you that no Celtic side I have ever seen has used such methods nor played in the manner you played tonight." [Speech at official banquet following a bruising

defeat in Budapest, 1964.]

[3] "I can see no sense in playing the tournament in Chile, a remote country in which I understand it takes one year to become acclimatised." [Opposing a proposed venue for the World Cup, 1960.]

Kenmure, Rev. Vera
(c1904-73)

Congregational minister, the first woman to be ordained a minister in Scotland. Born in Glasgow, she was educated at Hillhead High School, Glasgow University, and the Congregational Theological College in Edinburgh, where she was the first woman student. Her first charge was Partick Congregational Church, Glasgow, where she was ordained in 1928. Six years later a dispute arose within the congregation about her suitability to remain a minister after the birth of her son. She resigned the charge, but more than 200 members who had wanted her to stay helped her to set up a new congregation, Christ Church, and later followed her to Hillhead Congregational Church. She became Congregational minister at Pollokshields in 1954, retiring in 1968.

Kerr, John
(d 1972)

Cricketer who played his first game for Greenock in 1900, while still at school, and was selected to play for Scotland 39 times. In 1921 he became the first Scot in Scotland to hit a century off Australian bowling, scoring 147. He scored four other centuries for his country, all against Ireland, including a record of 178 n.o., and scored 41 centuries for Greenock. He was honorary president of the Scottish Cricket Union.

Kidd, John D.
(c1904-73)

Councillor, one of the more colourful in Edinburgh's post-war history. Born in Perth, he developed a successful road haulage business in the north of England. He was rich enough to retire comparatively young and in 1964 came to live in Edinburgh. Two years later he entered local government as a Tory councillor and won a reputation for reactionary comments and eye-catching stunts. An opponent of permissiveness, he was particularly outspoken about "long-haired students" and once addressed a student gathering wearing a long wig.

King, Sir Alexander Boyne
(1888-1973)

Cinema owner, born in Glasgow, though he regarded his home as Banffshire (where his mother was born). He received an elementary education. From an early age he displayed a passion for work, selling morning rolls to supplement the family budget. In his own words he "entered the theatrical profession" at the age of 12, as a programme-boy. In 1913 he turned to the emerging cinema industry and acquired a chain of cinemas. He became known as "the uncrowned king of the cinema in Scotland" and served the wider interests of the industry as president of the Cinematograph

Exhibitors' Association and chairman of the Films of Scotland Committee. He was knighted in 1944, his investiture taking place in an air-raid shelter so confined that the monarch scarcely had room to use his sword. An intensely patriotic Scot, he took a prominent part in organising the Empire Exhibition in Scotland in 1938 and was commandant of the Scottish team for the 1958 Commonwealth Games in Cardiff.

Kinnaird, 12th Baron
Kenneth FitzGerald Kinnaird
(1880-1972)
Landowner, educated at Eton and Trinity College, Cambridge. He served as a captain with Scottish Horse during the first world war. In 1923, on his father's death, he became 12th baron of the line. He was a Perth county councillor, Lord Lieutenant of the county, and Lord High Commissioner to the General Assembly of the Church of Scotland from 1936 until 1938.

L

Lilley, Francis James Patrick
(1907-71)
Politician and industrialist, educated at Bellahouston Academy, Glasgow. He entered local politics in 1957 and was a member of various committees of Glasgow Corporation before being elected Conservative MP for Glasgow Kelvingrove, 1959-64. He made a successful career in business as chairman of F.J.C. Lilley, a group of civil engineering and public works contractors. Latterly he lived in Jersey.

Lindsay, Sir William O'Brien
(1909-75)
Colonial civil servant and lawyer, born in Kent but with family roots in Dairsie, Fife. He was educated at Harrow and at Balliol College, Oxford, where he was a notable sportsman, and qualified as a barrister at Gray's Inn. During the second world war he served as an officer in the Sudan defence force, having entered the Sudan civil service before the war. Later he became the youngest and last white chief justice of the Sudan and was awarded the KBE when he retired from that post in 1955. During riots in Khartoum he succeeded in stopping what might have developed into an ugly situation by calmly walking across the firing line. After Sudan became independent he was appointed political secretary to the Sultan of Oman and later joined a Nairobi law firm as advocate and partner. Shortly before his death he married his third wife, Michaela, widow of Armand Denis.

Linklater, Eric
(1899-1974)
Novelist, son of Robert Linklater, of Dounby, Orkney. Born in Wales, he spent much of his childhood in Orkney. He was educated at

Aberdeen Grammar School and Aberdeen University, where his medical studies were interrupted by service in the Black Watch during the first world war. After the war he continued his studies, graduating in literature, and became assistant editor of *The Times of India* in Bombay. He returned to Scotland as assistant to the professor of English literature at Aberdeen University. He then spent two years in the United States as a Commonwealth fellow. In 1933 he married Marjorie McIntyre and stood as a nationalist candidate in a by-election. By then he had published eight books and established his reputation as a novelist. During the second world war he commanded the Orkney fortress as a major in the Royal Engineers, later working for the directorate of public relations at the War Office. He was rector of Aberdeen University from 1945 until 1948.

Essay by John MacRitchie

Over a long and distinguished career, Eric Linklater wrote 23 novels, 11 plays, some 30 short stories and novellas, three children's novels, and about 30 works of non-fiction with subject matter encompassing Scottish history, military history, biography, philosophical dialogue, criminology, literary history and travel, in addition to journalism and editorial work; but his own life-story was packed with incident, much of which found its way into his fiction.

Linklater excelled in his command of language. Each novel differs from its predecessors in setting and tone. "To match a hundredth part of the variety of life, the writer should go to work in a hundred different styles," he believed, so sometimes he is satiric, sometimes he is elegiac, sometimes he writes in imitation of the Norse sagas, sometimes he writes with the fervid mannerisms of an Italian peasant. The brilliance of his style reflects the fertility of his invention. He is most often referred to as a comic novelist, which he certainly was, but there is a tendency for critics to under-rate him because of his comic gifts, and to assume that he only wrote comedy: he is not a writer who can be pigeon-holed. His early novels in particular were best-sellers and a sniffiness about his popularity may also be one reason for his critical neglect. Although he is arguably the foremost Scottish novelist of the century, much of his best work has been allowed to go out of print.

However, there may be difficulty even in regarding him as a Scottish writer. He was Welsh by birth, born in Penarth on 8 March, 1899, but more significantly (he claimed) he was conceived in Orkney, and in later life always presented himself as an Orcadian. In his volume of autobiography, *The Man On My Back*, he traces his family tree back to Viking ancestry. The magic of Orkney recurs in some of his best short stories, and in his novels it is a place of sanity and healing. By the age of 10 his family had relocated there.

After attending Aberdeen Grammar School, his medical studies at Aberdeen University were interrupted by service with the Black Watch in the first world war, and his second volume of autobiography, *A Year of Space*, describes his horrific experiences as a sniper in no-man's-land. After the war he graduated in English literature, specialising in eloquent Elizabethans such as Ben Jonson, and had a spell as a journalist with *The Times of India*. He spent his late twenties as a Commonwealth fellow in the USA, an experience which he satirised in his novel *Juan in America* (1931). This was his longest and biggest-selling novel, which borrowed stylistic elements from Smollett's picaresque novels and Byron's *Don Juan*, and it tore into the hypocrisy of Prohibition America with terrific force. Linklater tried out every comic trick in the book, from subtle wordplay to slapstick farce, and the rapid pace just about made up for the apparent arbitrariness of structure.

His next novel, *The Men of Ness* (1932), could not have been more of a contrast. It was a deliberate pillaging of Norse sagas, told with stark simplicity in Viking style, eschewing Latinate terms, a tale of pagan valour with at its centre the little unheroic Viking, Gauk. Francis Russell Hart, in *The Scottish Novel*, has suggested that at their most typical Linklater's heroes are simply concerned with survival, but if there is a common characteristic to his novels it may be that they all feature a central character in search of contentment. For some, this may take the form of a wild whirl across Prohibition America; for others, such as the eponymous hero of *Magnus Merriman* (1934), contentment only comes when the farce is over.

In *Magnus Merriman*, Linklater satirised his experiences standing in a by-election as a candidate for the National Party of Scotland, though he denied the more extreme elements of the story were autobiographical. A prime mover of the Scottish literary renaissance, he could not resist poking fun at its notables such as Hugh MacDiarmid and Wendy Wood, but the scenes of buffoonery in Edinburgh now stand up less well than the concluding chapters set on Orkney, when Magnus finds out what he really wants from life.

In the remainder of Linklater's pre-1939 novels, the quality is very uneven, ranging from the embarrassing *The Impregnable Women* (1938) and *The Sailor's Holiday* (1937), which is frankly poor, to the sustained brilliance of *Judas* (1939), an examination of the nature of cowardice and betrayal which found a prose style of economy and vividness to match the subject matter. Appearing shortly before the outbreak of war, it had no time to win the readers it deserved.

Linklater had a busy war, initially commanding fortress Orkney as a major in the Royal Engineers, then writing pamphlets for the War Office, culminating in the official history of the Italian campaign, which saw him with the troops at Monte Cassino and the Allied entry into Rome. He rediscovered the hidden art treasures of Florence – alone in a room with Botticelli's "Primavera" he kissed her, the quintessential Linklaterian moment. Out of his experiences in Italy came the novel for which he may be best remembered, *Private Angelo* (1946), the moving story of an unheroic peasant bemused by war. Again, the story determines the style, which is at once amusing and childishly innocent, but also robust enough to record war's horror.

In the 1950s Linklater made repeated attempts to succeed as a dramatist, only to realise that his real gift was as a novelist. Perhaps most typical of his novels of the '50s is *Position at Noon* (1958), which takes as its starting point the observation that young men always blame their fathers for their own shortcomings. He traces the Vanburgh family back over 200 years charting their appalling bad luck, in a witty, delightful take on English social history. Linklater's comic peers were quick to appreciate him: P.G. Wodehouse claimed that discovering his novels was "one of the great moments in my life"; and Evelyn Waugh described *The Merry Muse* (1959) as "a rare treat". *The Merry Muse* is very black comedy, in which the find of a bawdy book by Burns prompts wild shenanigans in Edinburgh, including two disastrous funerals.

Yet Linklater followed this up with *Roll of Honour* (1961), which can only be described as an extended prose poem, a threnody for his schoolfellows who died in the war. Anthony Burgess, recognising a kindred spirit, described Linklater as shamefully undervalued, one of the finest craftsmen of the century, and this is borne out most remarkably of all in Linklater's last novel, *A Terrible Freedom* (1966). Here he attempts an experimental mixture of dream-fantasy and reality which defeated most critics of the day. The baffled reception this novel received persuaded the author to devote the remainder of his career to non-fiction. This included a final volume of autobiography, *Fanfare For A Tin Hat* (1970) and various books of Scottish history, but it is for what his biographer Michael Parnell has described as his "magnificent series of novels" that he will be best remembered. A fat volume, *The Stories of Eric Linklater* (1968) proved his mastery of that demanding form.

Eric Linklater died on 7 November, 1974, and is buried in Harray churchyard, Orkney. A short poem he wrote in the 1930s characterises his sense of humour and philosophy of life: "The older man grows/The quicker Time flies/So the longer he lives/The sooner he dies."

Personal memoir by Andro Linklater (son)

When I was a child in the 1950s, my father's reputation as a writer had passed its peak. He was one year older than the century and his great fame had come in the 1930s and 1940s with a succession of best-selling novels beginning with *Juan in America* and ending with *Private Angelo*. Nevertheless his reputation remained sufficiently powerful to breed in me a distinct expectancy of recognition. In the company of strangers voices above my head would say "This is Eric Linklater's boy" or a face would duck down to my level and assert brightly, "So you're the great man's son", and I would feel the spread of a wider penumbra than a small boy could throw. To be Eric Linklater's son then seemed no hardship.

With my father on hand, however, the expectancy was shot through by a fearful apprehension that something might go wrong. Like some infant Duke of Norfolk superintending a coronation, I felt it imperative that his importance be acknowledged by those around him. My worries reached a peak when he appeared in public – on a local *Matter of Opinion* panel where he was bound to be contradicted, or on the radio where the interviewer would surely fail to catch his jokes, or on television where the camera would reveal him, as indeed it did, with his flies undone. To be his son in those circumstances was to feel his dignity threatened at every turn.

To some extent these were the natural misgivings of any child seeing his parent perform in public, but they also had a source in Eric's own apprehensions. Beneath his exuberant exterior ran a layer of uncertainty. My father disliked his physical appearance and emotional inhibition, and from adolescence had fought to overcome these shortcomings, as he perceived them to be. Anything which reminded him of them was liable to provoke a fury quite disproportionate to its overt cause. There was a manner in which people *should* behave and a way in which things *should* be done, and it was crucial that the people or things around him should measure up to the standards he had set himself. Thus my Norfolk-like concern for appearances echoed in some degree that of the monarch.

From our different standpoints we were both familiar with the ideal. It came when he was in the company of men he admired, for the most part those who added writing to other accomplishments: soldiers, such as Robert Henriques or Bernard Fergusson; a doctor such as O.H. Mavor (James Bridie); and above all Compton Mackenzie whose additional guises defy brief description. With them he became the person he wanted to be, extravagant in affection, hospitality and discourse.

When they came to stay the house swelled in sympathetic grandeur. The dining-room table grew in length, the cellar was harvested of bottles, and dark corners of the hall sprouted sheaves of roses, lupins or gladioli. From a mingled sense of drama and terror the butcher produced his best mutton, my mother her best cooking, and the four children their best behaviour. It was a pleasure to be present on such occasions, and to offer a second helping of carrots was to stand on the edge of glory.

Eric then made a splendid companion. His conversation was served by a Jacobean wit and a prodigious memory crammed with reading and experience, but most importantly admiration unstoppered his feelings so that his friends were bathed in their warmth. Driven by the gale of his personality their talk grew boisterous and its direction unpredictable. Allusion served for explanation, personal experience stood in for definition. A quotation from Racine comprehended France and war was caught in the memory of a battle. Like wizards they leapt from one conversational peak to another, and wherever they landed an entire mountain of knowledge was assumed to stand beneath their feet.

There was something of Cinderella in this gaiety and the departure of the guests represented the chimes of midnight. Then the saddle of mutton turned to rissoles, the claret bottles became a water-jug, and in place of the glittering talkers sat four bespectacled, unattractive children. I surmise that nothing reminded Eric more forcibly of his secret faults than his children, for he strove repeatedly and angrily to mould us to a less irritating form.

In memory these attempts have their focus on the long-polished table in the dining-room from one end of which he sat facing the window so that its westerly light illuminated the pink, imperial dome of his bald head and made his spectacles gleam like mirrors. Meals took place in an atmosphere which I recall as being so charged the squeal of a knife on china or the slurrup of soup on lip could trigger an explosion. "If you can't eat like a civilised human being," he bellowed, "you can finish your meal at the bottom of the garden." At his most irritable, he had a habit of addressing us through my mother as though she were the NCO of a slovenly platoon he had to inspect. "Marjorie! Have you seen this boy's tie? Does he have to come to table looking like a slum child?" or, on the occasion I first tried to carve a chicken, "Marjorie! What's that bloody boy been doing? The bird looks as though it's been attacked with a Mills grenade."

When he shouted, his voice had a percussive force at which I usually cried, as much for my own failure as his anger. Despite straining every Norfolk nerve, things could not be prevented from going wrong. There were sudden unannounced purges against the smell of peeled oranges or grapes pulled from the stalk, and if these were avoided paralysing interrogations exposed my ignorance about people, places and dates.

The other children, being older, had presumably run this gauntlet before me, and our collective failings must have seemed part of a conspiracy against him. For all his shouting, deficiencies continued to appear on every side. Plates were served cool when they should have been hot, drinking water was tepid instead of cold, and spoons were dull instead of sparkling. There was, in consequence, no mistaking who was at the centre of the conspiracy – the woman responsible for plates, spoons, children and, most infuriatingly of all, for boiled potatoes which either dissolved to flour or split as crisply as apples. "Good God, woman, look at this!" he bawled in disbelief. "After 23 years of married life you *still* haven't learned to boil a potato." And despite the years, he would still be goaded into slinging the potato at my mother, though either because she was only a silhouette against the light, or out of good manners, he usually missed.

The emotional drama left no one untouched, and viewed on the distorting screen of memory, meal-times have a decidedly operatic quality. Conversations are shouted arguments, unforgivable accusations are hurled across the table, people break down and cry, exits are made to the sound of slammed doors – my elder sister once exited with a slam which dislodged a full-length portrait of my maternal grandmother from the wall and two painted plates from the sideboard. Acknowledging a force as elemental as himself, my father relapsed briefly into silence.

I do not present this as the whole truth – the sunnier moods are absent, and as we grew older and tougher, and thus more acceptable, they often predominated – but it is accurate as to the intemperate quality of his frustration. For a child it was impossible to understand that the violence of his emotions was inseparable from his writing, and that what enraged him in life could become comedy in fiction. In fact I remember my embarrassment at the age of seven when I first read *The Pirates in the Deep Green Sea*, a book which he wrote for my brother Magnus and me. There for all to see was my father in the person of the ferocious pirate, Dan Scumbril, who terrified half the North Atlantic with his blazing temper and loud voice. "Split my liver with a brass harpoon," thundered Dan Scumbril, and I quailed, not with fright but shame that my father's rages should now be known to everyone. When, so far from being thought the worse of, he was congratulated on the creation of an exceptionally comic character, I logged it as one more of those bewildering quirks of existence which had to be accepted even though they made no sense.

As it happens, it is more complex than most childhood matters to understand how fiction transforms reality. In my adolescence and early twenties, I found – as did most of my contemporaries to judge by reviews and comments – a lack of sensitivity in his resort to comedy. It was too obviously the right thing to do, not to take the world very seriously – even his nightmare of service on the western front in the first world war was presented in *The Man On My Back* in comic form.

Yet, when I read his books today it seems to me that what underlies his writing is not an absence but an excess of feeling. A violent sentiment runs through his most extravagant comedy so that it dances on the edge of blackness or slips abruptly into tragedy. The variety of his approaches to fiction which once irritated his critics – the rollicking of *Juan in America* followed by the gut-spilling *Men of Ness*, the macaroni jollity of *Private Angelo* and the sombre *Roll of Honour* – now appear much more a piece. A word which he liked was inenarrable, or untellable, and what strikes me is the persistent attempt to convey the inenarrable exorbitance of his feelings.

Had he been born with a poet's head, with tragic brows and an aquiline nose, he would have had a mask to suit his inner being. As it was, the sergeant-major's jaw was surmounted by a massive skull and a nose which he explained as the outcome of 800 years of peasant ancestry exposed to the bulbous gales of Orkney. The physical ideal was subverted before he began, and his spirit met a similar stumbling-block in the weighty Victorian values instilled by his parents. It was little wonder that he raged so furiously, sometimes to be free of the encumbrances, sometimes to make sense of them.

They bred in him a lust for beauty – for the sense of liberation which it conferred and for the model which it offered of the way things should be. No moment exposes him more clearly than when in wartime he found himself alone in the room where Botticelli's "Primavera" had been stored for protection, and stretching up on tiptoe he pressed his lips to those of Spring. He married a beautiful wife, he built and bought houses for their views rather than their suitability as homes, and he purchased pictures even faster than poverty required him to sell them. He kept Highland cattle for their shaggy grandeur, and allowed a succession of elegant, self-possessed Siamese cats to step with impunity across his writing-paper. Even the aggressive pattern of his tweed jackets I suspect of answering some aspiration which he felt to be bold and carefree.

His laugh was always loud and in old age his tears grew copious. He cried at memories of soldiering, at a pipe tune or a reading of *Danny Deever*. Perhaps they sprang in part from an old man's sentimentality, but I also remember the remark made by a neighbour, Donald MacGillivray, a supreme piper and teacher of piping. When he played *The Lament for the Children* Eric was not the only one moved to tears, but it was for him in particular that the piece was performed. "I always like playing for your father," Donald said. "You see, he has the soul for it."

From Linklater's *The Man On My Back* [autobiography, 1941]

[1] "I threw my second bomb, more usefully than the first, and turned to run. I ran so very fast that, although I was the last by a long way to leave the trench, within two hundred yards I had passed several of those who preceded me; including an officer who was looking back with an expression of reluctance that, in the circumstances, appeared strangely ill-timed.

I continued to run till in a mingling of righteous indignation and utter dismay I felt on my head a blow of indescribable force. It was a bullet, and probably a machine-gun bullet; for the rifle-fire of the German infantry was poor.

When I recovered consciousness the surrounding landscape appeared entirely empty. But I could not see very well, and perhaps I was mistaken. A few shots, that were evidently hostile, gave me a rough direction, and with clumsy fingers I took from a pocket in the lining of my tunic a little package of field-dressings. I could not undo it, but stuck it whole on the back of my head, where I judged the wound to be, and kept it in position with my steel helmet, that a chin-strap held tightly on.

Scarcely had I made these arrangements when, my sight growing more foggy, I fell into a water-logged trench. It was deep, and full to the brim, and the sides were so well revetted that I had great difficulty in getting out. I was nearly drowned, indeed, and lost my good rifle there. But the cold water revived me, and now my only feeling of discomfort was extreme weariness. So I threw off my equipment and my tunic, and found progress a little easier. Presently, after walking, as I thought, for many miles, someone came to help me, and I saw a cluster of men in kilt and kilt-apron, who looked familiar. I waved my hand to them. It was the very last, the ultimate remnant of the battalion, and already they were forming for the counter-attack. In the afternoon they recaptured Voormezeele."

[2] "I had decided to live in Orkney for a number of reasons, and one of them was my belief that Scottish writers should live in their own country. My political adventure on behalf of Scottish Nationalism had been ill-judged and ineffectual, but my belief in Scotland, my fondness for it, were none the less genuine, and from the slow exodus to the South, that was draining it of strength, I could subtract at least one. Another reason, which may discount my patriotism – but I wish to be honest – was that in Orkney, as I thought, I could work without much interference at my chosen trade, which above all else was what I wanted. I am in truth a weak-willed and gregarious creature, a temptable thing, and solitude was the only guard I knew against easy amusement and the voice of friends. In Orkney as in a monastery, I said, I shall not easily be seduced."

From Linklater's contribution to Scottish Country *[1935] about an abandoned island in Orkney*

"A school teacher in Gairsay – but there is no school there now – once told me that the ghost of a woman was sometimes to be seen near his hall. She wore a yellow gown, that seemed to hold and reflect a cold light as she walked. Now Sweyn [swordsman and seaman], coming home from raiding in the western seas, brought with him a princess from Man or Ireland, and saffron was the royal colour of Ireland. She may not have liked the rough life in Gairsay, and the noise of eighty men-at-arms [kept by Sweyn]. Or when Sweyn went out to Dublin, and his ships came back without him, her grief may have been so bitter that even death could not quieten it. There are other ghosts in Orkney, but none lonelier than the Irish girl in her cold yellow frock. For now when she walks – if walk she does in these later days – there is none to see her, since the island is deserted by all but sheep, save in a month or two of summer."

Longmuir, Very Rev. Dr James B.
(1907-73)
Church of Scotland minister, born in Larkhall and educated at

Dalziel High School, Motherwell, and Glasgow University. He was ordained and inducted at Swinton, Berwickshire, in 1934, and became principal clerk to the General Assembly in 1955. Elected moderator in 1968, he was the first principal clerk to hold that office for more than 50 years. He was Dean of the Chapel Royal and a chaplain to the Queen in Scotland.

Essay by
R.D. Kernohan

"He was impressive because he never tried to impress." Although supremely competent rather than brilliantly gifted, James Longmuir had a power of character and capacity to be trusted which made him a very influential churchman.

He was a father rather than a leader of the church, a minister who managed to deploy great pastoral gifts even after he became a full-time administrator and senior manager of the notoriously unmanageable Kirk. He was a reluctant yet immensely successful church bureaucrat.

He had his year as moderator of the General Assembly (1968-69) but knew the office's limitations too well to attempt too much. He also had the prestige of a chaplain to the Queen, latterly as dean of the Chapel Royal in Scotland, and was great and good enough to serve on the Royal Commission on the Constitution (the Kilbrandon commission). But it was as principal clerk of the General Assembly that he exercised his influence – usually a gently conservative and moderating one, accepting and guiding change rather than provoking it. He reigned from 1955 to 1972 – years which saw the Kirk consolidate post-war revival and expansion before its slide into decline. He also helped set the tone which ensured that admission of women to the ministry and eldership was a calm and almost painless process.

Jim Longmuir was a Lanarkshire lad who set out to be a lawyer, graduating in law at Glasgow before turning to divinity. He settled congenially into a pastoral ministry and the quieter ways of Berwickshire, as minister of Swinton (1934-52) and then Chirnside, where he remained even after becoming principal clerk. Only in 1962 did he yield to trends of the time demanding a full-time bureaucrat as principal clerk and secretary of the Assembly's general administration committee.

He had become a Territorial Army chaplain before the second world war and his parish ministry was interrupted by army service which took him to France, Italy and Austria. He was mentioned in despatches. Other distinctions included the Territorial Decoration and – in 1959 – appointment as CBE.

Lovell, James
(c1913-72)
Theatre director, born in Canada, though he spent all of his career in the British theatre. He began as a trainee designer in repertory at Manchester. At the time of his death, from head injuries as a result of falling down an unlit tenement stair, he was artistic director of Dundee Rep. He first came to Dundee in 1966 as a guest director and was appointed artistic director in 1970. He produced two documentary-style plays with local themes – *The Tay Bridge Disaster*, 1968, and *McGonagall, McGonagall*, 1969 – as well as many plays from the classical repertoire. His death came a few days after the re-

opening of the theatre following a fire. He was so grateful to the men who had saved the theatre that at the end of the performance he stood at the door with a collecting box on behalf of a firemen's benevolent charity.

Michael J. Barry wrote in *Scottish Theatre* magazine

"His idiosyncrasies frequently puzzled new acquaintances. Actors being directed by him for the first time were often dumbfounded by his habit of expressing chunks of text and intricate directions concerning psychological motivation as a vigorous hand-movement and "dah-di-dah-di-dah-di-dah!" followed by a quick wheel away to someone else's problem. Once they got on his wavelength, however, most actors found him both helpful and invigorating to work with... Jimmy was adept at creating shows in rehearsal – a sort of on-the-spot driving inspiration that lay behind some of his best work."

Low, Sir Francis
(1893-1972)
Journalist, born at Finzean, Aberdeenshire, and educated at Robert Gordon's College, Aberdeen. He joined the *Aberdeen Free Press* in 1910, at the age of 17. In 1916 he was commissioned in the 4th battalion of the Gordon Highlanders, and served in Mesopotamia with the 6th battalion of the Hampshire Regiment. After the war he returned briefly to the *Aberdeen Free Press* as chief reporter, but left Scotland in 1922 to work for *The Times of India*. As the paper's editor, 1932-48, he guided it through the most tempestuous years of India's modern history and turned it into an important forum of national opinion. He was knighted in 1943.

M

Macadam, Sir Ivison
(1894-1974)
Administrator and editor, son of a professor of chemistry at Edinburgh University. He was educated at Melville College, Edinburgh, King's College, London, and Christ's College, Cambridge. During the first world war he served with the City of Edinburgh (Fortress) Royal Engineers and was officer commanding the RE in the Archangel, North Russian expeditionary force, earning three mentions in despatches. He was a key figure in the establishment of the National Union of Students. In 1929 he began a 26-year association with the Royal Institute of International Affairs (Chatham House) as secretary and director-general. He was editor of the *Annual Register of World Events*, 1947-73.

McCallum, David
(c1897-1972)
Violinist, born in Kilsyth, whose first appointment as orchestral leader came with the Scottish Orchestra in 1932, under Sir John Barbirolli. Four years later he left Scotland to work in London, though he briefly rejoined the Scottish Orchestra after the war. In 1948 he was appointed leader of the London Philharmonic

Orchestra, founded a year earlier. His son is the actor David McCallum.

Mac Colla, Fionn
Thomas J. Douglas Macdonald
(1906-75)
Novelist, born in Montrose of a father from the Black Isle and a mother from the Mearns. He trained as a teacher, taught briefly in Ross-shire, and lectured at the Scots College in Palestine before returning to Scotland in 1929. His first novel, *The Albannach*, in which he used the Highlands as the setting for a critical study of contemporary Scotland, was published in 1932 and earned glowing reviews, particularly from C.M. Grieve (Hugh MacDiarmid) who maintained that Mac Colla had been kept back by "a horde of his intellectual inferiors". *And the Cock Crew*, which followed in 1945, had the Clearances as its backdrop. Mac Colla, whose religious background was Plymouth Brethern, converted to Roman Catholicism. An ardent nationalist, he saw the Union and Calvinism as twin enemies hostile to the spiritual well-being of Scotland. His autobiography, *Too Long in this Condition*, combined passion with naivety in equal doses.

From Mac Colla's Too Long in this Condition [1975]

[1] "From very early years I had a profound distrust for 'respectability' and regarded it as the deadliest of the virtues. In any case I had found in my going about among both urban and rural populations, that most of the most colourful people, the people with the richest personalities – and with the greatest charity, understanding, and mercifulness of judgment – were those whom [the Kirk] disdained to own."

[2] "There was forced on my notice at a very early age what would now be called the brain-drain: emigration, the energy drain, the ability drain, the drain of skill, was in full swing. And although I was too young to formulate it in those terms I realised it as what I might call the character drain and the personality drain, the temperament drain. Such able people, the sight of whom was a joy to the eyes, whose voice was joy to the ears and immediately set up a responsive quiver in the breast, whose presence with that of others – but most often rather *more* than others – made the stimulation and the adventure of each day, were continually disappearing as if overnight, and the answer knocked on one's heart – gone to Durban, or Buenos Aires, or Adelaide or my God Stockport or O God not Montreal! Anyway it all added up to *forever*, which was difficult – yes, and bad – for a small child to have to 'take' again and again and again: it made for insecurity."

Macdonald, Agnes M.
(d 1973)
Lexicographer, whose work with W. & R. Chambers began in 1944. She worked first on a completely revised edition of the company's *Etymological English Dictionary*, then on the later stages of the 1952 edition of the *Twentieth Century Dictionary* edited by William Geddie. In 1958 she succeeded Geddie to the editorship. She amassed a considerable amount of new material, taking account of the revolutionary changes in language in the middle decades of the

20th century, finally producing her revised edition of the dictionary in 1972, for which achievement she was awarded the OBE. It was said of her that she gave to British lexicography a well-nigh Johnsonian devotion.

MacDougall, Leslie Grahame
(1896-1974)
Architect, educated at Merchiston Castle School, Edinburgh University, and the School of Architecture at Edinburgh College of Art. A son of Patrick Thomson, of the Edinburgh store, he changed his surname when his wife became chief of the Clan MacDougall in 1953. He set up in practice in Edinburgh in 1926 and designed a wide range of buildings, including the Royal Bank of Scotland headquarters in St Andrew Square, Edinburgh. In 1946 he became an academician of the Royal Scottish Academy. He was a past president of the Royal Incorporation of Architects in Scotland.

MacGregor, Stuart
(c1936-73)
Novelist, poet and physician, who studied medicine at Edinburgh University. His novel, *The Myrtle and the Rose*, was published in 1967 and a collection of his poetry brought together in the volume *Four Points of a Saltire*. He died in a car crash in Jamaica, where he held a staff post in the university department of social and preventive medicine at Kingston. A second novel, *The Sinner*, was published posthumously.

McIntosh, Ian Donald
(1908-75)
Teacher, born in Forres. He was educated at Inverness Academy, Aberdeen University, and Trinity College, Cambridge. From Bradfield College, where he began his teaching career as an assistant master, he moved to Winchester College. In 1953 he returned to Scotland as headmaster of George Watson's College, Edinburgh. He was headmaster of Fettes College, 1958-71.

Mackenzie, Sir (Edward Montague) Compton
(1883-1972)
Novelist, born in West Hartlepool, son of Edward Compton, a well-known actor, and his American wife, Virginia Bateman. His birth was registered in the name Mackenzie after his paternal grandfather, Charles Mackenzie, who had taken the stage name of Henry Compton and who claimed descent from an Episcopal minister of Cromarty.

Having taught himself to read at 22 months (or so he boasted), he was educated at St Paul's School, London, and Magdalen College, Oxford, leaving university with a grant from his father of £150 a year for five years to enable him to pursue a career in literature. Two of the allotted years had been used up before he finally placed a novel, *The Passionate Elopement*, which was published in January 1911. It was the first of more than 100 books which included, as well as fiction, a prodigious output of essays, poetry, biography and travel.

Sinister Street was begun in the following year while he was laid low by acute sciatica, a condition that plagued him for the rest of his life. The *Daily Mail*, which seldom noticed books, singled it out for praise, guaranteeing the novel an immediate commercial success. The stylish low-life adventure attracted the attention of Henry James who hailed Mackenzie as a rising hope of English fiction, though others attacked him for corrupting youth with the use of such daring words as "tart" and "bitch". Some libraries were reluctant to stock the book at first, and its American publisher insisted on bowdlerising the text.

He was received into the Roman Catholic Church in 1914. During the first world war he served in Gallipoli, where he enjoyed chasing spies, and worked for British Intelligence in Greece, later recounting his experiences in a memoir, *Greek Memories*, which led him to be prosecuted under the Official Secrets Act. He escaped with a fine.

By the 1930s he was no longer young, no longer considered daring, no longer the darling of the critics. But the then fashionable view of him as a pot-boiling hack failed to disturb either his enormous popularity with the reading public or his natural ebullience and good humour. He just stuck to the literary grind.

For a while he retired from public view to the Channel Islands. It was from this unlikely vantage point that Mackenzie began to be actively impressed by the merits of Scottish nationalism. In a shrewd presentiment of the second world war, he outlined to an audience in the Usher Hall, Edinburgh, his plan for a Scottish-Irish entente which would act as a barrier against barbarism. This was perfectly in tune with the growth of nationalist sentiment, particularly among the young, at that time and in 1931 he was elected rector of Glasgow University, the first Catholic rector of a Scottish university since the Reformation. In 1933 he rented a cottage at Northbay, Barra, and later bought a house on the island. His love of the Hebrides inspired his whimsical comic novel, *Whisky Galore*, a tremendous hit both as book and film though not nearly so substantial a work as his sextet, *The Four Winds of Love*, published between 1937 and 1945.

Mackenzie scarcely counts as a Scottish writer, though he remains a considerable British one. But for many years after his death he was remembered with affection in Scotland, and particularly in Edinburgh where he lived for part of the year towards the end of his life. He acquired a double ground-floor flat at 31 Drummond Place and transported there his library of thousands of books, which he had been collecting since he was a small child, and which now overflowed from the library into the corridors and basement. Mackenzie was much feted by the Edinburgh literary and artistic establishment and became the city's best-loved figure. Although he failed in an early half-ambition to follow his parents into the professional theatre, he remained a consummate actor with impressive powers of mimicry. Friends who visited Drummond Place marvelled at his "being" a West Highland policeman, an Irish country priest, a government minister, and a simpering peer of the realm, all within five minutes. He was a great lover of Siamese cats and of the gramophone.

From his Edinburgh base he worked on his multi-volume autobiography and embarked on numerous journeys to speaking engagements all over the country. He died on St Andrew's Day and was buried on his beloved Barra on a foul December day. His old friend Calum Johnston, aged 82, played a lament on the bagpipes, then himself died.

From Andro Linklater's *Compton Mackenzie: A life* [1987]

"'Monty laid up his treasure in the hearts of his friends,' wrote Bob Boothby in an obituary, and in the years since his death the warmth of their affection has evidently not dimmed. For them his power to charm the passing moment into intense experience gives him a pre-eminence that cannot be challenged.

His reputation as a novelist is less securely based. In the books written before the First World War he created an adolescent mood which will never be forgotten, and the comedies of Capri and the Western Isles contain parodies which will always seem more convincing than their originals. It is fruitless to wish that he had devoted himself to these strengths and been less prone to distraction and extravagance. He had almost every gift that a great writer requires except the belief that writing is of supreme importance.

His books enabled him to be the sort of public figure he wished to be. They brought him fame and financed, although only just, a dramatic and romantic way of living. Through them he could express his outrage and amusement at the outside world, and repeatedly, in reminiscence both fictive and factual, he used them to render his past permanent. But writing was never an end in itself. Like those other great causes, Catholicism and Nationalism, it became part of the background, a setting for his life as a whole.

In the end it is clear that his true genius was theatrical, but that instead of confining his talents to the stage he created around him a stage on which he could represent himself. However wrong it may be to compare a man's life to a work of art, the comparison is difficult to avoid in the case of Compton Mackenzie. In the quixotic, extravagant performance of his own life he achieved his real masterpiece."

From Wilfred Taylor's *Scot Easy* [1955]

[1] "One of the many nice things about Sir Compton is that he does not dwell in the glory of past achievements. I once said to him that someone had written that it was a pity he didn't produce another *Sinister Street*, a book which had made a notable impact on a whole generation. He shrugged his shoulders impatiently and said, 'Ach! Any bright young man at Oxford could write a *Sinister Street*. I have done that and why should I do it again? It takes far more skill than people realise to turn to a completely new medium and write funny books.' It wasn't true, of course, that any bright young man could write another *Sinister Street*, but I did agree with him that it requires a great mastery of technique to write popular funny books."

[2] "All his life, since he was a very young man, Sir Compton has been successful. He takes his success for granted and he has enjoyed it but has never allowed it to corrupt him. To trade on his reputation would be unthinkable. He is far too preoccupied with the present and the future to worry about the past. He is a happy man who knows he has led an extraordinarily rich life."

From Ivor Brown's *The Way of My World* [1954]

"I like to think of talkers in terms of the stream. Listening to Sir Compton Mackenzie has caused me to believe that the Mackenzie River in full spate is one of the richest floods of our time."

MacKenzie, Rev. Kenneth
(c1921-71)
Church of Scotland missionary, born in Strathpeffer and educated at Dingwall Academy. He was a missionary in Malawi, 1946-56, and became not only an authority on African affairs but a leading opponent of apartheid. On his return to Scotland he was minister of Old Restalrig Parish Church, Edinburgh.

Mackie, George W.
(1911-71)
Golfer, educated at Loretto School, who was known to his fellow competitors as "Squiggles". An accomplished amateur competitor, he won the Gleneagles Silver Tassie in 1939 and played for Scotland in the home international series in 1948 and 1950, captaining the Scottish team a few years later. He was captain of the Royal and Ancient Golf Club at the time of his death.

MacKinnon, Georgina Russell Davidson
(1885-1973)
Company director and farmer, educated in London and at Wick Academy. She was chairman of the Drambuie Liqueur Company and a farmer of pedigree Jersey cattle, as well as a celebrated hostess. In 1968 she entertained to tea the entire Gurkha detachment appearing at the Edinburgh military tattoo. When the nine-hole golf course at Linlithgow, near her home, was threatened with closure because the farmer who owned it wanted to plough it up, she promptly bought the land and made additional ground available so that the course could be extended to 18 holes.

Maclagan, Professor William Gauld
(1903-72)
Philosopher, son of a minister, educated at the City of London School, Exeter College, Oxford, and Edinburgh University, where he began his academic career as an assistant in the Department of Logic and Metaphysics. He was professor of moral philosophy at Glasgow University, 1946-69. In 1961 he published *The Theological Frontier of Ethics*.

McLaren, Moray David Shaw
(1901-71)
Author, playwright and critic, born in Edinburgh, son of a surgeon, educated at Merchiston Castle School, Edinburgh, and Corpus Christi College, Cambridge. He continued his studies in Paris. A convert to Roman Catholicism, he contemplated studying for the priesthood, and although he abandoned this ambition remained a devout Catholic. His first job was as assistant editor of the *London Mercury* under Sir John Squire. He entered the BBC in 1928, joined *The Listener* on the foundation of the magazine the following year, and in 1933 returned to Edinburgh as the BBC's first programme director for Scotland. After two years he transferred back to London as assistant director, talks, then worked for features and drama, but he was turned down as head of the BBC in Scotland – some claimed for religious reasons. An enthusiast for all things Polish, he was attached to the Foreign Office in 1940 as head of the Polish region

political intelligence department. After the war he returned to live in Edinburgh and write. His varied output included novels, short stories, biographies and travel books, as well as the *Shell Guide to Scotland*. For one of of his books, *The Highland Jaunt*, he toured Scotland on a horse. Among his plays, *One Traveller Returns* redomiciled Hamlet in a Scottish mental asylum. It was said of him that he was a romantic, a dreamer and a defender of lost causes, a man who brought style to living. He was married to the actress Lennox Milne.

John Grierson on McLaren

"I read the other day that someone wrote 'like polished walnut'. One thing you can say about Moray McLaren is that he does not write like polished walnut. He just lets go and there are his words all over you...As a stumblebum myself I am fascinated by the free-wheeling ease with which he does it. 'No hands,' says he, and he's up the hill and down the dale of the words as footloose, free and unfurrowed in the forehead as if he had taken a double first from a psychiatrist."

From Wilfred Taylor's *Scot Easy* [1955]

[1] "He [McLaren] has told me that he knows no Greek but I feel he would have been completely at home among the philosophers with the tongue-twisting names. He shares their passionate determination to get down to the grass roots and to present the human dilemma in eloquent and elegant language."

[2] "It was Moray who was responsible for Macpherson's Law, in my opinion one of the great and comforting discoveries of modern philosophy...Moray first glimpsed the Law in all its grandeur when he was an undergraduate at Cambridge. As he told me, he was lying on a *chaise longue*, wearing a brocaded dressing gown, in his room one night when a sudden sunburst of insight came to him. He had been reflecting on the curious fact that whenever a round of drinks had to be paid for McLaren had to foot the bill, or whenever a taxi-driver, having driven a number of convivial souls home, demanded his fare, McLaren, being the last, had to fork out. The more he ruminated the more convinced he became that these things happened not fortuitously but as an expression of a great design. In the lesser misfortunes and afflictions of life McLaren had to be sacrificed on the altar."

From McLaren's *The Highland Jaunt* [1954]

"Though I completely trusted my air-minded and prison-breaking companion I was extremely uncomfortable. I had torn a hole in my waterproof leggings the last time that I had mounted; and that hole was on the windward and rainward side of me. My left leg became waterlogged, my riding-gloves turned to pulp, and (gloomy thought for the future in these remote parts) my parcel of snuff which I had carried in a large so-called grease-proof packet got soaked through. Snuff that has been watered and then dried is useless; and snuff is to me what ordinary tobacco is to the smoker. The cold even at this period of the Autumn was intense, and we could not see more than a hundred yards in front of us. Through the rain a stag rose up in front, and after stamping contemptuously drove his hinds off. I did not quite like this; for though my companion was equal to any modern emergency I did not think that even he could cope with an angry male red deer in the middle of the rutting season; nor did I fancy myself in the role of a matador in so remote a spot."

From McLaren's *Understanding the Scots: a guide for South Britons and other foreigners* [1972]

"When all is said and done, if we are going to have a national get-together day, the birthday of a poet is not a bad date to choose. As a man who makes his living by his pen I have always been pleased and rather proud that the largest public monument to any Scotsman (to any man) in the Capital of Scotland should have been put up to a novelist, Walter Scott. One may or may not approve of the preposterous architecture of this monument in Princes Street, but one does approve of the sentiment that erected it. One may not approve of the forms many Burns day celebrations take, but it is something to be grateful for that it is a poet's birthday which is being celebrated and not a politician's."

Thoughts of McLaren

[1] "The paradox of Scotland is the combination of its high intellectual quality and its perpetually present barbarous background. The savage is always nearer to the front of any Scotsman's mind than in an Englishman's."

[2] To be a student at Glasgow University today [1932] is, to my mind, more enviable than to be the wisest and most cultivated don in all Oxford or Cambridge."

[3] "I know too well in my own nature that sense of reserve in the presence of a stranger which can come over any Scotsman so suddenly. It is the result of being a member of a small race that has always had to struggle for its independence and whose enemies have always lain in the South."

Maclean, Brigadier Alasdair Gillean Lorne
(c1902-73)
Soldier and producer, who grew up on Mull and was educated at Wellington. After two years at Sandhurst, he joined the Cameron Highlanders in 1920. He served in the army for 33 years, including postings to Burma and Japan, commanding the 1st battalion, Queen's Own Cameron Highlanders during the second world war. Later he served as ADC to the Viceroy of India. When the Edinburgh International Festival was established, there were attempts to establish a small military tattoo on the Castle esplanade. In 1950 Maclean became its organising director and set out to establish the annual event on a more ambitious scale. He retired from the army in 1953 and was at once appointed full-time producer, travelling the world in search of items for the programme. His other interests included piping and curling, and he was chairman of the Scottish Official Board of Highland Dancing.

McLean, Lex
Alexander McLean Cameron
(c1907-75)
Comedian who began by acting as a "feed" in halls and little theatres from Arbroath to Rothesay. In 1948 he took his own show on the road. He became the mainstay of the Pavilion Theatre, Glasgow, Scotland's last commercial theatre, where it was said that his robust comedy act was as blue as the jerseys of his favourite football team. At the height of his popularity he could command £2,000 a week. He lived in Helensburgh where, by his own account, "it's so posh the men go for fish suppers with their brief cases". He never gave his age away.

Essay by
William Hunter

Latecomers at a Lex McLean show suffered as his stooges, especially if they were unlucky enough to be bald or fat or had stayed too long in the bar. They became fair game for a laugh. It was his best knack as a comic. For he had a rare skill to make himself appear to be part of his audience in an energetic way which was often aggressive. He said: "You've got to hit them with the pail to make them forget all their problems." Besides, he had started as a stooge, feeding an earlier generation of funny men.

His stage foils he used well and often unselfishly from wee Jimmy Carr and Glen Daly, a Glasgow-Irish tenor, to Walter Carr, an actor, when the king of comedy had late, almost reluctant, success on television. His natural habitats were the Pavilion and Empress theatres, Glasgow, Edinburgh's Palladium, the Tivoli, Aberdeen, and the Gaiety, Ayr. With him old-time music hall passed away.

Born in Clydebank, he soon decided shipyard work was not for him. He took to show business as a musician, a piano player who picked up accordion and clarinet no bother. Later, in a chaos of hilarity, he could have his fans misty-eyed by singing a soppy song. He was darkly intense and good-looking for a Scotch comic (normally a disadvantage); a womaniser. Off-stage, he became withdrawn and looked sad. He seldom said much unless he had to.

He fought audiences. Undone by a torrent of patter, they could not help themselves from laughing. His bag of gags was bottomless. Defencelessness was induced by a percussive roll of wisecracks, topical allusions, fitba' insults, total nonsense, inspired ad libs, sudden asides, sheer rudeness, daft whimsy, personal sharpness that could cut to the quick. He embedded *mince* in the vernacular as a word of abuse.

Sexy Lexy became a nickname he learned to accept, not that he had much choice. Not that he told dirtier jokes than other comics, he indicated them better. He could signal a blue one with his eyebrows. His mastery of double meanings and lewd looks was complete. He could have 'em shrieking by silently mouthing the words. Even his most robust turns had in them golden moments of silence. When he appeared as a doll, or unmarried lady, the double entendres were end-to-end. Age was not allowed to curtail lusty appetite. As a venerably frail character, often an ancient shepherd, he would confess: "In the Boer war they put stuff in our tea to keep us from chasing the Zulu women. I think it's beginning to work."

Brief bouts of stage modesty endeared him. Coming to the front of the curtain to work alone after a production number, he would say for openers something like: "Awe right, now you can get tore into your caramels." He was a universal comic in the sense that his humour travelled as far as even England and was enjoyed by people of all sorts of social pretensions. He filled the Palladium during an Edinburgh Festival at a time when vaudevillians felt it only prudent to leave town.

His still mien when not working seemed a mystery. He looked, as he might have said, as if somebody had stolen his scone. Bringing laughter to others emptied him of his own.

Macleod, Robert Duncan
(d 1973)
Librarian, born in Greenock. He was first librarian to the Carnegie

United Kingdom trustees, helped to start library training classes in Glasgow, edited the *Library Review*, and promoted other library activities. As honorary secretary of Scottish PEN he made a vigorous contribution to Scottish culture as a whole. He wrote books on library history, a history of the Scottish publishing houses, and a biography of John Davidson.

From William Power's *Should Auld Acquaintance* [autobiography, 1937]	"Contemporary Scottish literature made a brave show at the exhibition of Scottish books held in Messrs W. and R. Holmes's bookshop in Dunlop Street under the auspices of the *Glasgow Evening News*, and opened by Hugh Walpole. Its organisation was largely due to my friend Robert D. Macleod, founder of the *Library Review*, a first-rate quarterly which is published in Coatbridge and which circulates in about thirty countries 'from China to Peru'. R.D. Macleod, who has done good work for PEN, combines Celtic fire with Norse realism, and prefers to work rather than talk."
From Macleod's *The Scottish Publishing Houses* [1953]	"We must honour the old pioneers, many-sided men, who combined in their work the arts of printing, publishing, bookbinding and bookselling, and who were also in instances truly great scholars. The best of them, like old Andrew Myllar, travelled far to learn their lessons; Robert and Andrew Foulis we know to have travelled on the continent four times."
From Macleod's *John Davidson* [1957]	"John Lane of the Bodley Head early appreciated his [Davidson's] quality, and Davidson worked hard and soon found a circle of friends that took him to Fleet Street where he is said to have become one of the most popular figures of the time. But these were years of desperate struggle. There were those who knew of his embarrassments. Others did not. He may have wassailed with his cronies, but all the time a rather desperate spirit was developing in him..."

McMichael, Hugh
(c1901-71)
Political journalist, son of an Edinburgh town councillor, educated at George Watson's College and George Heriot's School. He entered journalism as a youth and joined *The Scotsman* in 1922. With his appointment as parliamentary correspondent 10 years later, he began a long career at Westminster, reporting the premierships of both Ramsay MacDonald and Harold Wilson. For a time, he was also the paper's London editor.

McMillan, William
(1887-1977)
Sculptor, born in Aberdeen and educated at Gray's School of Art and the Royal College of Art. He was elected a member of the Royal Academy in 1933. His works include the George V Statue, Calcutta; the Beatty memorial fountain in Trafalgar Square; statues of King George VI in Carlton Gardens, London, of Sir Walter Raleigh in Whitehall, and of Lord Trenchard at the Victoria Embankment.

McNeill, Florence Marian
(1885-1973)
Folklorist and cookery writer, born in Orkney, a daughter of the manse. After graduating at Glasgow University she spent two years

in France and Germany. While in London as a social worker, 1913-17, she became an organiser in the women's suffrage movement, was secretary of the Association for Moral and Social Hygiene, and conducted an inquiry into the protection of girls in English and Welsh towns. Further travels followed – to Greece, Egypt and Palestine – before she returned in Scotland in 1926. She worked for a time on the staff of the Scottish National Dictionary. In 1929 she made her name as the author of *The Scots Kitchen* in which she brought together many traditional Scottish recipes. Between 1956 and 1970 she produced a four-volume work on Scottish folklore, *The Silver Bough*. Her other books included a history of Iona and a semi-autobiographical novel, *The Road Home*. She was closely involved in the movement for self-government, founded the Clan MacNeil Association of Scotland in 1932, and was a prime mover in the revival of the tradition of New Year revels at the Tron Kirk in Edinburgh.

Recipe from McNeill's *The Scots Kitchen* [1929]

KIPPER CREAMS
Kippered herring, eggs, salt and pepper, thick cream or white sauce, parsley
Remove the skin and bone from a plump kipper and rub the flesh through a sieve. Add two egg yolks, pepper, little or no salt (if the fish is highly cured), two tablespoonfuls of thick cream or white sauce, and the well-beaten white of one egg. Mix well and turn into little paper cases. Bake in a moderate oven to a light golden brown. Sprinkle with finely chopped parsley and serve on fish paper, or turn on to small round oatcakes made hot and crisp in the oven and buttered.

From McNeill's *The Road Home* [1932]

"Morag was not long in realising that in college, as in the world outside, there was a tendency for people to divide into two camps, the sheep and the goats. The sheep were the douce, decorous ones, the steady workers; their motto, selected for them by the goats:
  'How doth the little busy bee
  Improve the shining hour'
The goats were the worldly-minded ones, the slackers; their apologia, made by one of their number in the pages of the University Magazine:
  'The ne'er-do-weel, who never cared a jot,
  The first-class Honoursman, who thought he thought,
  Have passed alike from pulpit and from pub,
  And equal daisies mark their funeral plot.'
A few sheep and goats browsed amicably together on the border of their respective pastures, but on the whole the flocks kept apart and eyed each other with more or less disapproval.
Morag having spent most of her life in the sheep-fold, where she had frequently chafed at her barriers, felt strongly tempted, now that the gate was ajar, to slip out to the other side. She was not at all sure that she was a goat, but at least, she thought, it would be amusing to run about in a goat-skin."

MacNicol, Rev. Dr William
(c1885-1972)
Minister, born in Alexandria and educated at Glasgow University. He began his ministry as assistant at the Barony Church, Glasgow, and was later inducted to the Chapel of the Gairioch. He served as

a chaplain in France during the first world war. In 1925 he became minister at Longforgan, a charge from which he retired in 1963 after an active ministry in the Church of Scotland of 51 years. He was at various times secretary of the business committee and principal clerk of the General Assembly. At the age of 81, a year after the death of his wife, he re-married his former secretary.

Macphail, Dr Katherine
(1888-1974)

Physician, born in Coatbridge, third of four daughters of a doctor, who took her medical degree at Glasgow University in 1911. At the outbreak of the first world war she went to Serbia with the Scottish Women's Ambulance Unit and worked among the wounded in Kragujevac. She moved to Belgrade to help fight the typhus epidemic, caught typhus herself, and was invalided back to Scotland. Nothing daunted, she returned to the Balkans later in the war and ran medical clinics for the women and children living in remote mountain villages behind enemy lines in Macedonia.

When peace came to Belgrade, many thousands of children were in need of help. Dr Macphail, with £25 in her pocket, set up a makeshift hospital in a disused, bug-ridden army barracks and soon had beds for 30 patients as well as a large out-patients department. Save the Children, hearing of "the sturdy young Scotswoman for whom the impossible was a challenge and difficulties existed only to be overcome", decided to support the hospital financially and, at critical moments, helped it to survive.

From its tiny beginnings, her initiative grew into the Anglo-Yugoslav Children's Hospital, for many years the only children's hospital in the country, which treated 170,000 children and trained hundreds of Yugoslav nurses before it was sold to the Ministry of Public Health in 1933.

Dr Macphail, with the money raised by the sale, built a special hospital at Sremska Kamenica, 50 miles from Belgrade, for children suffering from tuberculosis of the bones and joints. During the early stages of the second world war, with Yugoslavia threatened by invasion, she heroically stayed at her post until 27 March, 1941, when the government was overthrown. A week later bombing began near her hospital. When she attempted to leave the country she was interned by the Italians, but was eventually repatriated to Scotland.

In 1945 she led a Save the Children team back into Yugoslavia and resumed her work at Kamenica. She had developed a deep feeling for the country and its people, and fully intended to devote the rest of her career to the hospital, but the post-war government refused to tolerate a privately run hospital and in 1947 it was taken over by the state. Dr Macphail, for whom this was a source of grief, had no alternative but to return to Scotland. Kamenica continued as a working hospital, even if few of its visitors knew why a Scottish lion rampant was patterned in red on its mosaic floor.

Professor Svetislav Stoyanovic said "The name and personality of Dr Katherine Macphail, this modest and generous, tenacious and resolute Scotswoman, as enduring as the granite of her beautiful homeland, have become part of the national and medical history of Serbia."

Macphail's account of attempted escape from Yugoslavia, April 1941, in *The World's Children* magazine [1942]

[1] "Our journey by train, which lasted two days and two nights, was uncomfortable and crowded. At all the little railway stations raw peasant youths making their way to the regiments crowded in and there was no possibility of sleep for any of us. As we neared Sarajevo someone came along the train and told me that a baby had just been born. I went along and found the mother with her newborn baby in her arms looking pale and exhausted. She had with her another small child and a sick husband sitting helplessly by. She told me he had been turned out of the civil hospital two days before to make room for the military, and that her husband was an advanced case of tuberculosis. He was so ill he looked as if he had only a few days or hours to live. That morning their little house in the centre of Belgrade had been bombed to pieces and they had fled with a few of their household goods and were going to his native village in the mountains of Bosnia. I roused a large soldier in the compartment who had slept through the whole proceeding, so as to let the woman lie down and recover from her exhaustion. The last we saw of them was at a wayside station, a pathetic little group patiently waiting for some means of transport to take them up to their mountain village."

[2] "As night drew on we settled in our strange quarters [in an out-of-the-way village] to wait, and some went to bed and others sat about on top of their suitcases. We had no lights and were scattered about in dark, poverty-stricken houses. The people were kind to us and shared with us everything they had to eat, which was a strange soup and black bread. Then at 11 o'clock that night we heard voices calling us to collect at the village inn as we were to embark at once. We gathered together by the light of candles and then began our exit into the pitch dark night. We had four miles to go to the quay...When we arrived at the quay we could dimly make out the rigging of two motor sailing ships which the Yugoslavs had put at our disposal to take us out to the open sea to meet the hoped-for destroyer. We were embarked, crowded into a small space, and many of those who had hoped to go with us had to be left behind, with many regrets...We reached the mouth of the Gulf by dawn but on the horizon there was no sign of the destroyer, which never came, and so we landed again at Herzignovi, the little port which we had left the day before, and resigned ourselves to be taken prisoners by the Italians who took possession of the town the next day."

Macpherson, Sir John
(1898-1971)
Colonial civil servant, born in Edinburgh and educated there at George Watson's College and Edinburgh University. His service with the Argyll and Sutherland Highlanders during the first world war gave him a spinal injury which caused him great pain for the rest of his life and forced him to wear a steel corset. As a result of the wound he was also completely deaf in one ear. He spent two years in the Colonial Office in London before a succession of important and politically sensitive posts abroad, including chief secretary of Palestine and governor of Nigeria. In Nigeria his efforts to lay proper foundations for independence earned him widespread respect. In particular he saw that Nigerians were trained in sufficient numbers for senior civil service posts. In 1956 this devoted

servant of the Commonwealth was appointed permanent under-secretary of state for the Colonies. Debonair of manner, he was described in one obituary as "a Scot of Scots, endowed with all the toughness and tenacity of the best of his race".

Macrae, Dr Angus
(1893-1975)
Physician and medical administrator. Born in Lochearnhead, a son of the manse, he was educated at McLaren High School, Callander, and George Watson's College, Edinburgh. During the first world war he was wounded and taken prisoner while serving with the 4th Seaforth Highlanders. After the war he resumed his studies, graduating in medicine at Edinburgh University, and joined the National Institute of Industrial Psychology as an investigator. In 1935 he began a long association with the British Medical Association, first as assistant secretary, then as deputy secretary, finally succeeding Dr Charles Hill, MP, as secretary in 1950. He retired in 1958.

McWilliam, Sir John
(1910-74)
Local politician and public servant, a native of Clydebank. He moved to Fife to become managing secretary of the Kirkconnel, Lochgelly and Dunfermline Co-operative Societies. In 1950 he was elected to Fife County Council and became county convener. Among his other public offices, he was the first chairman of the Countryside Commission for Scotland, chairman of the Forth Ports Authority, and deputy chairman of Glenrothes Development Corporation. He was knighted in 1970.

Mains, John
(c1913-72)
Local politician and public servant, born in the Gorbals district of Glasgow, who left school at 14 to serve an apprenticeship and went to sea as a marine engineer. When his name was put forward as a Labour candidate for Glasgow Corporation, he was dismissed from a job at the government-owned Blantyre industrial estate because workers in nationalised industries were not allowed to take part in politics. Nevertheless he turned out to be a highly successful leader of the Labour group in Glasgow. In 1969, when he assumed the leadership, his demoralised party held only 38 seats out of 111. By the time of his death it had increased its representation to 79. In 1957 he led the city's mass radiography campaign against tuberculosis, more than a million people being screened compared with a target of 250,000. As education convener he took charge of the expansion of the school building programme, an achievement for which he was awarded a fellowship of the Educational Institute of Scotland. He was equally effective as parks convener, overseeing the creation of 500 acres of new parks and setting up many children's playgrounds. He pushed through the decision to get rid of "keep off the grass" signs and allowed Sunday games in the parks. When he died only nine weeks after being elected lord provost, he was lauded as a man of the people, in many ways typical of the city he served.

Mansfield and Mansfield, 7th Earl of
Mungo David Malcolm Murray
(1900-71)

Landowner and politician, educated at Christ Church, Oxford. Before he succeeded to the earldom he entered the Commons as Lord Scone, Unionist member for Perth, and was instantly recognisable as the one wearing the silk hat on the second bench below the gangway. He founded the top hat club, an organisation of young MPs whose objective was to improve the sartorial appearance of Parliament. His other passions included agriculture, of which he had a practical knowledge, the preservation of game (he deplored the methods employed by deer poachers) and foreign affairs. He sat on many committees, nationally as well as locally, serving such diverse interests as children, mental patients, birds, salmon, and cacti. A frequent correspondent to the press on subjects varying from murder to party politics, he championed the cause of such organisations as the British Society of Monarchists, the Society for Individual Freedom and, less contentiously, the Church of Scotland, as Lord High Commissioner to the General Assembly, 1961-62. He owned banana plantations in Jamaica, which he visited periodically. His principal residence, Scone Palace, was damaged by fire in 1942 and he spent 12 years restoring it. One of his obituaries stated that he was a Scot notably representative of his class.

Mar, 30th Earl of
James (Clifton) of Mar
(1914-75)

Premier earl of Scotland, educated at Marlborough. He farmed in Kenya for 20 years, returning to Scotland in 1965 when he succeeded to the title on the death of his cousin. His first marriage ended in divorce and two years later he married the widow of a major in the Indian army. While living in Haddington with his second wife he helped out his friend, the landlord of the George Hotel, becoming a temporary barman for a short period. Among the recreations he listed in *Who's Who* was "kicking pigeons". The earl died after falling from the window of his fifth floor flat in Knightsbridge. His wife told the Westminster coroner that he had drunk five large whiskies the night before, about his usual amount, and they had gone to bed about 10.30. Early the next morning she was aware of him sitting on the edge of the bed for a while. Then she heard a door open and about five minutes later wondered what he was doing and got up. The window of the sitting room was wide open. She looked out and saw her husband sprawled on the road 50 feet below. She said the earl was healthy, financially secure, and had no thought of taking his life. The coroner concluded that there was insufficient evidence as to the exact circumstances of the fall and an open verdict was recorded.

Martin, Maj.-Gen. John Simson Stuart
(1888-1973)

Soldier and physician, educated at Oban High School, in Australia, and at Edinburgh University. He entered the Indian medical service in 1912, becoming regimental medical officer to Sam Browne's cavalry. When the first world war began, he was sent to

Mesopotamia, captured by the Turks at the siege of Kut-el-Amara, and held for three years. Afterwards he returned to India and played an important part in the reorganisation of the country's medical service. During the second world war he was responsible for the medical needs of 60,000 men of the 14th Army and for a rapid and massive expansion of hospital facilities. Retiring to Skye in 1945, he bought and farmed a 5,000-acre estate.

Matthew, Sir Robert Hogg
(1906-75)
Architect, educated at Melville College, Edinburgh, and Edinburgh College of Art. He joined the Department of Health for Scotland in 1936 and was appointed chief architect and planning officer in 1945. The following year he left Scotland to take up a similar post with London County Council. He returned to Edinburgh as Forbes professor of architecture at Edinburgh University, 1953-68.

Essay by
Miles Glendinning

Sir Robert Matthew was Scotland's most important architect of the post-1914 era, a major participant in the establishment of Modernist concepts of architecture and planning in Britain and the Commonwealth, and a significant player in international architectural and cultural diplomacy during the Cold War and decolonisation periods.

Robert, the strong-willed eldest son of J.F. Matthew, partner of Robert Lorimer, was steeped from childhood in the crafts-influenced values of the "Traditionalist" architectural dynasty of turn-of-century Edinburgh, and witnessed during his youth the designing of the late masterpieces of that movement, such as the Scottish National War Memorial (1924-27). However, after studying architecture at Edinburgh College of Art, Matthew became committed to the very different architectural doctrine of the Modern Movement, with its collectivist social principles of rationalist design, state patronage and strategic planning, and its forcible rejection of the *laissez-faire* values of 19th-century architecture.

In 1936 he joined the Department of Health, the section of the Scottish devolved government administration which oversaw housing and planning. There he indefatigably promoted the cause of Modernist architecture (rising by 1945 to the post of DHS chief architect), beginning work in 1944 with Sir Patrick Abercrombie on the Clyde Valley regional plan, the foundation of the drive for Modern regional planning and new towns in Scotland.

In 1946 the young Matthew seized a further opportunity for a dramatic advance in his career when he secured the post of architect to the London County Council, then arguably the most prestigious public architectural post in the British Empire. He set about making the LCC a pioneer of Modern architecture in Britain, exploiting both the grand status of the Royal Festival Hall project (1948-51) and the social prestige of the renowned housing projects (such as Roehampton, from 1949) produced by the *avant-garde* young designers attracted to his department. In 1953, having turned the LCC into a hothouse of innovation, he returned home to Scotland, taking up academic posts at Edinburgh University and College of Art, and beginning his own private practice (his first job being the now-demolished Turnhouse Airport, 1953-56, a "regionalist" Modern design in rubble and timber).

It was from the late 1950s that he entered the period of his greatest influence. His private practice, from 1956 in partnership with the former government architect Stirrat Johnson-Marshall, burgeoned into one of the first large Modernist multi-disciplinary private practices geared towards state-sponsored social building: it involved itself in the full range of projects, from power stations and new universities to urban redevelopment areas – including the controversial rebuilding plans for Edinburgh's George Square (executed from 1960).

From the early 1960s Matthew launched into a career as an architectural diplomat dedicated to the proselytising of social-democratic values in the built environment; he presided over the International Union of Architects (UIA) from 1961, at a time of Cold War tensions between "east" and "west" members, and founded the Commonwealth Association of Architects (from 1965), with its decolonising and emancipatory aspirations. From the late 1960s, with the growing public crisis of confidence in Modern architecture and replanning throughout the west, Matthew returned to his Lorimerian and Traditionalist roots by becoming increasingly involved with conservation issues at home in Scotland: his greatest achievement in this final period of his career was the foundation of the Edinburgh New Town Conservation Committee, in 1970.

Maxwell, Maj.-Gen. Sir Aymer
(1891-1971)

Soldier, educated at the Royal Military Academy, Woolwich. Commissioned in the Royal Artillery in 1911, he served in both world wars and won the MC. He was chairman of the British Legion, Scotland, and convener of the County Council of the Stewartry of Kirkcudbright, the fifth member of the Maxwell family to hold this post. He was knighted in 1957.

Mercer, Sir Walter
(1890-1971)

Orthopaedic surgeon, born at Stow, Midlothian, where his father owned a tweed mill, and educated at George Watson's College and Edinburgh University. He was one of the pioneers of cardiac surgery in Scotland, a distinguished president of the Royal College of Surgeons of Edinburgh and author of a standard textbook on orthopaedic surgery.

Essay by
I. F. MacLaren

Sir Walter Mercer was one of the most distinguished Scottish surgeons of the 20th century who, through his astonishing clinical versatility and almost uncanny operative dexterity, became a legendary figure in his own lifetime.

During the first world war he saw service as a regimental medical officer in some of the bloodiest battles on the western front and part of his time in the trenches was spent with a battalion of the Royal Scots Fusiliers commanded for several months by Winston Churchill. Towards the end of the war he was seconded to the surgical division of a base hospital and this was the start of what was to become a brilliantly successful surgical career.

In 1921 he obtained the fellowship of the Royal College of

Surgeons of Edinburgh and four years later he was appointed to the staff of the Royal Infirmary of Edinburgh as assistant surgeon in the wards of Professor John (later Sir John) Fraser. In the professorial unit he had responsibility for the treatment of all fractures and most of the orthopaedic cases but he did not restrict himself to this specialised field and soon he developed a reputation for outstanding technical skill in many different areas of surgery. In 1932 he published his famous book *Orthopaedic Surgery*, which ran to six editions in his lifetime and was translated into several foreign languages. For many years this was the foremost British didactic text in orthopaedics and it was a remarkable achievement for a single author.

Mercer was a popular and effective clinical teacher at the bedside but, although his formal lectures were meticulously prepared and always well delivered, he did not greatly enjoy this mode of teaching. The development of his reputation and its extension far beyond the confines of Edinburgh greatly enlarged his private practice but the demands of this were never allowed to encroach upon the time he devoted to his work for the Royal Infirmary and other voluntary hospitals.

In the 1930s he was the foremost Scottish exponent of the new specialty of thoracic surgery and having in 1938 become surgeon in ordinary to the Royal Infirmary with charge of his own wards he was one of the first surgeons in Scotland to achieve the successful operative treatment of congenital cardiac disease.

His workload during the second world war, with many of his younger colleagues away serving in the armed forces, was prodigious and covered every field of surgery except for neurosurgery. In modern times there has never been a "general" surgeon who more thoroughly deserved that descriptive term but such was his reputation in the specialty of orthopaedic surgery that in 1948 the University of Edinburgh appointed him as the first incumbent of the newly established Law chair of orthopaedic surgery.

Until 1951 he continued with his general surgical activities but thereafter devoted himself solely to orthopaedic surgery and to the development in Edinburgh of a first-class academic department which is his lasting monument today. His other outstanding professional achievement was his presidency, from 1951 to 1956, of the Royal College of Surgeons of Edinburgh, and he has a strong claim to be regarded as the greatest holder of this office in modern times. He transformed the college from being an inward-looking and somewhat parochial institution concerned only with examinations into a vigorous and vibrant centre of higher surgical education with a prestige and influence which today extends worldwide.

During his presidency there occurred the 450th anniversary of the college's foundation in 1505 and he was responsible for the planning and organisation of the outstandingly successful celebrations which marked this important occasion. Honours and distinctions came to him thick and fast. In 1956 he was knighted, but perhaps the two honours that gave him the greatest personal satisfaction were the vice presidency of the British Orthopaedic Association and the presidency in 1963 of the Watsonian Club.

"Wattie", as he was known to his friends, colleagues and students throughout his life, was a slightly built trim figure of a man with a brisk manner and a dry, pawky sense of humour. He inspired the utmost loyalty in all who worked for him and many young surgeons whom he trained achieved notable success.

He was a keen curler and golfer, a skilled fisherman, and an excellent shot, but the sport at which he excelled in his younger days was tennis. His wife, Maisie, whom he married in 1923, was an equally talented tennis player; indeed it was through their partnership in a tournament that they first met. Sir Walter was also a serious philatelist with an impressive collection built up over many years, and he was a recognised authority on Scottish postal history to which, following his retirement in 1958 from the chair of orthopaedic surgery, he was able to devote a considerable amount of time. As he approached his 80th birthday, his physical activity declined but his mind remained fully active until not long before his death in 1971.

Wattie Mercer occupies an honourable place in the history of Scottish surgery and his name will be long remembered in the Edinburgh medical school and by the Royal College for which, as its president, he did so much. He was a caring and compassionate doctor with the gift of inspiring his patients with total confidence and they held him in the same high regard as did his colleagues and his students. He was one of the very last of the great general surgeons and we shall certainly not see his like again.

Middleton, George
(1898-1971)

Trade unionist, born in the Townhead district of Glasgow. He served with the Medical Corps on the Somme late in the first world war. After the war he was actively involved in the communist movement and took part in the hunger marches of the 1920s and '30s. Beginning as a pastry cook in the St Enoch Hotel, Glasgow, he moved from one job to another between the wars, gradually establishing himself as a trade union leader, originally with the Union of Shop, Distributive and Allied Workers. He joined the Labour Party in 1948 and the following year was appointed general secretary of the Scottish Trades Union Congress, a post he held until he retired in 1963. One of Scotland's better known faces, he was once described as the "ugliest looking man ever to appear on television", but delighted in repeating the insult. In his final years he adopted a new if unlikely public persona as chairman of the Herring Industry Board.

Essay by Andrew Hargrave

George Middleton's style, character and political stance were shaped in the harsh environment of pre-war years – mass unemployment, class conflict, the shadow of Nazi Germany, the Spanish civil war, the second world war, and the east-west split that followed.

Born on the north side of Glasgow, son of an Aberdeen printer, Middleton was apprenticed to a baker, hated it, and left for a variety of jobs, interspersed with frequent bouts of unemployment. He worked as a labourer, as a Co-op insurance agent, and with Russian Oil Products (raided in 1928, a reflection of the climate of the day).

Meanwhile he joined the Communist Party, stood in the 1929 general election and also in municipal elections. In the mid-1930s he was full-time industrial organiser of the party: it was then that he became a leading figure in Glasgow Trades Council.

Before and during the war he stayed loyal to the Communist Party, with all its twists and turns, opposing conscription and the "imperialist war", until the Soviet Union itself was invaded. After the war Middleton, a man of powerful if at times limited vision and burning ambition, increasingly felt his party membership blocking his way to the top in an atmosphere of deepening chasm between east and west. In 1948 he became chairman of the STUC general council and was one of the 62 applicants for the post of general secretary vacated by Charles Murdoch after less than two years. The short-leet included James Jack, then a departmental secretary, who succeeded him 14 years later. In the final run-up Middleton beat his long-time adversary, David Currie, by a single vote.

In many ways Middleton was fortunate during his term of office. Post-war reconstruction was in full swing, unemployment at its lowest level ever, the prestige and influence of the trade union movement enhanced. Although Labour was out of office for most of his tenure, there was a powerful consensus on many issues, including the public ownership of utilities and coal, the National Health Service, and full employment.

On the other hand, the STUC was little known on the UK stage and even in Scotland its influence was limited. Middleton's early years as general secretary were spent impressing the trade union movement and general public that this was the wrong image. Disbanding and then re-constituting the powerful and left-wing-dominated Glasgow Trades Council, only a couple of years after demitting its secretaryship, was an early sign of Middleton's determination to show that the STUC was indeed "in charge".

However, Middleton was not satisfied with the STUC confining itself to traditional trade union matters. As he – and the Labour opposition – could not halt the legislative process, he allied himself with erstwhile opponents, including employers' organisations, the Scottish Council (Development and Industry), the Scottish Board for Industry (largely a talking shop for employers and trade unions) and even the steel bosses to get the show for structural change on the road. The main objective was threefold: first, to divert some of the expansion in new industries (e.g. the motor industry) to Scotland – Bathgate, Linwood, and Ravenscraig were monuments to Middleton's tactics of ruthless determination combined with persuasion and a powerful instinct for behind-the-scenes manipulation; then to provide the infrastructure, especially roads, to support these developments, including the Forth and Tay road bridges, and at the same time launch major campaigns against the erosion of the rail network; finally, to bring about major institutional changes – foundations for the Highlands and Islands Development Board (set up in 1965) and even the Scottish Development Agency (set up in 1975) were laid during Middleton's time.

On the other hand, he was dead against political devolution: one wonders if he was influenced by the fact that a Scottish Assembly was being promoted by the miners with whose communist leaders he often clashed on the floor of Congress. At the same time,

Middleton was instrumental in introducing and fostering contact with the Soviet Union and Eastern Europe in the form of exchange visits, delegations to Congress, etc. There was certainly an ambivalence in his attitude: at heart he was a Marxist, in practice he fought home-grown communists (some of whom never forgave his "defection") while trying, with some success, to bridge the east-west divide.

Middleton continued to play a role in Scottish public life during the eight years of his retirement, first as vice-chairman of the Scottish Economic Planning Council set up by the Labour government in 1964, and later as a popular chairman of the Herring Industry Board. Opponents called him unprincipled and ruthless: but most, supporters as well as opponents, agree that George Middleton put not only the STUC but Scotland "on the map" and, in the process, elevated the STUC to top decision-making levels. He hardly exaggerated when he remarked in a report: "Congress projected itself into every domain of economic activity".

For all his bonhomie and outgoing personality, George Middleton remained an intensely private person to the end. He was reluctant to talk about his pre-STUC past: on his retirement he refused this writer any co-operation for a television profile.

From Keith Aitken's The Bairns O' Adam: the story of the STUC, on Middleton

[1] "A bulky, vigorous man with a grin like a deflated football."
[2] "Not uncommonly for one schooled in the Scottish Communist tradition, Middleton's idealism was underpinned by a robust practical belief in the need to focus on attainable rather than distant objectives."
[3] "He projected a bluff, rugged common sense to which a Scottish audience instinctively warmed."

Thoughts of Middleton on his retirement

"Trade unionism to me has always been a movement dedicated to causes and interests with a powerful bond of friendship and understanding existing among those who comprise its membership. No other movement is comparable to that of the trade unions either in cohesion or camaraderie."

Miller, John
(1911-75)
Artist and lecturer, educated at Glasgow School of Art and Hospitalfield Art College, Arbroath. He returned to Glasgow School of Art as a lecturer in drawing and painting and was promoted to senior lecturer in 1972. Every year he took part in the exhibition of the RSW, of which he was once president. He specialised in landscapes, still life and the seascapes visible from his home at Rhu, overlooking the Clyde. His work is included in the permanent collections of Glasgow, Dundee and Paisley Art Galleries.

Milligan, Rt. Hon. Lord
William Rankine Milligan
(1898-1975)
Judge of the Court of Session, son of the Very Rev. George Milligan, of Glasgow, educated at Sherborne. Service in the HLI during the final two years of the first world war interrupted his studies, which were resumed at University College, Oxford. Renowned as an athlete, he was a member of the combined Oxford-Cambridge relay

team which set a world record for two miles in Philadelphia in 1920, ran for Scotland in the same year, and was elected president of the Oxford University Athletic Club. He was admitted to the Faculty of Advocates in 1925, successively Solicitor-General and Lord Advocate, 1951-60, and for the final five years of that period sat as Conservative MP for Edinburgh North. A ready wit, he was known as the joker in the pack of the Scottish bench.

Milne, Sir David
(1896-1972)
Civil servant, born in Edinburgh, a son of the manse, educated at Daniel Stewart's College. His studies at Edinburgh University were interrupted by the first world war, in which he served with the 9th Royal Scots. He was wounded in France. After the war he completed his degree and in 1921 entered the Scottish Office, which at that time was based at Dover House in London. In the mid-1930s Milne headed the new unit of the Scottish Office established at Drumsheugh Gardens in Edinburgh, the first decisive step in the transfer of power to Scotland. He was appointed secretary of the Scottish Home Department in 1942 and permanent under secretary of state for Scotland four years later. He was known as a patient, tactful administrator. Shortly after he retired in 1959 he became the BBC's national governor for Scotland, and in 1964 he chaired a committee of inquiry which investigated the typhoid outbreak in Aberdeen.

From Milne's
The Scottish Office –
and other Scottish
government
departments [1957]

"It is perhaps worth mentioning here that the overwhelming majority of civil servants in the Scottish Office are Scots – born and educated in Scotland and working in Edinburgh. An Englishman once expressed surprise that his first official contact with the Scottish Office had been a voice on the telephone saying 'Oskins ere', but no one walking along the corridors of St Andrew's House would doubt what country he was in. Moreover, the importance of the decision to concentrate the four departments in one building should not be underestimated...undoubtedly the machinery of administration runs all the more smoothly for the countless informal discussions that take place in the rooms, in the corridors or in the canteen (or, as it is rather grandly called, the dining club) of St Andrew's House."

Minto, Countess of
Marion Cook
(c1897-1974)
Charitable organiser, elder daughter of G.W. Cook, a Montreal businessman. She married the 5th Earl of Minto in 1921 when he was ADC to the governor-general of Canada. Largely as a result of her energetic leadership, the Roxburgh branch of the Red Cross sent 5,000 parcels a week to prisoners of war during the second world war. She undertook a wartime goodwill mission to her native Canada, which resulted in many food parcels, dressings and clothing being sent to Britain. When Scotland's Gardens Scheme began in 1931, she was its first convenor. It was the countess who raised the alarm when fire destroyed Melgund House, Minto, in 1955. Her husband survived her by barely a year.

Minto, 5th Earl of
Victor Gilbert Lariston Garnet Elliot-Murray-Kynynmound
(1891-1975)
Landowner and godson of Queen Victoria. He joined the Lothians and Border Horse Yeomanry in 1910 and commanded the Hawick troop until 1913, when he became a lieutenant in the Scots Guards. Five years later he went to Canada as ADC to the Duke of Devonshire, the Governor-General. He was a member of Roxburgh County Council and Deputy Lieutenant of the county, and played an active part in the farming of his 25,000 acre estate near Hawick.

Moffat, Abe
(1896-1975)
Coal-miners' leader and champion of the old age pensioner. Born in Fife, he went down the pit at Lumphinnans as a pit boy at the age of 14. In 1926, the year of the general strike, he joined the Communist Party. He held a variety of offices in both the Scottish and national miners' executive, becoming Scottish president of the union in 1942, and was invariably at the forefront of demands for better wages. His loyalty to the Soviet Union endured all tests and provocations: in 1956, the year of the Hungarian uprising, he topped the poll in voting for the executive of the British Communist Party. His brother, Alex, was elected Scottish vice-president of the NUM in 1957 and together the Moffats ran the union leadership north of the border until Abe retired in 1961. Alex succeeded him as president. In retirement, Abe campaigned for the Scottish Old Age Pensions Association as vigorously as he had done for the miners.

From Moffat's My Life with the Miners [1965]

[1] "Like every other young boy in a mining village, I knew that my pit clothes with piece-box and flask were ready six weeks before I left school, as mining was the only occupation available, and still is in many mining villages.

Within six weeks of commencing work in 1910 at No. 1 Pit, Lumphinnans, I experienced the hazards and risks of miners when I suffered an accident. Fortunately, the large stone that fell did not really strike my body. It was only the tail end of the stone that caught my foot, otherwise it might have been more serious. There was no ambulance available at the time, and my eldest brother Jim had to carry me home on his back from the colliery. Even today I can see my mother's face when I was carried into the house. Grief and pain were in her face as she looked at me, a boy with my black face (we had no pit-head baths to wash in, even when an accident took place). My schoolmaster came to see me and put it to my father that I might return to school; but for the second oldest brother in a family of eleven children this was an impossibility. So after I recovered from the accident I resumed my occupation at the coal face along with my father and eldest brother."

[2] "We had a Frenchman who was a miner and lived in the same village. His name was Laurence Storian. Very short in height, he was an ardent Communist, and he played a part in convincing my eldest brother Jim and me that we should become members of the Communist Party. That was in January, 1922. From the Communist Manifesto I learned that the Communists had no interests separate from the interests of the working class, and in the fight for

immediate aims they took care of the movement for the future, to ensure a continuation of the struggle for the complete emancipation of the working class on the basis of working-class power...I joined the Communist Party at twenty-six years of age, and I have never regretted making this decision."

[3] "...if anyone wants to see miners and their families enjoying themselves, despite hard times (and that goes for today), then they should visit a mining village in Scotland for Hogmanay. It won't matter if you are the biggest stranger in the world, you will be made welcome. In Lumphinnans, I have seen fifty people in our own house, and Helen would make a special dumpling and cook potted meat so that nobody was hungry during the night. When the bells rang at 12 pm, the bottles would get drawn, sometimes before 12, and then the singing and dancing would go on until eight and nine o'clock in the morning. And although I am now sixty-seven years of age, I, my wife and family still carry on this tradition, as it is still done in every mining village."

[4] "Although out of practice, I still appreciate my violin, and can still play the beautiful melodies of 'Bonnie Mary of Argyll' and 'Rowan Tree', which were always my favourite tunes, and several Scottish reels and strathspeys. I appreciate that it was a big sacrifice on the part of my father and mother to spend £5 to purchase a violin for one of their family. That was a great deal of money then. It was a good violin 100 years old when my father bought it, which means it is well over 160 years old now."

Moore, Lt.-Col. Sir Thomas
(1886-1971)
Politician, born of an Irish father and a Scottish mother, educated in Ireland. He joined the regular army in 1908, served in France, Ireland and Russia, was twice mentioned in despatches, and was awarded the CBE. After retiring from the army, he became Unionist MP for Ayr, 1925-64, and sponsored nine acts of Parliament, including one dealing with the humane slaughter of animals. He claimed to have served all the leading animal protection societies in Britain, including the RSPCA of which he was vice-president.

Moran, Frank
(c1885-1975)
Journalist and golf correspondent, who joined *The Scotsman* at the age of 19 and became the doyen of British golf writers. In his early days he reported Saturday afternoon football matches for the *Evening Dispatch*. This was so long ago that he sent the half-time scores back to the office by carrier pigeon. In 1913, while he was working for *The Scotsman* as a general reporter, the correspondent who should have covered the Irish open golf championship for the paper took ill and Moran was given the opportunity to take his place. As a result of this break, he became the paper's golf correspondent shortly afterwards and with a few other pioneers helped to transform reporting of the game from a colourless recitation of scores and weather conditions into a more graphic account of the play. Hogan's victory in the 1922 Open championship was one of the many notable events he reported. He succeeded Bernard Darwin as president of the Association of Golf Writers and

finally retired as golf correspondent, at his own request, on his 80th birthday, while continuing to write a column for his newspaper. He was awarded the MBE.

From Moran's
Golfers' Gallery [1946]

[1] "Andra [Kirkcaldy] used to have a freely expressed contempt for the card-and-pencil golf and was wont to declare that the matches were the 'life's bluid o' the game'. He was certainly a doughty fighter in the money matches. His reply to a member of the R. and A., who asked him if he was not nervous when playing for a big stake before so many people, sums up the Kirkcaldy attitude and character: 'Nervous men should never back themselves. It would be like pickin' their ain pockets. I never gave the crowd a thocht and the money only made me stick to the lead when it came my way.' Andra, in short, was tough. The only time his nerves gave way, he used to say, was at Tel-el-Kebir."

[2] "The crowd who went out with [Abe] Mitchell on the final day [of the 1920 Open championship] to see him win had the shock of their lives; they saw him begin his third round by missing a putt of 18 inches. It was not so much the actual miss as the manner of it that was significant. Mitchell hit the ball about six inches. Looking back on the sensational sequel I again see that putt – the first surprise crack in the Mitchell security. It was like the touch that sets an avalanche in motion, for Mitchell piled up mischances from there to the climax of the fifth hole, where he took an 8."

Moray, 19th Earl of
Archibald John Morton Stuart
(1894-1974)
Farmer, educated at the Royal Naval College, Osborne, and Dartmouth. He entered the Royal Navy in 1907, served in destroyers during the first world war, and took part in the battle of Jutland. After he retired as a lieutenant commander in 1923, he went to Bechuanaland to farm, returning to Scotland in 1943 when he succeeded his brother to the title. Another brother was James Stuart (Viscount Stuart of Findhorn).

Morren, Sir William Booth Rennie
(1890-1972)
Policeman, born in Aberdeen, son of the chief constable of Roxburgh, Berwick and Selkirk. He was a captain in the Royal Scots during the first world war. Following his father into the police, he became chief constable of Edinburgh, 1935-55, and played an important part in the development of the police wireless. He was knighted in 1952.

Morton, Alan
(1893-1971)
Footballer, Scotland's most brilliant outside left and one of the "Wembley wizards" forward line which trounced England 5-1 in 1928. He signed for Queen's Park in 1913 while studying mining engineering and joined Rangers in 1920. After he retired as a player in 1933, he continued his association with Rangers for a further 38 years as a member of the club's board, finally severing his connection six months before his death. He was the only player

invited to the dinner celebrating the Scottish Football Association's golden jubilee.

Essay by Bob Ferrier

Arguably the greatest of the many hundreds of footballers who have played for Rangers in the club's long history, Alan Lauder Morton was the most brilliant of wingers, and dominated the British game in the 1920s in the way that Stanley Matthews and George Best were to do in later decades.

Only 5' 4" tall and seldom more than nine stones in weight, and throughout his career a part-time player, Morton was surprisingly strong and took the rough with the smooth against big unruly defenders without complaint. He had a quite powerful shot with either foot, but was a goalmaker rather than a goalscorer. One bewildering facet of his play was the "floating lob", a cross which seemed to stop and hang on the face of the crossbar, provoking indecision in the minds of goalkeepers.

In the famous "Wembley wizards" match of 1928, in which Scotland beat England 5-1, each goal of the hat-trick scored by Alex Jackson, the outside right, came from Morton's crosses. It was at this match that Ivan Sharpe, a prominent English critic of the day, dubbed Morton the "wee blue devil".

He was born in Glasgow in 1893, one of the five sons of a coalmaster. Alan was to become a mining engineer, a profession which he followed throughout his football career. Training "after hours", he maintained a high level of fitness. In his teens he joined Queen's Park to "keep his brother Bob company", and in 1920, when he joined Rangers, he was already an experienced international player, with caps against Wales and Northern Ireland. Over a dozen years he won 31 caps for Scotland at a time when three international matches per season was the norm. From 1921 to 1932 he played 11 times against England. The match of 1926, which England won 1-0 at Old Trafford, was spoken of as "the year Morton didn't play". His international appearance total stood as a record until it was broken by George Young of Rangers after the second world war.

Alan Morton was a prim, trim man. He'd turn up for training at Ibrox straight from business wearing a suit and bowler hat, often carrying an umbrella. Inevitably he was dubbed by Rangers fans the "wee society man", their tag for the man who came to the door every week collecting penny premiums for "the policy". He could also look after himself. If he felt that his famous left-wing partner Bob McPhail was neglecting him – McPhail had a tendency to swing the play to the right – he'd call out, "Robert, Robert, I'm over here, don't forget me!"

In all he played a total of 742 competitive games – 244 for Queen's Park, 498 for Rangers – and scored 166 goals. He was often the scourge of Celtic, whose players always treated him with respect and admiration. Rangers fans, on their way to and from Old Firm matches in horse-drawn brakes, would sing:–

> "Oh, Charlie Shaw, he never saw, where Alan Morton put the ba'
> "He put the ba' right in the net, and Charlie Shaw, he roared and gret,
> The Celtic fear, the Rangers cheer, we'll keep the league flag flying yet".

The tune was "Oh, Tannenbaum" and Charlie Shaw was the famous Celtic goalkeeper.

Alan Morton played seven matches at the start of the 1932-33 season, then announced his retirement. He was immediately made a director of the club and remained one until his death in 1971, aged 78. His portrait in oils, in Rangers' football uniform, hangs in solitary splendour to this day in the marble entrance hall to Ibrox Stadium.

Morton of Henryton, Lord
Fergus Dunlop Morton
(1887-1973)
Judge, whose family came from Troon, educated at Kelvinside Academy and St John's College, Cambridge. After being called to the English bar in 1912, he served as a captain in the Highland Light Infantry during the first world war and was awarded the MC. He pursued his subsequent legal career south of the border, as a judge of the Chancery Division, 1938-44, and as a Lord of Appeal in Ordinary, 1947-59. His only significant connection with Scotland was as captain of the Royal and Ancient Golf Club, reflecting his addiction to a game in which he had been steeped since childhood.

Muirhead, Brigadier Sir John Spencer
(1889-1972)
Solicitor, educated at Fettes College and the Universities of Oxford and Glasgow, who served his law apprenticeship with Maclay, Murray & Spens. He rose to command the 51st (Highland) divisional signal company, RE, during the first world war and was awarded the MC and DSO. After the war he was senior partner of Baird Smith, Barclay and Muirhead, Glasgow, and lectured in Roman law at Glasgow University. In 1950 he became the first elected president of the Law Society of Scotland, and was influential in implementing legal aid in Scotland.

Mulcahy, Rt. Rev. Dom Columban
(1900-71)
Monk, abbot of Scotland's only Cistercian monastery for 22 years and a leading advocate of Christian unity in Scotland. He joined the Cistercians at Roscrea, Ireland, in 1923, and was ordained as a priest five years later. In 1948 he presided over the foundation of Sancta Maria Abbey, Nunraw. He retired in 1969 but remained at Nunraw as an ordinary member of the community.

Essay by
Donald McGlynn

Abbot Columban (Samuel) Mulcahy played a key role in Christian ecumenism in Scotland between 1961 and 1966. In the 20 years he was abbot of the Cistercian monastery of Nunraw, Haddington, he presided over the construction of a new monastery. The collaboration of countless people from all walks of life, and all faiths, was reminiscent of the building of medieval cathedrals. Addressing 1,500 people at the laying of the foundation stone in 1954, the abbot put his life's endeavours in the perspective of faith. "It is necessary to stress that in the eyes of monks, any achievements are only secondary and subsidiary. The chief purpose of monks is the personal service of God."

He was born in Thurles, Co. Tipperary, Ireland, in 1900. A Quaker grandmother's influence may have coloured the deeply religious character of the family. Of eight children, four girls became nuns and the youngest boy, Samuel, aspired to become a missionary in China. Towards the end of his theological studies with the Columban missionaries, a slight speech impediment may have weighed his decision to join the "silent" order of Cistercians. In 1923 he entered the monastery of Roscrea which was hoping to make a foundation in China. He took the name Columban. He was ordained priest, taught philosophy and directed young student monks. An appointment to the order's office in Rome in 1947 was cut short by his election as abbot of Nunraw which brought him to Scotland.

The rallying call of Pope John XXIII for the churches to be "open to the signs of the times" was not likely to galvanise the Catholic Church or the Church of Scotland into hasty moves towards unity. If "the future belongs to those who see it first", then Dom Columban was at that happy point of an historic junction of man and moment.

In 1961 leading men and women of the Church of Scotland and the Episcopal Church responded to abbot Columban's invitation to attend the annual meeting of the Roman Catholic Council of Religious Superiors of which he was chairman. He was a diminutive figure. With disarming good humour he opened the meeting, "Friends – Romans – Countrymen". The telling pauses were greeted with applause which put people at their ease. In the interest of informality and friendly dialogue the media were excluded. The reaction of the press was to sensationalise this historic encounter between members of the different churches as "a secret meeting" with innuendos of a Roman take-over. Ministers rushed to distance themselves from the event. There were impassioned letters to the press. These voices were but echoes from a past of intolerance. The actual participants remained enthusiastic and soon their initiative gained official approval. The General Assembly of the Church of Scotland gave its first tentative acceptance of such inter-church meetings in 1962. In the Catholic Church, in 1968, the move culminated with its *Bishops' Directory* described as "Scotland's ecumenical charter".

As the 1960s progressed unexpected problems faced the abbot. A television documentary on Nunraw Abbey in 1967 portrayed a scene which was very different from the thriving optimism of the 1950s and early 1960s. In the presenter, Malcolm Muggeridge, Dom Columban found a "soul-mate" who shared his concern for the changing attitudes in society, in the church, and in the monastic community. He continued to be in demand as an ecumenical speaker after his retirement as abbot of Nunraw in 1969. In a tribute on radio after his death, the Rev. Roderick Smith of the Church of Scotland, a friend and collaborator in ecumenism, acknowledged him as "a man of God". The building of a monastery in the Lammermuir hills, and the building of the churches in closer relationship, are fitting memorials to such a man.

Murray, Charles de Bois
(1891-1974)
Lawyer and author, son of a Glasgow merchant, educated at Glasgow Academy and Glasgow University, where he graduated in

law. During the first world war he served in France and Belgium with the infantry and the Tank Corps. He was called to the Scottish bar in 1919 and the English bar three years later. His books include a biography of Forbes of Culloden, a textbook on wills, and studies of Scottish government and European post-war regeneration.

From Murray's *Duncan Forbes of Culloden* [1936]

"Later in the same year we have four letters from Duncan to his brother. One of them contains a very unkind reference to his own son – 'This day after a very hard pull I got the better of my son at the gouf in Musselburgh Links; if he was as good at any other thing as he is at that, there might be some hope for him.' Duncan was a generous and big-hearted man. Indeed very few people have achieved his success at so cheap a price in enemies, and the reason for his well-earned popularity was that he never forgot a friend. But with his own son (in early manhood at any rate) he was not a success. He was not gentil for his son, and later on in the Culloden Correspondence we shall find a really deplorable letter, addressed to his son's tutor, in which Duncan achieves a colourable imitation of Polonius. If and as far as letters reveal the heart, John Forbes the uncle was much fonder of the boy than his own father was. But in fairness one ought to remember that Duncan married early, and lost his wife early, and that perhaps affected his attitude to his son. Of his wife, Mary Rose, daughter of an Inverness-shire laird, we know almost nothing. One would like to think that she was a pretty girl with bright eyes and a quick mind. All that is known, however, is that Duncan never married again, in spite of the well-meant advice of his brother."

From Murray's *How Scotland is Governed* [1947]

"In the opinion of the present writer it would be far better to abolish licensing restrictions altogether, and to allow the sale of wines and spirits to be conducted in the same way as the sale of any other commodity. The grant of a valuable commercial privilege to some persons, and its refusal to others, is utterly indefensible in principle, and therefore the system would appear almost certain to lead to subterfuge and corruption. Then again, canalising the drinking of whisky and beer into fixed hours and at fixed places, where non-alcoholic drinks, let alone food, often cannot be had, would seem of all possible methods, that best calculated and most likely to lead to excess."

Murray, David
(d 1973)
Racing driver and entrepreneur. Educated at the Royal High School, Edinburgh, he qualified as a chartered accountant, but his passion was motor racing. After the second world war he was invited to race Maserati cars on the continent. His career came to an abrupt end at Nurburgring when his car turned upside down and he was trapped beneath the wreckage. Undaunted, he went on to fulfil his ambition to run his own Scottish racing team: Ecurie Ecosse was born. Murray chose the dark blue of Scotland as team colour and persuaded Esso to back the venture. Although drivers were selected not so much for their ability than for their ownership of suitable sports cars, Ecurie Ecosse scored success after success and won the Le Mans 24-hour race in two successive years. But when his drivers began to do less well, Murray's private finances suffered. At the end

of 1967 he failed to appear for a public examination in bankruptcy and fled to the Canary Islands. He died after suffering multiple injuries when a car he was driving collided with a bus.

Murray, David
(c1902-75)
Industrial journalist and authority on the iron and steel industry. Born in Motherwell, he began work as a rivet heater but went on to Glasgow University where he graduated in engineering. During the second world war he was attached to the Ministry of Information with responsibility for steel conservation. After the war he became a prominent figure in industrial journalism and broadcasting, and wrote a number of books on the steel industry. He stood for Parliament three times – once as a "Home Ruler", once as a Liberal, and once as an Independent.

N

Neill, A(lexander) S(utherland)
(1883-1973)
Teacher and educational reformer, born in Angus and educated at Kingsmuir village school, where his father was headmaster, and at Forfar Academy. After an unsuccessful attempt to become an apprentice draper, he returned to the strict supervision of his father as a pupil teacher at Kingsmuir. He was aged 15. Later, in an examination for entry into a teacher training college, he finished 103 out of 104 candidates – an experience which gave him a bitter distrust of the exam system and helped to shape his subsequent philosophy of education. With all hope of a college place dashed, he accepted a teaching post at Bonnyrigg, where he was told on his first day to strap any child who dared to whisper in class. Here, and in other Scottish schools where he taught, he was increasingly repelled by the brutal use of corporal punishment.

He became an undergraduate at Edinburgh University, edited the university magazine, and developed an interest in socialism. In 1913 he arrived in London with the intention of becoming a journalist. He went straight to Fleet Street hoping to bump into famous editors. He bumped into none. But he did get a job on the *Piccadilly Magazine*, until its closure forced him back to Scotland and to the headship of Gretna public school.

It was at Gretna that Neill's rebellious nature finally emerged. One day he put the strap in the stove that heated the school, vowed never to use it again, and kept his word. He declared as his chief aim to allow the children to have as much freedom as possible: "I want a bairn to be human, and I try to be human myself". His book, *A Dominie's Log*, was an immediate success. However, he soon found himself writing another entitled *A Dominie Dismissed*.

After army service during the first world war, he taught at King Alfred School, Hampstead. By then he had determined to set up a school of his own with democratic government and no punishment (nor rewards, for that matter) and with the emphasis on creativity and self-expression. In 1921 he went to Dresden to run the international department of a school there, but soon moved to Saltzburg where he realised his ambition of opening his own school. He brought it to England in 1924, establishing it first at Lyme Regis in a house called Summerhill and then at Leiston in Suffolk, retaining the original name.

Neill completely rejected the authoritarian techniques of most other private schools in favour of a free and easy atmosphere in which pupils governed themselves, attended lessons as and when they wished, and were encouraged to be familiar with the staff. The pursuit of academic standards was so actively discouraged that critics condemned Summerhill as anti-intellectual. However Neill's unorthodox approach proved highly successful, particularly with the difficult children of relatively rich parents, many from the United States.

The craggy iconoclast loathed Shakespeare and religion in more or less equal measure. He once told Robert Graves that he stropped his razor on the Bible to show what he thought of it. "Thank God I am an atheist," he declared. For a while he believed in the Soviet idea. He smoked both cigarettes and a pipe, had a liking for whisky (though never to excess), and took a cold bath every morning. To strangers he tended to appear dour. His favourite book was *The House with the Green Shutters* by George Douglas Brown, an author for whom he developed an obsession. When he received an honorary doctorate from Exeter University in 1968 the citation described him as "perhaps the most distinguished figure in progressive education". His first wife, who helped him with the development of the school, died after a prolonged mental illness. He re-married a young woman who had come to help with the cooking, and they had a daughter when Neill was aged 63.

John Aitkenhead, who modelled Kilquhanity School, Galloway, on Summerhill, wrote about Neill in *The Scottish Review* [1998]

"As headmaster [at Gretna] he had to keep a 'log' recording all that was happening in his school. But there was a condition: he must not criticise the system that was employing him. Neill continued to be openly critical of the system and of the government of the day which had been promoting what was called the 'Great War'. He openly shared his opinions with the pupils, especially the adolescents about to leave school. He told them it was not their war, but that the government was using them. He explained that boys of their age in Germany were not their enemies. It was the governments of both countries whose plans for Empire control had them conscripting the young men.

Neill knew quite well that the parents of his pupils probably agreed with him but were afraid of the local farmers and other employers. Anyway, he was sacked and promptly published *A Dominie Dismissed*. His views were basically pacifist, but he said he didn't have the courage to become a CO (conscientious objector). So he 'joined up' and soon found himself in the army of occupation in Germany."

From Neill's *A Dominie's Log* [1915]

[1] "I have been thinking about discipline overnight. I have seen a headmaster who insisted on what he called perfect discipline. His bairns sat still all day. A movement foreshadowed the strap. Every child jumped up at the word of command. He had a very quiet life. I must confess that I am an atrociously bad disciplinarian. Today

Violet Brown began to sing 'Tipperary' to herself when I was marking the registers. I looked up and said: 'Why the happiness this morning, Violet?', and she blushed and grinned. I am a poor disciplinarian."

[2] "These bairns of mine will never know how to find truth; they will merely read the newspapers when they grow up. They will wave their hats to the King, but kingship will be but a word to them; they will shout when a lawyer from the south wins the local seat, but they will not understand the meaning of economics; they will dust their old silk hats and march to the sacrament, but they will not realise what religion means."

[3] "I am determined to tear all the rags of hypocrisy from the facts of life; I shall lead my bairns to doubt everything."

Thoughts of Neill

[1] "I want to raise people who know their own mind and can think for themselves."

[2] "I'd be very disappointed if a Summerhill child became prime minister. I'd feel I'd failed."

[3]"Pioneering is a washout, man. I am getting weary of cleaning up the mess that parents make." [Letter to Bertrand Russell]

[4] "I don't fear death. I fear ceasing to live, and of course the method of dying."

Neven-Spence, Colonel Sir Basil Hamilton Hebden
(1888-1974)

Landowner, physician and politician, member of a Shetland landowning family, educated at Edinburgh Academy and Edinburgh University, where he graduated in medicine. He became a lieutenant in the RAMC in 1911. Three years later he was seconded to the Egyptian army and the Sudan government with the rank of major, served in Darfur and Palestine, was twice mentioned in despatches, won several decorations, served as a magistrate and as a government bacteriologist, and finally reverted to the British army. In 1927 he was elected a fellow of the Royal College of Physicians of Edinburgh. He became Unionist MP for Orkney and Shetland in 1935 and held the seat until 1950, after which he was Lord Lieutenant of Shetland. Among other public offices he was chairman of the Scottish committee of the Nature Conservancy.

Newman, Professor Sidney Thomas Mayow
(1906-71)

Conductor, pianoforte recitalist, teacher and music administrator, born in London, who studied music at Oxford University and at the Royal College of Music, where he learned composition under Vaughan Williams. As Reid professor of music at Edinburgh University, 1941-70, and as conductor of the Reid Orchestra, he was an influential figure in Scotland's musical life, serving on the council of the Edinburgh Festival and as a director of the newly-founded Scottish Opera. An enduring legacy of his work was the restoration of St Cecilia's Hall, Edinburgh's original concert room.

Nicol, Rev. Anderson
(1906-72)

Minister of the Church of Scotland, born in Stevenston, Ayrshire, and educated at the High School of Glasgow and Glasgow University. His first charges were Dunbarney and Braid (Edinburgh). Between 1943 and 1946 he was a chaplain in the Royal Navy. In 1948 he became minister of the West Church of St Nicholas, Aberdeen, where he remained for 19 years. He was a member of the Broadcasting Council for Scotland and held various appointments in the Scout movement. His last charge was at St Fillans, Perthshire. In 1964 he was appointed a chaplain to the Queen in Scotland.

Nisbet, Professor James Wilkie
(1903-74)
Political economist, educated at Hutchesons' Grammar School, Glasgow, and Glasgow University. He was appointed an assistant to the Adam Smith professor of political economy at Glasgow University and later became a lecturer in the department of political economy at St Andrews University. After 12 years he was promoted to the chair of political economy and retired from the post in 1970. He was chairman of the Scottish Consumers' Council, 1954-68. Among his books were biographies of Thomas Chalmers and Adam Smith. A member of the Royal and Ancient Golf Club, he won the club's Calcutta Cup tournament in 1946.

Noble of Ardkinglas, John
(c1910-72)
Patron of the arts, second son of Sir John Noble and brother of Michael Noble, former Secretary of State for Scotland. As chairman of the BBC Scottish music advisory committee for five years, he led the fight against plans to disband the BBC Scottish Symphony Orchestra. He was founder chairman of the Scottish Crafts Centre and president of the Saltire Society.

O

Orr, John Boyd
Boyd Orr of Brechin, 1st Baron
(1880-1971)
Scientist, born in Ayrshire, founder of the Rowett Research Institute, one of the most influential campaigners for a more healthy diet, and winner of the Nobel Peace Prize in 1949.

Essay by
Walter R.H. Duncan

Nutritional physiologist, first director of the Rowett Research Institute, first director-general of the United Nations Food and Agricultural Organisation, chancellor of Glasgow University, social reformer and Nobel peace prize-winner, John Boyd Orr was born on 23 September, 1880 at Kilmaurs, Ayrshire, the son of Robert Clark Orr and Annie Boyd. A middle child in the family of seven, he attended school at West Kilbride and later Kilmarnock Academy, before returning to West Kilbride as a pupil teacher. He graduated in arts at Glasgow University (MA, 1903) and was a school-teacher for three years. He re-entered Glasgow University, graduating BSc (1910) and MBChB (1912). He then obtained a Barbour scholarship to enable him to work with E.P. Cathcart, head of physiological chemistry in the Institute of Physiology. He graduated MD (1914) with honours, being awarded the Bellahouston gold medal for his thesis.

With modest funds from the development commissioners, a joint committee of the University of Aberdeen and the North of Scotland College of Agriculture planned to establish an "Institute of Nutrition" at Aberdeen under Cathcart. Cathcart meanwhile had been offered a chair of physiology in London and recommended Orr be appointed by the joint committee in his place. Orr arrived in Aberdeen in April 1914 as a researcher in nutrition. There was no institute. He presented to the joint committee a scheme for an adequate institute and the news that he had committed all the capital sum available to the building of a laboratory at Craibstone.

Orr had trained in Glasgow University's OTC and joined the RAMC at the outbreak of the first world war. He served as a medical officer in the trenches, winning an MC at the Somme and DSO at Passchendaele. He was commissioned in the Royal Navy in 1918.

Orr returned to Aberdeen in January 1919 and pressed for a new research institute. The government agreed to pay half the cost and Orr persuaded John Q. Rowett to provide funds and a new site for the Rowett Institute, opened in 1922. In the ensuing years, the Reid Library, the Duthie Farm, the residential Strathcona House and the Imperial Bureau of Animal Nutrition which published *Nutrition Abstracts & Reviews*, were tribute to his perseverance and his persuasive powers.

Perhaps because he was almost 40 years old, Orr was a man in a hurry. He was impatient at the slowness of decisions by committee. He himself was direct, a hard but fair taskmaster, who could enthuse even the most junior of staff and 50 years later these early workers, long retired from active work, were still fiercely loyal to the institute and to Orr. F.C. Kelly of the Chilean Iodine Foundation, writing in 1973, describes how he, just graduated in science, walked in on Orr on a Friday afternoon in 1923 and asked for a job. He was told to start on Monday and asked to study the nutritional role of the element iodine and its metabolism in relation to that of the other mineral elements in the body. This became his life's work.

Under Orr the institute became a nutrition centre of international renown and he himself was elected a fellow of the Royal Society in 1932 and knighted in 1935. Orr's research work at Glasgow was on starvation, water and protein metabolism. He saw at first hand the poor health and physique of many in the conscript army and in 1918, with Cathcart, studied the energy expenditure of the infantry recruit during training. At the Rowett Institute he turned his attention to the study of minerals in pastures, to the nutrition of farm animals, and to the study of the health and diet of the Kikuyu and Masai peoples in Kenya.

During these early years, Orr visited the Middle East, Africa, India, Australasia and Canada and reported on the state of agriculture. He was a member of the research grants committee of the Empire Marketing Board, a fellow member being Frank MacDougall, economic advisor to the Australian High Commissioner in London. The work on animals at the institute brought improvements in the production of meat, wool and milk and improved knowledge on pastures and food mixtures. Orr could persuade farmers of the value to their stock of his application of sound nutritional principles, but few believed that the same was true of children.

In 1924 "The importance of mineral elements in the nutrition of children" appeared and in 1927 he showed by experiments the value of milk in the health and growth of British children. This led Orr's lifelong friend, Walter Elliot, an early postgraduate student at the Rowett Institute, and by then under-secretary of state for Scotland, to introduce legislation to provide milk for children in Scottish schools and directly benefit the ailing dairy industry. In 1930 a report on the diet of 607 families in seven Scottish towns was published. Orr continued to draw attention to the poor state of health and nutrition of the British people and advocated a national food policy linked to an agricultural policy and one which had concern for human need. In 1936 he published "Food, Health and Income" which claimed one third of the British population was too poor to buy enough food to maintain health. He was already involved in a League of Nations technical commission on nutrition and David Lubbock, a member of the Rowett staff, was a member of a committee which reported in 1937 on "The relation of health, agriculture and economic policy".

In 1936 the Carnegie Trust made a grant to the Rowett Institute. David Lubbock headed the "Carnegie survey of family diet and health" carried out at 16 centres in England and Scotland in 1937-39. More than 1,000 families took part and more than 3,000 children were medically examined. Detailed information was provided on household socio-economic circumstances and diet. The dietary information was analysed at the Rowett Institute to produce per capita consumption of calories, fat, protein, carbohydrate, minerals and vitamins for each household. The outbreak of war delayed the main analysis but "interim conclusions" were made available to the government and influenced war-time food policy. At the outbreak of war most of the Rowett staff enlisted in the forces, the farm was geared to maximise food production, and the biochemistry department organised and carried out the analyses for Scottish wartime food surveys. In 1945, at the war's end, Orr retired. The Rowett Institute by then was very rundown with an ageing staff.

Orr embarked in the 1930s on a series of broadcasts and popular articles on national food policy and then on war-time food policy. In 1940 with David Lubbock he published "Feeding the people in wartime", outlining ways of maximising food production at home, reducing non-essential food imports, and diverting milk and vitamin-rich supplements to expectant and nursing mothers, infants and growing children. They advocated rationing for protein-rich foods and price controls. The early war-time food surveys showed that the poorer classes did not take up their full rations of the more expensive foods. After two years of war, however, with full employment, money was there to buy full rations. Health improved, the circle was complete, Orr's findings of 1936 were banished for a generation.

When the coalition government was formed in 1940 Orr was invited to join the cabinet scientific sub-committee on food policy. In 1941 he became first president of the newly formed Nutrition

Society and in the following year travelled to the USA to take part in renewed discussions on a world food plan. Later Frank MacDougall was able to present Orr's ideas to President Roosevelt, who called a conference at Hot Springs, Virginia, in 1943 to give effect to the "third freedom" – "freedom from want". From this stemmed the Quebec Conference of 1945 which brought into being the Food and Agricultural Organisation of the United Nations. Orr was not a British delegate at either of these meetings but attended Quebec as an unofficial member. He was asked to address the conference and gave a rousing speech asking that FAO be given power and funds to address the urgent needs of the hungry. Orr was invited to become director-general. Frank MacDougall became one of his advisers and David Lubbock his personal assistant.

Jean A.S. Ritchie, dietician and MSc of the University of Chicago, had come back to Scotland and was an ambulance driver when she first met Sir John Orr in 1941. Three days later she was at the Rowett Institute. She ran the scientific food survey in poor areas of the Scottish cities to find out whether industrial workers could buy their food rations on their pay and feed their families properly. She transferred to the Ministry of Food, then was recruited into UNRRA, working in post-war Europe. In late 1946 she went to Washington to the nutrition division of FAO, again working under Orr until he resigned. Writing in 1995 she states that Sir John was a great "inspirer". He would call the staff in Washington together to talk about FAO's role and work, and say in rousing tones, "Come on my lads and lasses, there's so much to do and we must all work even harder." And everyone would be almost rising in their seats with support and determination.

During the later war years Orr became even more well-known as a broadcaster and contributed to publications looking forward to post-war Britain. He made significant contributions to the Paul Rotha films *World of Plenty* (1943) and *The World is Rich* (1947). In 1945, elected to Parliament as an Independent MP for the Scottish Universities, he was also rector of Glasgow University. In 1947 he was appointed chancellor there, a post he filled with distinction until his death.

Orr had retired to his farm in Angus when he became director-general of FAO, 1945-48. His first task was to gather statistics on population growth, food production and food stocks, and ability to move these. The first returns showed a projected shortfall for the winter of 1946-47 and, FAO having limited powers, an International Emergency Food Council was set up in May 1946 to deal with the situation. Thus encouraged, Orr continued planning a World Food Board, a supra-national body with powers to buy and hold food stocks, to give interest-free loans to promote the technical development of agriculture, to finance food supplies to needy countries. "The cooperation of all nations on a world-wide project of developing the vast potential resources of the earth for the benefit of the wealthy as well as the poor nations would make cooperation easier in political spheres and be an important step in the evolution of the United Nations Organisation as a World Government without which there is little hope of a permanent peace." These proposals were discussed at the Copenhagen Conference in 1946 and had the support of the US delegation. A preparatory Commission on World

Food Proposals was set up to report the following year. By September 1947, things had changed. The financial implications for Britain were serious, there were problems in the United Nations Council as the power blocs became suspicious of each other, and the prospects of that body becoming a world government diminished. Orr's major proposal was shelved and he resigned a disappointed man. Nevertheless he had given FAO a tremendous start.

In 1949 Orr was created Baron Boyd Orr of Brechin Mearns and in the same year he was awarded the Nobel peace prize. Typically he donated the cash award to the National Peace Council, the World Federal Government, and other organisations. He took up some financially rewarding directorships and was a member of the British Council for the Promotion of International Trade, which was considered to be a cover for fellow travellers but whose aims were in line with those of Orr, who considered commercial, scientific and other non-political links useful for the promotion of world peace and also helped to keep open trade channels between the USSR, China and the UK. Orr was a welcome visitor to both communist countries. He travelled widely in Europe, especially in Poland, and was an advisor on agricultural affairs to both the Indian and Pakistani governments. He also visited Israel, Egypt, Japan and Cuba. Lady Orr was his constant companion. *The White Man's Dilemma* (Orr and Lubbock, 1953), published in many languages, is a statement of his position on a world food board and world government and he championed these projects to the end of his life. Fittingly his last public engagement was in September 1970 at the opening of a large extension to the Rowett Institute.

Orr received honorary degrees from 12 universities in Britain and abroad, as well as many medals and marks of distinction. In 1968 he was made a Companion of Honour. As a young man he was a member of the Free Church, whose tenets of mission and service were surely fulfilled in a lifetime devoted to the welfare of his fellow men. In 1915 he married Elizabeth Pearson Callum. They had two daughters and a son who was killed on active service. He died on 25 June, 1971, at his home in Brechin. His barony became extinct.

It is now 50 years since Orr resigned his FAO post. There are more mouths to feed, and large areas of the earth are unproductive due to civil war, drought, poor agricultural practice, and debt. His dream of a world food board and world government remains unfulfilled.

The Rowett Institute recovered from its wartime rundown and prospered under Sir David Cuthbertson and Sir Kenneth Blaxter, committed to animal nutrition research with generous government support. Today, under Professor Philip James, research is once again concerned with human nutrition and there are more than 50 postgraduate students on campus from all corners of the globe. John Boyd Orr's vision has stood the test of time: the Rowett Institute has come full circle with its current emphasis on the food chain. Research is geared to defining the nutritional needs of man so that the producers can be properly informed as to the type of food that is required.

From Orr's
Food and the People
[1943]

"The discovery that some commonly occurring diseases arise from the *absence* of specific substances in the food was revolutionary. It had always been assumed that diseases not due to heredity were due to the *presence* of germs or other toxic agents. A new field of research was opened up. Investigation was carried out to ascertain whether deficiency in the supply of known substances might not be a source of disease. It was found that many diets in common use were deficient in some of the minerals, e.g. calcium and iron, with resulting ill-health and poor physique. The foodstuffs rich in vitamins and minerals became known as the protective foods because they protect against the deficiency diseases. Important examples of these are milk, eggs, fruit and vegetables, especially green, leafy vegetables."

From Orr's *The White Man's Dilemma* [1956]

"There is a reason, though it is largely subconscious, for the reluctance of those in power to co-operate in abolishing hunger and poverty. The power of money depends not so much on the absolute amount a man has, as on the relative amount to other men. If all men were wealthy, a wealthy man would have no more power than anybody else. If, however, a few men are wealthy, and the rest are so poor that they are dependent on the wealthy for getting work to earn the price of food, then the wealthy can obtain both service and, at least, the outward show of submission. So as soon as the poor are assured of food and the other physical essentials of life, they have taken the first and by far the most important step to liberty. The power of money over their lives is broken. They no longer need to cringe to live. As an American writer put it, 'when you clean up the slums the servant problem gets tough'. The same problem has arisen in the 'welfare State' of the United Kingdom. This does not mean that people are no longer willing to work. Everyone wants more than merely the physical necessities of life. It is the people above the poverty level who work hardest. But if assured of the necessities of life they can work with the 'glorious feeling of being independent' of another human being for the right to live."

P

Parker, William Mathie
(d 1973)
Author and historian, born in Renfrewshire and educated at Edinburgh University. An authority on Sir Walter Scott, he undertook much of the research for a 12-volume edition of the letters of Scott. His *Modern Scottish Writers* included studies of Robert Louis Stevenson and J.M. Barrie.

From Parker's *Modern Scottish Writers* [1917]

"There was one specially commendable trait in Stevenson's character that ought never to be overlooked in estimating him. He was never disgruntled by life. There was scarcely any side of life but what he faced fearlessly, almost boldly. There was no flinching with him; and though he sometimes treated it with undue levity, he saw life clearly and saw it whole, and he thought kindly of it. He set his ship in the teeth of the wind from whatever quarter it might chance to blow, and his optimism was steadily enviable through the storm and stress of an invalid life. Because a small measure of health, and ultimately of life, was granted him by Providence, he had, as compensation, an irrepressible zest for life."

Primrose, Sir John Ure
(1900-74)
Local politician, farmer and company director, son of a United Free minister, educated at Kelvinside Academy, Glasgow, and Stanley House, Bridge of Allan. He was a naval lieutenant during the first world war and a sergeant-major in the Intelligence Corps during the second. In 1921 he took up farming and became active in the NFU locally. He was lord provost of Perth, 1945-54. Among his public offices he took a keen interest in bodies connected with air transport and persuaded his fellow councillors to establish Scone as the first municipal airport in Britain. He was chairman of the Scottish committee of the White Fish Authority and of the Scottish Motor Traction Co. Ltd.

R

Ramensky, Johnny
(c1905-72)
Safe-blower, also known as John Ramsay, a recidivist who nevertheless enjoyed the public's affection and became something of a legend. Although he carried out countless robberies, he was careful always to avoid violence and earned the nickname "Gentle Johnny". He was imprisoned many times and escaped many times. On one of his five escapes from Peterhead, he eluded re-capture for 10 days. He protested that he escaped for propaganda purposes – in order to draw attention to the mistreatment of fellow prisoners. In 1942 his skill as a cracksman came to the notice of British Intelligence, which was anxious to acquire German documents and equipment. Ramensky was freed from prison to join a parachute commando unit, dropped behind enemy lines, and made a number of effective raids. He was also invaluable as a trainer of his fellow commandos in the art of cracking safes. After this lawful interval he returned as zealously as ever to a life of crime. In April 1972, now only three years short of 70, he was arrested after being found on the roof of a shop in suspicious circumstances. He received yet another term of imprisonment – 12 months – and was serving his sentence in Perth Prison when he collapsed. He died in Perth Royal Infirmary. He was the hero of at least two folk songs – one by Roddy Macmillan, *Let Ramensky Go*, and another by Norman Buchan, *The Ballad of Johnny Ramensky* which contained the following lines: "He has slipped frae the darkness an' intae the light/Tae the green fields around him he has taken his flight/For one breath o' fresh air, just one glimpse o' the sun/But Johnny Ramensky nae freedom has won."

Rankin, John
(d 1973)
Politician, educated at Allan Glen's School, Glasgow, and Glasgow University. He was a teacher and lecturer in industrial history and economics before entering politics. In 1922 he became Eastwood Parish Council's first Labour member. He was elected to Parliament

in 1945, the year of Labour's post-war landslide, as member for the Tradeston division of Glasgow. Later he represented Govan. In 1961 he was one of 15 Scots who signed an appeal for £100,000 to enable a plebiscite on Scotland's constitutional future to be organised. When he died he was believed to be Scotland's oldest MP (though reluctant to state his age) and with his colleague William Hannan (of Maryhill) the longest-serving MP.

Reay, George Adam
(1901-71)
Fisheries expert and pioneer of food science and technology, educated at Robert Gordon's College, Aberdeen University, and Emmanuel College, Cambridge. He began his career as a research officer with the Food Investigation Organisation, joining the Torry Research Station, Aberdeen, when it opened in 1929. He was director of the station, 1958-64.

Reid of Drem, Lord
James Scott Cumberland Reid
(1890-1975)
Judge, one of the most brilliant of his era, who went to the House of Lords as a Lord of Appeal without first having served on the Scottish bench. Born in Drem, East Lothian, where his father combined the practice of a Writer to the Signet with farming, he was educated at Edinburgh Academy, Jesus College, Cambridge, and Edinburgh University. When he was called to the Scottish bar in 1914, he was the first advocate to be admitted in uniform. He served with the Royal Scots in the Machine and Gun Corps and did not begin his legal career until after the war. Between 1931 and 1948 (with the exception of a brief interval in 1935-36) he sat as a Unionist MP, first for Stirling and Falkirk Burghs, then for Glasgow Hillhead, as well as practising law. He took silk in 1932, was appointed Solicitor-General four years later, and became Lord Advocate in 1941. Between 1945 and 1948 he was dean of the Faculty of Advocates. He gave up his Parliamentary seat when he was made a life peer and went to the Lords. Known for his incisive mind, he presided over several complex inquiries, including the Malaysian constitutional commission and the committee on the registration of title to land. His judgments were often hailed by his peers as models of brevity and lucidity, setting sound precedents for future generations. He once asked a barrister pleading before him, "You have now spoken for three days. How much more of our time are you going to waste?" But this was an exceptional lapse into impatience.

From *Scots Law Times*

"Probably Scotland has never before sent to the Lords a man so well equipped by nature and temperament to determine legal questions on appeal."

The Times on Reid's retirement

"Lord Reid was in control in the heady decade of the sixties when traditional social and legal assumptions were coming under incessant challenge. During that period he guided the House of Lords down the middle path between a slavish acceptance of old judicial concepts and the radicalisation which some critics were demanding."

Reid, Sir Edward (James)
(1901-72)
Banker, elder son of the 1st baronet of Ellon, whom he succeeded in 1923. He was godson of King Edward VII, his mother having been maid of honour to Queen Victoria. Between 1911 and 1917 he was the King's page of honour. Educated at King's College, Cambridge, he joined the board of Baring Bros & Co., retiring in 1966 after 40 years. In 1930 he married Tatiana, daughter of Alexander Fenoult, who had been a colonel in the Russian imperial guard. He was honorary president of the Clan Donnachaidh Society.

Reid, Admiral Sir (John) Peter (Lorne)
(1903-73)
Naval commander and signals expert, born in Aberdeen, second son of the 1st baronet of Ellon, educated at the Royal Naval Colleges of Osborne and Dartmouth. He was twice mentioned in despatches during the second world war. After the war he earned a series of swift promotions, serving as third sea lord from 1956 until 1961. He retired to East Lothian, where he became a county councillor and vice-lieutenant of the county. His wife, Jean, was the only daughter of Sir Henry Dundas, 3rd baronet of Arniston, and Beatrix, daughter of the 12th Earl of Home.

Reith, John Charles Walsham
Lord Reith of Stonehaven
(1889-1971)
Creator of the BBC, born in Stonehaven, fifth son of a prominent figure in the United Free Church, the Very Rev. Dr George Reith. Reserved and aloof, a very bad mixer, he was only 13 when his father told him it seemed he would have to live on a desert island. He was educated at Glasgow Academy and Gresham's School, Norfolk, but missed university because his father, who believed that every man should have a trade, was determined that he should be a mechanical engineer. For several years Reith divided his time between studies at the Royal Technical College, Glasgow, and an apprenticeship with the North British Locomotive Company, rising at 4.45am and seldom getting to bed before 11pm. Despite this dedication, and his utter determination not to be a mediocrity, he was not mechanically minded.

When the first world war broke out he joined the 5th Scottish Rifles and had what he later called "a thoroughly happy war", although as a teetotaller he was not much sought after socially. "There were various dinner parties but all company affairs, and I was not bid to any," he noted. The happy war, in which he fell foul of his commanding officer, ended at the battle of Loos in which he was shot in the side of his face by a sniper. As a result of the wound he was compelled to leave the front line and spent 18 months in the United States negotiating contracts for munitions. Back in Britain in 1918, he fell in love with Muriel Katharine Odhams, the driver of his colonel's car. They married in 1921.

After the war, while working as general manager of Beardmore's plant at Coatbridge, he flirted with the idea of becoming an MP. He sounded out both the Liberals and the Labour Party, but was generally undecided about his future. One evening in the

Presbyterian church he attended, the minister preached a sermon about the Lord requiring a man to fill a gap, and added: "Maybe there's somebody in this congregation tonight that might be called to fill a considerable gap." Reith regarded this as an extraordinary premonition and wrote in his diary: "I still believe there is some great work for me to do in the world."

It was shortly afterwards that he spotted an advertisement in the *Morning Post* for the job of first general manager of the BBC. He wrote his application in the Cavendish club, in London, and gave it to the hall porter. As an after-thought he looked up Sir William Noble, chairman of the interviewing panel, in *Who's Who* and discovered that Noble was an Aberdonian. He quickly retrieved the letter and added the postscript: "No doubt you would know some of my people in Aberdeen." A departure from Reith's austere code of self-reliance, it none the less did the trick: he got the job and began work on 30 December, 1922. Four years later the company received its royal charter.

Reith likened his task to blazing a trail through virgin forest, overcoming disease and danger, opening up and developing what had been barren and desolate. In another grand metaphor he expressed broadcasting as a drawn sword cleaving the darkness of ignorance. His enormous enthusiasm was infectious, and his influence on the emerging BBC all-pervasive as well as profoundly beneficial. He became the architect of its worldwide reputation for high-quality public service broadcasting, giving education, religion and culture an importance equal to that of news, information and entertainment. Its engineering quality set international standards. In 1936 he was responsible for inaugurating television in Britain.

Occasionally the high moral tone on which he insisted exposed Reith to ridicule. One day he entered a deputy's office and complained that an artist called Daisy Kennedy was performing that night. When the deputy asked if there was anything wrong with that, Reith replied: "Haven't you seen the papers? She was divorced yesterday. We can't have a divorced woman performing." However, when they were not infringing his Presbyterian values he took little day to day interest in programmes once he had determined the strategy and laid down the percentages for music, light entertainment, talks, etc. His work was largely strategic, concerned with the politics and economics of the organisation.

His lasting achievement, in the words of a leader in *The Times* when he resigned, was to make the BBC "a great liberating influence" in the face of sceptics, and there were many, who saw little future for the new invention.

The driven Calvinist deep within his psyche insisted that he should be "fully stretched". By 1938 the BBC stretched him no longer. Increasingly unsettled and restive, "for the single and simple reason that there was not enough to do", he was invited by Neville Chamberlain, the prime minister, to become chairman of Imperial Airways. "Foolish of course to have left the BBC," he wrote later, "stupendous folly to have left one of the most responsible and rewarding posts in all the world." Forbidding any presentation, indeed any form of farewell, he took the lift down to the entrance hall of Broadcasting House, where his wife shook hands with the senior commissionaire. Reith, touched by this gesture, left the building in tears. His impetuous departure – a kind of abdication, as one commentator pointed out – haunted him for the rest of his life.

In 1940 he became National MP for Southampton and minister of information, later minister of transport, later still minister of works and a peer. However he was ill-suited to the political life and Churchill dismissed him. He joined the Royal Navy as a lieutenant commander in the RNVR and exercised an important role in masterminding the D-Day landings.

His post-war work included chairmanships of the Commonwealth Telecommunications Board, New Towns Committee, Hemel Hempstead Development Corporation, National Film Finance Corporation and the Colonial Development Corporation, but he continued to long for a national post of greater importance and lustre which never came. In Scotland he derived pleasure from his appointment as Lord High Commissioner to the General Assembly of the Church of Scotland, somewhat less from his rectorship of Glasgow University. He died a frustrated visionary, in his own estimation a failure. "Life's for living," he said during his Glasgow rectorial address, "and that's what I missed."

Looking back in his old age, he regretted that he had never had the capacity to suffer fools gladly or to employ the compromises that further the ambitions of others.

Personal memoir by
Marista Leishman
(daughter)

John Reith was an outstanding actor – even though he could only play one part; that of John Reith. All his life he worked for the effect for which his height, his craggy looks, the Denis Healey eyebrows (without the kindly humour) and appalling scar usefully combined. Wherever he went he devised a sort of stage set: the playing field scale of his desk top was curiously devoid of papers and of the paraphernalia of process and the pens and inkwells were arranged with geometrical precision. He quaintly believed that to get to Heaven your affairs must be in perfect order. He had a gold fountain pen which lay across his desk like a telegraph pole – making the point that nothing cheap would do. Behind his enormous desk chair he strode quickly to and fro. His audience – because that was the form that meetings with Reith took – had uneasily to follow his movements back and forth and feel vaguely disadvantaged.

"You were," said Malcolm Muggeridge in a televised interview, "one of the top three people in Britain at the time..." In that short time between his appointment in 1922 to manage the then British Broadcasting Company – "when," as he said, "I worked out of a sort of broom cupboard" – and his enigmatic departure 17 years later, he became a colossus who bestrode the world. He had, in his view, been singled out for special attention. "I would say that the Almighty was there in my appointment to the job and was there in the execution of it." (Was this some divine intervention whimsically withheld for Haley, Jacob, Curran, and Greene?)

But other less beneficent forces were also at work. One was Winston Churchill whose singular processes during crises Reith curiously understood and whose warlike spirit his own resembled. There could not be room for them both, and he wrote to Churchill as from "someone whom you broke and whose life you ruined". "Old Wuthering Heights" Churchill called him, thus capturing the rugged ferocious look of a prophet of doom mournfully brooding over a world gone wrong.

His Highland ancestor Jeannie Stewart of Tomintoul put it another way. She had married into the family and noted: "There niver was a Reith man yet wha hadnae his back tae the wa'". Reith exploited his Scots origins. There was his five-year engineering apprenticeship with the North British Locomotive Company in Springburn – an inappropriate move urged by his unworldly minister father, unable to comprehend the commotion that was his youngest son. The Kincardineshire village wheelwright, the tollhouse keeper, and especially the general manager of the Clyde Navigation Trust – they were for him his significant forebears. But it was to the Cairngorm mountains and the Rothiemurchus forest where he spent his boyhood summers that he returned in spirit; those place-names enhanced his Scottish accent with the rolling r's which he made to reverberate around the chamber of the upper House and other London platforms. But of Scottish culture he was practically innocent, unmoved by any urge to put anything back into Scotland. A Londonised BBC emerged. Regional accents in broadcasting were out and BBC regional offices looked to the centre.

Near London he leased a middling grand house and, ever the establishment man, he kept up an elaborate Edwardian life style with servants inside and out. But he was an eccentric also, and having got the setting right felt no need himself to conform. One day he disappeared just before a formal lunch party. In response to my mother's question to the head parlour maid she coloured and said, "My lady – his lordship is in the coal cellar tidying it out." At which he appeared, grotesquely black from head to foot.

Family conversation was sparse. Occasionally at lunch he would make a statement; but it was more likely to be about the bones in the fish pie or the weeds in the path and the gardener's incompetence. Hardly the stuff of dialectic. You didn't converse with Lord Reith: you listened respectfully, trying from time to time to poke in your bit, only to feel that it hadn't actually lodged anywhere. Anyway, he was deaf.

His appointment as her majesty's Lord High Commissioner to the General Assembly of the Church of Scotland, with residence in the Palace of Holyroodhouse and a retinue, enabled him to feel "adequately circumstanced" for once. Their graces received a visit from their grandchildren. In full regalia he bent down towards his grandson of seven years. "Well, Mark," he said ominously, "what have you to say to me?" The boy looked steadily up at him. "Well grandfather", he said, "how can I have anything to say to you until you have asked me a question?" At this robust response a sudden engagement called his grace elsewhere, his entourage hurrying along behind him.

In all his appointments Reith worked as a pragmatist with the benchmarks "Will it work?" "Is it efficient?". His leadership was only so good as there were people who could flourish under benevolent paternalism. When, with the war clouds gathering, he precipitately left the BBC in 1939, he probably did so in the hope of a War Office appointment under Chamberlain. Or was it another piece of audacious drama, which he calculated would cause the BBC governors to entreat him to return? They didn't. He developed a sort of hate list of those distinguished figures most deserving of his contumely: Churchill, Earl Mountbatten, Field Marshall Montgomery, Bertrand Russell. And then came his son-in-law to be. "Never mind Reith," said one of his few enduring friends to Murray, "Walsham always was impossible." And so he was. He had the most frightful problem with himself. He who could with little fuss shoulder enormous responsibility for affairs had little idea what to do for himself or his family. He noted in his diary how "a crushing, awful, unspeakable remorse comes on me when I think how far I've failed". He became clogged in self-pity.

His was a troubled spirit that seems still to inhabit the high tops of Ben Macdui and yet seeks peace in the little graveyard below in the old kirk of Rothiemurchus.

Times leader the day after Reith's death

"His conception, which has been admired, studied and occasionally applied in other countries of the world, still has its home base at Broadcasting House. It is a still operative principle. The corporate personality of the BBC still gets, and will continue to get, a twitch on the thread from that angular Scots engineer, of unabashed earnestness and unbending strength, who, having survived a sniper's bullet in 1915, felt himself to be elected by Providence to do something great in the world. He did."

From Peter Black's *The Biggest Aspidistra in the World* [1972]

[1] "He was essentially a romantic Roundhead, who felt that he was fulfilling the purpose for which he had been born only when he was working himself half to death leading a cause that did the public good, in a bracing kind of way. That such a man, pre-eminently equipped for a big task, should have been knocking around London looking for something to do at the moment when the BBC was looking for a chief executive is a coincidence extraordinary enough to make you suspect that Providence may have had a hand in it, after all. But it is misleading to imply that he cuffed and kicked and badgered broadcasting into going the way he wanted. The team he steered, the directors he served, thought as he did."

[2] "He grasped immediately two of the things that made broadcasting unique. Because it was a live communication mistakes were not only probable but certain, and they would be impossible to retrieve or even to limit. And unlike the theatre and cinema the wireless did not offer the customer a choice between a score of different plays and films but made the choice for him. It was, said Reith, exclusively a table-d'hôte menu."

Reith's account from *Into the Wind* [autobiography, 1949] of the Duke of Windsor's abdication broadcast

"I slipped out of the chair to the left; he was to slip into it from the right. So slipping, he gave an almighty kick to the table leg. And that was inevitably and faithfully transmitted to the attendant multitudes. Some days afterwards I was invited to confirm or deny a report that, having made the announcement, I had left the room, slamming the door. It was even suggested that, by so doing, I was not just forgetful of microphone sensitivity, but was indicating disapproval of what was to follow. I had left the room, but no microphone would have noted it."

Letter from Reith to Churchill

"I have, like you, a war mentality, and other qualities which should have commended themselves to you. Even in office I was nothing like fully stretched and I was completely out of touch with you. You could have used me in a way, and to an extent, you never realised. Instead of that there's been the sterility, humiliation and distress of

	all these years, eyeless in Gaza, without even the consolation Samson had in knowing it was his own fault, and that's how and where I still am."
Letter from Churchill to Reith	"So far as my administration's concerned, I've always admired your abilities and energy and it was with regret that I was not able to include you in the considerable reconstruction of the Government in February 1942. Several times since then I've considered you for various posts which became vacant, but I always encountered considerable opposition from one quarter or another on the grounds that you were difficult to work with...If you think I can be of service to you at any time, pray let me know, for I'm very sorry that the fortunes of war should have proved so adverse to you, and I feel the State is in your debt."
Reith's advice for a young man starting out in life	"Tell him to be a man of principle and ideal. Warn him of conflict between principle and expediency. Expediency not necessarily wrong; perhaps the only way to secure a just end; abominably wrong if it means betrayal of principle. To have a sense of humour; to profit from discouragement. To realise that it is often stronger to yield than to resist. To be ambitious, eager to excel, but conditioned by worthiness of aim. To have an opinion of himself and his capacity, if merited; but not to flaunt it."
Thoughts of Reith	[1] "I used to think, particularly when there was a wind and a sound of music in the trees, that there was a message for me, but I couldn't quite make it out." [2] "I was tremendously over-serious, I think. I doubt if I've ever been young. I don't think I took the potential enjoyment of life as most people of my age would and did." [3] "Despotism tempered by assassination." [The best form of government] [4] "A potential social menace of the first magnitude." [Television] [5] "A passionate desire for truth in oneself, one's actions, in one's believing. And kindness." [His set of values] [6] "I hear you." [His typical response when the remark he had just heard was either untrue or not worth answering]

Rice, Professor David Talbot
(1903-72)
Authority on Byzantine art, educated at Eton and Christ Church, Oxford. When he came down from Oxford, there were no centres for advanced study of his subject: Rice was prominent among those who promoted its cause. In 1925 he joined the staff of the Oxford expedition to Kish, Mesopotamia, excavated in Cyprus the following year, and in 1927 became field director of the British Academy excavations in Constantinople. The same year he married Tamara Abelson, a specialist in Russian art. Later he travelled extensively in the near East, including a journey to Mount Athos with Robert Byron, the results of which were published in their book, *The Birth of Western Painting*. In 1931 he helped to organise an important exhibition of Persian art at the Royal Academy. Then he was appointed lecturer on Byzantine and near Eastern art at the Courtauld Institute in London. At the age of 30 he came to Scotland as professor of the history of fine art at Edinburgh University, a post

he continued to hold until his death. He played an active part in Scottish cultural life, serving on the Arts Council and as senior trustee of the National Galleries of Scotland. During the second world war he was head of the near Eastern section of the intelligence directorate at the War Office. Among his many books was *The Appreciation of Byzantine Art*, published posthumously.

Scotsman obituary

"He belonged to a world which is fast disappearing, a world in which scholarship was a pursuit compatible with being a country gentleman; where travel was a work of art; where duty was a kind, the highest kind, of *noblesse oblige*."

From Rice's *Teach Yourself to Study Art* [1955]

"In a word, the reason [that we should look at pictures] is that we want to be taken away from ourselves and out of the limits of the everyday world in which we live. The artist, whether he be poet, painter, or musician, has the power to transport us, if we will allow him to do so, when we read his books, look at his pictures, or listen to his music with an open mind. Each man will find himself more in sympathy with the works of certain artists than with those of others, for neither all men nor all artists are moved by exactly the same things. But when the sympathy is there, the artist will be able to inspire the spectator, so that for a time at least he forgets himself and all his troubles in the contemplation of the work before him. But it is something more than mere forgetfulness that results, for man's spirit is at the same time recreated. All that is most spiritual in his make-up is aroused and inspired. He is transported into a new world, and when he has once visited it he will inevitably desire frequently to revisit it, and to seek the awakening of the same emotions again. Like all great emotions, those engendered by art are not always happy, and to seek only the oblivion of Nirvana is to ask the impossible. But the emotions will always be on a high plane, above common experience, and outside the run of everyday life."

Richardson, Robin
(1915-75)
BBC producer. He was responsible for many influential literary and cultural programmes on radio, notably *Arts Review*, a discursive critical forum unique in its day. A witty and erudite figure, he was also an active promoter of the arts in Scotland.

Riddell-Webster, General Sir Thomas Sheridan
(1886-1974)
Soldier, educated at Harrow and Sandhurst, who joined the army in 1905 and served with distinction in both world wars. In the first he won the DSO and was mentioned in despatches. Between the wars, among a variety of appointments, he was ADC to the King. In 1942 he was appointed general officer commanding-in-chief, Southern India, created KCB in the same year, and was again mentioned in despatches. By the end of the war he had risen to become quartermaster-general to the forces at the War Office. After the war he was president of the British Legion (Scotland).

Robertson, Edith Anne
(1883-1973)
Poet, translator and biographer, born in Glasgow. Her work

included collected ballads and poems in the Scots tongue, translations of Walter de la Mare and G.M. Hopkins into Scots, and two biographies of St Francis Xavier.

Robertson, Jeannie
(1908-75)
Singer of traditional Scottish songs and ballads. Born in Aberdeen, she learned much of her considerable store of unwritten material from her parents, who were north-east travelling folk. She was discovered in her home city in 1953 by Hamish Henderson, of the School of Scottish Studies at Edinburgh University, who was collecting and recording examples of the oral Scots tradition. As a result of this fortuitous encounter she played an important part in the resurgence of interest in Scottish folk culture. Among her public appearances she shared a concert programme with Maria Callas and Sir Thomas Beecham. She married Donald Higgins, a piper, and their daughter, Lizzie, became a prominent traditional singer in her own right.

Hamish Henderson wrote

"Jeannie Robertson had a vast repertoire of songs, ballads, and stories, and was unique in reshaping and recreating them with a powerful, creative intelligence. She was a storyteller of genius, and spoke a form of Lowland Scots which was almost eighteenth century in character. She was a poet in song, a virtuoso of the art and an artist of the first order."

Robertson, Dr Robert B.
(c1915-74)
Physician, psychiatrist and author, born in Egypt, a graduate of St Andrews University. He served with the Red Cross during the Abyssinian war and later with the British army in India, Palestine and Italy, receiving an MBE for his work at Salerno. In 1950-51 he spent eight months as senior medical officer in a whaling fleet in the Southern Ocean. His book about this experience, *Of Whales and Men*, became a best-seller and was translated into a dozen languages. Latterly he was resident doctor on the island of Jura.

From Robertson's Of Whales and Men [1956]

[1] "Sometimes the whale is killed outright, but more often it either races away on the surface or dives deep as though to think over this disconcerting matter of an explosion inside its tummy."
[2] "Thor ambled back up the flying bridge, wiping his hands on his trousers, and glanced once, casually but a little sadly, at the mighty thing he had fought and killed. Perhaps, like myself at that moment, he was seeing the drama from the whale's point of view. Ten minutes before, this harmless monster had not known that man existed, and now it lay, smashed and upside down, without having known or comprehended why or how it had been attacked."

Robertson-Justice, James Norval Harold
(1905-75)
Film actor, born somewhere north of the border – *The Times* in his obituary giving "north west Scotland" as his place of birth, *The Scotsman* preferring Wigtownshire, another obituary making him a Dundonian. He was educated at Marlborough College and Bonn University. In his *Who's Who* entry he made no mention of his films,

describing his career as "undistinguished but varied, comprising some three score jobs in different parts of the world". Intended by his family for a diplomatic career, he entered journalism with the Reuters news agency. Later his booming voice, larger-than-life appearance, and natural ebullience enabled him to carve a niche in a distinctive type of film role of which the peppery surgeon Sir Lancelot Spratt in *Doctor in the House* was characteristic. He also appeared in *Whisky Galore* and *Scott of the Antarctic*. Twice rector of Edinburgh University, he was described on the citation for his honorary doctorate from that institution as "film star, journalist, engineer, farmer, sailor, policeman, racing motorist and bird-watcher". He claimed to be the inventor of a rocket-propelled net method of catching wildfowl for marking, and was the author of various papers on ornithology, ecology and conservation. For 20 years he lived in Sutherland and indulged his interest in falconry, afterwards dividing his time between Easter Ross and Hampshire. His agent described him as "a divine chap and a wonderful character".

Robson, Jack
(c1910-74)
Journalist and horse-racing tipster, who worked first for the *Evening Dispatch*, Edinburgh, where he acquired a reputation for spotting a winning horse. In 1941 he began a long association with India as a major in the 14th Army. After the war he became sports editor of *The Statesman*, Calcutta, returning to Edinburgh as senior racing correspondent of *The Scotsman*, where he wrote under the pseudonym of Major. He was largely responsible for winning the *Sporting Chronicle* nap table for *The Scotsman* in 1967. During one particularly hot streak his doubles forecast proved correct on 13 successive Saturdays.

Rogers, Mgr. Gerard
(c1909-75)
Roman Catholic priest, ordained in 1931, whose skill in canon law was widely recognised within the church. He began as an assistant priest in St John's, Gorbals, in the heart of the Glasgow slums, and progressed to the office of the Sacred Roman Rota, an important tribunal dealing with matrimonial cases, in which he succeeded Cardinal William Heard.

Rosebery, 6th Earl of
Albert Edward Harry Meyer Archibald Primrose
(1882-1974)
Soldier, politician, landowner and horse-breeder, briefly secretary of state for Scotland, whose father – who had been one of Queen Victoria's prime ministers – remarked of his heir's birth certificate: "Names enough in all conscience". The 6th earl was educated at Eton and Sandhurst and relinquished his commission in the Grenadier Guards to contest Gladstone's old seat, Midlothian, where he was returned in 1906 by a large majority over his Tory opponent. At the age of 24 he was the youngest member of the House. He sat as a Liberal MP for four years, but decided not to stand again. When war broke out he returned to the army, serving in France, Belgium and

England. He was wounded and received the DSO and MC.

On his father's death in 1929 he succeeded to the title and to the family estates, and his burly figure became a familiar sight in Edinburgh. The turf was one of his chief interests. He persuaded the Betting Levy Board to continue its grant to Musselburgh race course when it was threatened with closure and, as an owner, won the Derby twice – with Blue Peter in 1939 and Ocean Swell in 1944 – donating £1,000 from his 1944 winnings to help start the Scots Ancestry Research Society.

Early in the 1930s, he became so disillusioned with Lloyd George that he joined the National Liberals, becoming the party's president, but, influenced perhaps by his family's traditional distaste for the Tories, he never took the ultimate step of turning Conservative. For most of the second world war he served as regional commissioner for civil defence in Scotland. In 1945 he followed Tom Johnston as secretary of state for Scotland in Churchill's caretaker government, becoming the first peer to be appointed to that post for 40 years. His term of office lasted only two months, but it was not without political achievement: during it, Prestwick was designated an international airport. Tom Johnston, a political opponent, was an admirer, describing Rosebery as "an active restless enemy of all bureaucracy".

In the post-war era, he played a notable part in Scottish public life, particularly as a highly effective chairman of the Scottish Tourist Board. In 1971, at the age of 90, he presided at the annual general meeting of the Scottish National Blood Transfusion Association, whose president he had been since 1940. He was Lord Lieutenant of Midlothian for 35 years.

His 90th birthday was celebrated in January 1972 with a bonfire in front of Dalmeny House. By then he was the sole survivor of the 1906 House of Commons. To mark his birthday he presented to the National Library of Scotland a letter written by Mary Queen of Scots 15 days before her execution in 1587, having bought the letter at a public auction in 1945.

In his youth he captained the Surrey county cricket team for three seasons and was included in the Scottish side which met the Australians in 1906.

From Tom Johnston's *Memories* [1952]

"If you wanted a thrill of excitement, equivalent to say parachute jumping, you could always invite Lord Rosebery to motor you along Princes Street and make a circular dive through the traffic, and head for home again without mishap. Once I badly blotted my copy book with him. We were out at Dalmeny House, and he was proudly exhibiting a picture of a horse of his that had won the Derby. Almost with an air of reverence he ejaculated 'Blue Peter!'

'Indeed!' I commented politely, not knowing anything about its pedigree, its points, or its achievements.

'Yes,' he added. 'I was offered a big sum of money for that horse from America.'

'And why didn't you take it?' I innocently and courteously asked. But immediately I was aware I had said the wrong thing.

'I would die in the poorshouse before I would part with that horse,' declared his Lordship. 'Not for all the money in the world would I part with that horse!'

Obviously I had roused not only the sportsman but the affectionate owner; his horse had given him what was perhaps one of the most memorable triumphs of his life."

Ross, Sir David
(1877-1971)
Philosopher and university administrator, born in Thurso, whose father, John Ross, had been principal of Maharajah's College, Travancore. He was educated at the Royal High School, Edinburgh, Edinburgh University, and Balliol College, Oxford. In 1900 he began a long association with another Oxford college, Oriel, as fellow, lecturer and provost. He made an outstanding contribution to philosophy with his work on Aristotle, whose works he translated in the Oxford edition, and whose calm and dispassionate outlook mirrored his own. "If you can convince me" was his favourite phrase. A dedicated scholar, he seldom took a rest, even when on holiday, and had no time for small talk. Between 1941 and 1944 he was vice-chancellor of Oxford University.

Ross-Farrow, Algernon
(c1907-74)
Art dealer, educated at Glenalmond School and Cambridge University. An authority on old silver, he was instrumental in the return to Scotland of the Charles Edward silver canteen, taken from Culloden, which subsequently formed part of a private collection. He served on destroyers with the Royal Navy during the second world war.

Rowallan, Lady
Gwyn Mervyn Grimond
(c1899-1971)
Wife of Lord Rowallan (former Chief Scout) and sister of Jo Grimond (former leader of the Liberal Party), born in St Andrews. A keen sportswoman, she won the women's doubles and mixed doubles of the Scottish hard court tennis championships in the late 1920s. She was president of the Royal Scottish Society for the Prevention of Cruelty to Children.

Roxburghe, 9th Duke of
George Victor Robert John Innes-Ker
(1913-74)
Landowner, whose godparents were King George V and Queen Mary. Educated at Eton and Sandhurst, he succeeded to the title in 1932 at the age of 19, on the death of his father. He was a subaltern in his father's former regiment, the Royal Horse Guards. In 1968 he became county convener of Roxburgh. He lived at Floors Castle, Kelso, owned about 80,000 acres, and was a countryman in the traditional mould, a keen angler, hunter and shot. He married twice, his first marriage to the daughter of the Marquess of Crewe ending in divorce. He died after being taken ill while grouse-shooting on one of his estates.

Roy, Professor James Alexander
(d 1973)
Scholar and writer, son of a Kirriemuir minister, educated at

Edinburgh University and Giessen University, where he became a reader in English. He returned to Scotland as a lecturer in English language and literature at St Andrews University, 1908-20, before emigrating to Canada as professor of English at Queen's University, Kingston, 1920-50. During the first world war he served in the artillery and on the intelligence staff, GHQ. In 1919 he was attached as educational officer to the Peace Conference. He retired to Edinburgh.

Times obituary

"Roy was a Celt of incredible energy, warm, generous, often impulsive in his judgments of men and events, but a disciplined and learned romantic when he put pen to paper."

From Roy's
The Heart is Highland
[1947]

"It was one of those days they have only in Scotland in early May. And to see those days at their best one has to go to the West Coast to the town where Mamie lived in the days when she was called that. It rained and it poured. The water came rushing down the spout and battered and hammered on the beech hedges and the poplars and the apple trees; it formed itself into torrents and brooks and rivulets and streams and rushed down the road that led to the house where Mamie lived till it joined more brooklets in the streets that ran down to the sea. At the foot of the road where the rain waters met there was a tremendous whirring and gurgling and swirling and swishing and twining, just like a lot of old friends meeting again. And when the runlets from the garden and the streamlets from the farm-yard and the burns from the roadsides and the rills from the gutters had all said how do you do to each other they all paired off and tore down the street and raced to the sea. And that was the end of them so far as the people were concerned who lived where Mamie stayed."

Rusk, Robert Robertson
(1879-1972)

Educationist, born in Ayr and educated at Ayr Academy and the Universities of Glasgow, Jena, and Cambridge. He became principal lecturer in education at Jordanhill College of Education, and for five years headed the department of education at Glasgow University. After he retired he continued to work voluntarily for the Scottish Council for Research in Education as its director, finally giving up the post in 1958 at the age of 79. His influence on teacher training and educational research, not only in this country but throughout the Commonwealth, was considerable.

From Rusk's
The Philosophical Bases of Education [1928]

"The answer to every educational question is ultimately influenced by our philosophy of life. Although few formulate it, every system of education must have an aim, and the aim of education is relative to the aim of life. Philosophy formulates what it conceives to be the end of life; education offers suggestions how this end is to be achieved. Nowhere is this dependence of education on philosophy more marked than in the question of the curriculum."

Russell, Hon. Lord
Albert Russell
(1884-1975)

Judge of the Court of Session, born in Glasgow, son of Sir William F. Russell. He was educated at Glasgow Academy and Glasgow

University. Called to the bar in 1908, he took silk in 1931 and was Solicitor-General, 1935-36. During the first world war he served with the City of Edinburgh (Fortress) Company, Royal Engineers. In 1931 he won Kirkcaldy Burghs for the Unionists, but Labour regained the seat four years later, putting an end to his political ambitions. He was elevated to the bench in 1936 and retired as a senator of the College of Justice in 1960. As a judge one of his most famous cases concerned the use of the words "the old marriage shop" for runaway marriages at Gretna Green. He held that the legend or belief that irregular marriages had been performed in bygone days by a blacksmith acting as a so-called priest was unfounded in fact and should properly be characterised as a myth.

Russell, Sir Robert Edwin
(1890-1972)
Civil servant, born in Dublin and educated at Trinity College, Dublin, where his father was a fellow. He entered the Indian civil service in 1912 and was variously a district magistrate, chief secretary to the revenue department and adviser to the governor of Bihar. After 33 years he left India and came to live and work in Edinburgh as an assistant secretary in the Department of Health for Scotland. Later he presided at a number of public inquiries, producing reports of impressive and cultivated judgment. In 1956, when the Commonwealth Institute formed a Scottish committee, he was a popular choice as its first chairman.

Sir Robert Grieve said "When he came to settle in Edinburgh, his modest house in Grange Road was visited by eminent Indians coming to renew acquaintance with a man they regarded with affection and respect for his humane and courageous administration in the difficult period before independence."

S

Salvesen, Major Noel Graham
(c1893-1971)
Industrialist, educated at Edinburgh Academy and Oxford University. A captain in the 7th battalion of the Royal Scots during the first world war, he was badly injured in the Gretna Green railway disaster in which many soldiers were killed. Between the wars he became chief executive of Christian Salvesen, the company founded by his grandfather. A fluent Norwegian speaker, he worked for the Intelligence Corps during the second world war as security officer for the North of Scotland, and was responsible for interrogating Norwegians who had escaped to Scotland. With his two brothers, he established a chair at Oxford University.

Schilsky, Eric
(1898-1974)
Sculptor, born in Southampton, who studied at the Slade School of Art, London. After teaching at Westminster School of Art and the

Central School of Arts, London, he came to live in Scotland as head of the school of sculpture at Edinburgh College of Art, 1946-69. He was elected an academician of the Royal Academy and of the Royal Scottish Academy.

Scott, Professor John Waugh
(1878-1974)

Philosopher, born in Lanarkshire, educated at Hamilton Academy and at Glasgow University, where he later worked as a lecturer in moral philosophy. He then became professor of logic and philosophy at University College, Cardiff, from 1920 until his retirement in 1944. In the early 1930s he originated "The Homecroft" experiment, a mutual scheme for helping the unemployed by encouraging them to produce their own goods and services, and he was secretary of the National Homecroft Association for 18 years. Among his publications he wrote several books and papers on ameliorating the plight of the unemployed. He gave as one of his recreations in *Who's Who* "pestering modern economists for an authoritative ruling on C.B. Phipson's The Science of Civilisation".

From Scott's Self-Subsistence for the Unemployed – studies in a new technique [1935]

"Walking through the streets of Cheltenham one day during the winter of 1932, I perceived that a movement, or rather several movements, for unemployment relief were afoot in the town; because numerous small grocers' and chandlers' shops, fruiterers, dairies, etc., were displaying notices as I passed, intimating that they accepted the vouchers of various unemployment funds in payment for their wares. Finding one which professed to receive 'all' vouchers, I went in to inquire if they would accept those of our Homecrofting Group, then just commencing. In order to explain the difference between ours and all the others, I asked the good lady what she did with the vouchers, to which she naturally replied that she took them to the bank and received money for them. 'In the same way,' I said, 'if you take ours along to our headquarters you will receive potatoes for them.' But as one can quite well understand she was not very ready to do business. She did not particularly want potatoes. I mentioned some other commodities and services which we had on offer. But she was still reluctant – not sure she wanted any of them, and there the matter had to be left."

Scott, Very Rev. Dr. Robert Forrester Victor
(1897-1975)

Minister of the Church of Scotland, whose father was minister of Logie-Buchan, Aberdeenshire. On his mother's side there had been a minister in the family for each of 10 generations. He was educated at Morrison's Academy, Crieff, and the Royal High School, Edinburgh. After leaving school he served during the first world war with the 13th battalion of the Royal Scots in France, and was wounded in action three times. After demobilisation he resumed his studies at Edinburgh University and was ordained to the parish of Strathmiglo, Fife. In 1938, he became minister of St Columba's Church of Scotland, Pont Street, London.

Essay by R. D. Kernohan

Robin Scott (as he was generally known) was moderator of the Church of Scotland's General Assembly in 1956-57, both an admirable and much admired minister. He was the first minister from a church in England to be moderator. But he was most notable for restoring the Scots Kirk to a decent place on the skyline of London's west end.

He was minister of St Columba's, Pont Street (round the back of Harrods) from 1938 to 1960. During that time the congregation had its Victorian building destroyed in the 1941 blitz, improvised and borrowed accommodation for more than a decade, and handselled their new building designed by Edward Maufe. They didn't so much move in as move up, for Scott had conducted services in the basement-hall while the church took shape above it.

The building was opened in December 1955, its tower surmounted by a saltire below the Cross. It displayed comely dignity rather than dazzling beauty, but it had the good fortune to be built before modern architecture and materials got out of hand. Scott presided over the process, not only developing the congregation but making the most of its good connections in London – in the City, Whitehall, and even the Palace. The Queen (the later Queen Mother) laid the foundation-stone in 1950.

Scott moved to London in 1938 as "colleague and successor" to the more literary Archibald Fleming. He was a son of the manse from Logie Buchan who went from Morrison's Academy in Crieff to the ranks of the Royal Scots in the first world war, in which he was wounded three times. After the war he graduated at Edinburgh, where his student days were noted for what graver churchmen called "early exuberance of spirit", and was ordained to Strathmiglo, Fife in 1923. He next had nine years as minister of St Andrew's Dundee, before going to the Glasgow Barony Church in 1935.

On this occasion too he had been called, in a style abandoned by the modern Kirk, as "colleague and successor", still under the vast shadow of his predecessor John White, then retiring in theory but never in nature. Scott had time to make relatively little impact in Glasgow before going on to London.

St Columba's had done their research. At his welcome social he was confronted with three cards recording his presence (as lance-corporal Scott) in the 1914-18 soldiers' leave-club at which his wife, then Phyllis Graves, had been one of the "welcomers".

Early in the second world war he became an army chaplain but was later made an army information officer with a London posting which allowed him to keep an eye on the St Columba's congregation after the church was burned down. "He lovingly nursed the flame," said his session clerk in a tribute whose slight incongruity was outweighed by sincerity. It was then that Scott fully established himself, not only as St Columba's minister but as counsellor to a much wider Scots community in London, though the pastoral work was (and is) shared with the other Scots kirk in London, the historic Crown Court at Covent Garden.

He was an accomplished preacher whose admirers marvelled that anyone could say so much each week in so short a time. He was also helped by a kindliness of manner and a good singing voice. But he was made moderator of the General Assembly in 1956 more in recognition of his London achievement than through eminence in wider Kirk politics. The most memorable act of his moderatorship was an important bit of Presbyterian symbolism, the formal reception back into the Church of Scotland of the remnant of the

Original Seceders.

In 1960 he left St Columba's for the quiet parish of Auchterhouse, near Dundee.

Scott-Moncrieff, George
(1910-74)

Author, playwright and poet, born in Edinburgh. He spent his first five years "very happily" in Galloway, with sorties to Edinburgh and Lanark, before going south to live in Middlesex. Life for him there, he confessed later, was never so good as it had been before: he was always conscious of a difference of temperament between his own family and their southern neighbours. In London, he wrote a pamphlet entitled Balmorality, denouncing such Scottish institutions as the Church of Scotland. T.S. Elliot encouraged him in thin times by giving him books to review for the *Criterion* magazine. In 1932, convinced that things were happening in Scotland, he made his return, "prospectless and penniless, but full of high hopes in a cause". He was 22 and ready to man the barricades, but when he met the leaders of the SNP, he was disappointed by the spectacle of dour men in bowler-hats. He and his wife Ann, a children's author, settled down in a cottage in the hills near Peebles and he wrote a succession of books including *The Scottish Islands* and *The Lowlands of Scotland*, a play, *Fotheringhay*, about the final year of Mary Queen of Scots, and a collection of verse, *Book of Uncommon Prayer*. In 1939 he co-founded a joint Scottish-Irish quarterly, *New Alliance*, and kept it going throughout the war years, but he was first to admit that the hoped-for political renaissance which persuaded him back to Scotland in the 1930s failed to fulfil the aspirations he and others had for it.

From Scott-Moncrieff's *The Scottish Islands* [1952]

[1] "Although it has two low hills to west and south, Ben Hough and Ben Hynish, the main, immediate, and persistent impression given by Tiree is one of a tremendous flatness: on a fine bright day a brilliant green flatness contained beneath a great domed bowl of sky. There is a rare and exhilarating quality to the sense of space and light, often maintained by the winds that sweep unchecked from sea to sea; a cruel north wind, maybe, a saline, tonic wind tearing the skin from one's jowl as one battles along the shelterless machair. It is a terrific quality this of light, light pouring from the sky and bouncing back from the sea, enveloping everything, seeming shadow-free. Wind-spun clouds leap across the bowl of sky from horizon to horizon. Bright sands stretch along wide curved bays. Everything seems fresh painted."

[2] "As a whole, Stornoway people are extremely kind and friendly, assertive sometimes and intemperate in various directions, being not very sure of themselves. Many people have remarked on or written about the phenomenon of the Stornoway weekend, the contrast between the bacchanalian carousals of the Saturday night and the Sabbatarian solemnity of the Sunday morning. Indeed, the drama of the contrast would be hard to overlook. As a very shrewd citizen put it to me, the trouble with Stornoway is that there is too big a gap between those who drink too much and those who don't drink at all, in short, not enough true temperance. It is unfortunate that the only licensed premises in Lewis are all congregated in

Stornoway, so that the country people are put to the unfortunate shift of cramming their refreshment into the exigencies of the bus timetable."

From Scott-Moncrieff's *The Lowlands of Scotland* [1939]

[1] "At Dundonald, Dreghorn, and Tarbolton are some of the best classical kirks in rural Scotland, indicating an early nineteenth-century prosperity before taste had been overlaid by a too considerable wealth. The first sits amongst trees on high ground beside the Castle of Dundonald, at whose apparent barrenness Dr Johnson 'roared and laughed till the ruins echoed'. The second is hexagonal. The third has two sweeping stone stairs leading to the loft. All of them have good steeples."

[2] "The main Glasgow-Edinburgh road, which is as dreary as all trunk roads, to be left behind as quickly as possible, runs through north Lanarkshire. Here again the bings are visible although they and their miners' rows are by-passed. There is a grim beauty in bing-land in some lights and moods: and the process of covering with vegetation, slow because of the chemicals in the composition of the slag, suggests interesting results. The bings break the bleak flat moor back of Shotts: dead bings, live bings, the smoke of their increase rising from their sides; the moss dripping into the pits, the water pumped back to the moss. The cages swing up through the open trellis-work at the pit-head, dripping wet, as though with sweat from their speed and the fire in the earth's bowels. The doors slam open and the men march out and clank down the iron ladders: they wear tin helmets or leather caps, on some the little hanging lamp shows a spark through the daylight. To the stranger the blackened frank faces are astonishingly handsome, bright and cheerful in expression. In the showers they slap water over calloused bodies, search every smear, and pick the coal dust from between their toes."

Shepherd, Very Rev. Dr Robert Henry Wishart
(1888-1971)

Missionary, born at Invergowrie, Perthshire. He worked in the office of the North British Railway at Dundee before studying for the ministry at New College, Edinburgh. The shorthand he learned with the railway company he found invaluable when preparing sermons in later life. In 1919 he emigrated to South Africa and lived there until his death more than 50 years later. Originally a missionary of the United Free Church of Scotland, he came under the Church of Scotland on the union of the churches. He was variously chaplain, director of publications and principal of Lovedale Missionary Institution, 1927-58. In 1959 he became the third missionary to hold the office of moderator of the General Assembly since the 1929 union. His twin brother, Rev. Dr Peter Shepherd, was a medical missionary in Calabar and Bechuanaland for 25 years, and moderator of the General Assembly of the United Free Church (i.e. the minority which did not unite) in 1945.

From Shepherd's *Where Aloes Flame* [1948]

"Does it ever come home to the ruling race how strange must be the Bantu servant's lot in a European household? The host of appliances, many of them complex and hard to control; the European passion for great possessions and yet for spotlessness of rooms; the demand for working to schedule ruled by a clock; the late sitting up at night and rising in the morning – how far removed from primitive Bantu ways it all must seem to children of the veld."

Shillabeer, Paul
(c1899-1975)
Official photographer to the Edinburgh International Festival from its foundation in 1947. He began his career with the London firm of Elliot and Fry, but quickly set up on his own as a studio photographer and was elected a fellow of the Royal Photographic Society, serving on its council. During the second world war, after his studio in Eastbourne was bombed, he and his wife decided to settle in Edinburgh. He became official photographer to 27 consecutive Edinburgh Festivals, his collection of several thousand colour slides and monochrome pictures forming a unique pictorial record of the event. Each year he presented to the Festival Society a handsome volume of his best pictures.

Simmers, W. Maxwell
(c1904-72)
Rugby player and administrator, a commanding figure in Glasgow Academicals' back division, who played for Scotland 28 times between 1926 and 1932, captaining the national side in 1932. He was president of the Scottish Rugby Union, 1956-57. In his professional life he was a partner in S. Easton Simmers and Co., the firm of chartered accountants founded by his father, and chairman of Scottish Highland Hotels.

Smart, Professor William Marshall
(1889-1975)
Astronomer, born in Doune and educated at McLaren High School, Callander, Glasgow University, and Trinity College, Cambridge. He was an instructor lieutenant in the Royal Navy, 1915-19, serving in the grand fleet in HMS Emperor of India. After the war he took up an appointment as John Couch Adams astronomer and lecturer in mathematics at Cambridge University. He left Cambridge in 1937 to become regius professor of astronomy at Glasgow University, a chair from which he retired in 1959. For six years he was secretary of the Royal Astronomical Society, and for three years vice-president of the Royal Society of Edinburgh. One of his textbooks played a valuable part in the training of Royal Navy and RAF navigators. His three sons all became professors.

From Smart's
The Origin of the Earth
[1951]

"Let us not then exalt the scientific method unduly as the close preserve of the scientist nor, which is much more important, as the only means by which we attempt to discover the secrets of Nature. It is easy for the scientist to be a materialist if he sees only in the Universe the apparently relentless unfolding of natural law and forgets that there are domains where the laws of physics are irrelevant. But, more and more, scientists are realising that they are exploring only one section of the great world of Nature in all its manifold complexity; beauty, moral conduct, spiritual values, religious experience are all outside his domain, yet all come necessarily within man's scrutiny when he attempts to interpret the Universe as a whole and strives to discern purpose therein. A great work of pictorial art could be analysed by the scientist in terms of chemical constitution, atomic and molecular structure, the laws of physical optics and all the rest; he might reduce Beethoven's Fifth Symphony to a collection of mathematical formulae in the theory of vibrations; in neither case would his interpretation be more than bare bones, incomplete and unsatisfying.

From Smart's *The Riddle of the Universe* [1968]
"In the past the Earth must have been rotating more rapidly – the day would then be shorter than at present – and the Moon must have been nearer the Earth and thus more effective in its tidal effects so long as the oceans existed. Further back in time, before the formation of the terrestrial and lunar crusts, the two bodies can be conceived to be in a hot plastic state when mutual tidal actions operated even more effectively. Still further back in time, the Earth and the Moon can be imagined to be so close together as to suggest that the Moon had just broken away from the Earth, the composite body rotating in a period of about four hours according to Sir George Darwin's theory relating to the fission of a rapidly rotating fluid body. This theory has encountered various difficulties and now there appear to be two possibilities, either that the Earth and Moon were formed separately out of two fairly close condensations of cosmic matter, or that they were at one time two independent bodies whose motions brought them together in such a way that the Moon was captured by the Earth at an effective distance between them which, although not necessarily small, was however less than their present distance apart; in either case tidal action then ensued in the way described to bring the two bodies to their present distance and to impress on them their present rotational periods."

Smellie, Rev. Dr William Aitken
(c1904-73)
Church of Scotland minister, son of Dr Alexander Smellie of Carluke, a celebrated preacher. He was educated at Glasgow University, where he was president of the SRC, and entered the ministry as an assistant at Glasgow Cathedral. His first charge was Glencairn, Dumfriesshire. Later, when minister of St John's Kirk, Perth, 1937-72, he became deeply involved in the work of the church's central administration as convener of the home mission committee and of the home board of the General Assembly. He played a leading part in the Tell Scotland evangelism movement. Locally he was instrumental in taking various initiatives to preserve the historic church of St John's and contributed reviews of Perth theatre productions to *The Scotsman* for several years.

Smith, Dr Arthur Lionel Forster
(1880-1972)
Teacher, educated at Rugby, where he shared a study with William Temple, and Balliol College, Oxford, where his father had been master. In his youth he played hockey for England. Before the first world war, and briefly afterwards, he was a fellow and tutor of Magdalen College, Oxford. Once, when high-spirited students started to light a bonfire on the lawn at Magdalen, Smith came down in pyjamas and a bowler hat, said "I wouldn't, if I were you", and quelled a riot. Each Easter vacation he and Charles Fisher, a

fellow don, went to Italy on a walking tour. When asked why they wore short black coats and dark flannel trousers, and carried umbrellas on these expeditions, they replied that they wished to be ready for any eventuality from the heaviest rain to the politest society. During the first world war he served as a captain in the 9th battalion of the Hampshire Regiment. Later he was appointed adviser of education in Iraq for 10 years, helping to shape the new government. He was rector of Edinburgh Academy, 1931-45, preferring to stay in Edinburgh even when offered the headship of Eton.

Smith, Dr Arthur Robert
(c1933-75)
Rugby player and athlete, educated at Kirkcudbright Academy, Glasgow University, and Cambridge University. Powerfully built, yet with a graceful stride, he won the Scottish long-jump championship in 1953, but it was in rugby that he achieved international honours. He joined the national side against Wales in 1955, scoring a memorable try, and became the most-capped of all Scotland threequarters. In 1962 he captained the British Isles in South Africa.

Smith, Ian
(d 1972)
Rugby player, educated at Winchester, a lawyer by profession. He first played rugby for Jedforest. Capped 32 times for Scotland, he was a member of the national side's three-quarter line in the 1920s. In the match against France in 1925 he scored four tries, scoring another four against Wales three weeks later. He captained the Scottish team which won the international championship and Triple Crown in 1933.

Smith, Robert Paterson
(1903-71)
Industrialist, born in the Stewartry of Kirkcudbright and educated at the Ewart School, Newton Stewart. He qualified as a chartered accountant in 1925 and shortly afterwards emigrated to India, joining the Asiatic Petroleum Company, Calcutta. He worked for Burmah-Shell in India before returning to London, where he rose to become chairman of Burmah Oil, 1965-71.

Smith, Sydney Goodsir
(1915-75)
Poet, born in New Zealand, who came to Scotland in 1927 when his father, Sydney Smith, was appointed professor of forensic medicine at Edinburgh University. He studied medicine at Edinburgh, but abandoned this course and went instead to Oriel College, Oxford, before setting out on a career in the Scottish arts. An outstanding polymath, he combined the roles of poet, playwright, broadcaster, author, translator, painter, critic and wit, and somehow also managed to part of the furniture in Milne's Bar. His first collection of verse, *Skail Wind*, was published in 1941. Five years later he gained a Rockefeller Atlantic award and in 1951 he won a prize in the Festival of Britain Scots poetry competition. His masterpiece in

Lallans, *Under the Eildon Tree*, was published in 1948. Some criticised him for simply substituting Scots words for English, but his fellow poet Alexander Scott hailed the 24-part work as "the greatest extended poem on passion in the whole Scots tradition". His play *The Wallace* was performed in the Assembly Hall at the 1960 Edinburgh Festival and so aroused Scottish patriotism that at the end of the performance a few rose to their feet and sang 'Scots wha hae wi' Wallace bled' , though the embarrassed majority stayed in their seats. In January 1975 he sent a letter in *The Scotsman* replying to a poor review of his latest collection of poetry. He concluded: "I totter on into the night, bowed a wee, maybe, but certainly bloody." He died a week later.

Times obituary

"In his person he combined elegance and carelessness in a distinctive balance. If his clothes always looked untidy, they still looked as though they had at some point passed under the hand of the best tailor in Edinburgh."

Louis Simpson, American poet, wrote about Smith in *Memoirs of a Modern Scotland* [1970]

"One evening I met Sydney Goodsir Smith in the Paper Bookshop off George Square. We talked about poetry and he said: 'American poets are lucky. You can get published.' We talked about prose, and he said that the American tradition was the 'fiction of space', as in Mark Twain, Whitman and Wolfe. I told Smith that I didn't find American 'expansiveness' in his own poems, but wildness, as in his 'Meth-Drinker' poem, a wildness strictly controlled. Smith said he was a classicist: he wanted 'the concentration of feeling that explodes and goes straight upward.' I said he seemed more lyrical than MacDiarmid was nowadays. 'Don't compare me with MacDiarmid,' he said. 'I look at a man's shoes – MacDiarmid, at a man's dreams in the air.' By this time we had moved to a bar where Smith bought whisky for both of us and also three strangers. These people, good middle-class Scots, looked at Smith with a mixture of curiosity and some other feeling I could not place."

Sorley MacLean wrote

"[Sydney was] a romantic poet in the best sense of the word, for in his poetry experience is transfigured by passion, and especially by the most romantic and most complex passion of love."

Springer, Rev. Dr Oliver
(c1901-72)
Scotland's first coloured minister. Born in Trinidad, he emigrated to Scotland in his early thirties and, having trained originally as a chemist, graduated in medicine at Edinburgh University. He practised as a GP in Glasgow for 30 years before entering the ministry in Aberdeenshire. He was known as a faith healer.

Stalker, Philip
(c1900-71)
Journalist, born in Dundee where his father was professor of medicine, and educated at the High School of Dundee. After service in the RAF, he entered journalism in 1922 with the *Dundee Advertiser*. Two years later he went to *The Scotsman* and remained with that paper until his retirement in 1967. He was variously reporter, feature writer and churches correspondent, a familiar figure in the press benches at the General Assembly of the Church of Scotland. Among

his "scoops" was the return of the Stone of Destiny to Arbroath Abbey after it was taken from Westminster Abbey. "Pip" Stalker was the author of an official history of *The Scotsman* published in 1967. Another book, *The Spirit and Material*, reflected his preoccupation with eternity and space. He also wrote a series of nonsense verses, *The Elephant, the Tiger and the Gentle Kangaroo*.

Wilfred Taylor wrote

"It is difficult to write of Pip Stalker without using a term which nowadays is apt to invite mockery. He was, in every sense, a gentleman of the press."

Extract from Stalker's The Elephant, the Tiger and the Gentle Kangaroo [1971]

The Elephant, the Tiger, and the gentle Kangaroo
were loitering around one day with nothing much to do,
when suddenly the Tiger said,
'Queen Anne, Queen Anne, Queen Anne is dead!'
And leaning on the Kangaroo
he passionately wept, 'Boo-hoo!' –
a burst of grief which overcame
the Kangaroo, who did the same.
The Elephant, of course, can stand
a lot before he is unmanned,
but soon he gulped and murmured, 'If
you two don't stop soon I shall (*sniff*)
find difficulty (*sniff*) in keeping
from joining you (*sniff, sniff*) in weeping,
although I think you ought to know
Queen Anne (*sniff*) died some years ago.'

Stenhouse, Hugh Cowan
(1915-71)
Industrialist, born in Kilsyth and educated at Sedbergh, the youngest son of Alexander Rennie Stenhouse, founder of the Glasgow-based insurance-broking group bearing that name. After service in the RASC, of which he became a lieutenant colonel, he returned to the family business. In 1967 he succeeded Lord Fraser of Allander as treasurer of the Scottish Conservative and Unionist Party. Four years later Edward Heath's Conservative government appointed him non-executive chairman of Govan Shipbuilders, the company which rose from the ashes of UCS (Upper Clyde Shipbuilders). The unions responded positively to his straight talking and extrovert personality, but by a tragic paradox he was killed in a car accident three months later. He died at the height of his powers, before he had time to fulfil the promise of his last and most challenging appointment. His dynamism was much missed in Scotland as a whole. He strongly resisted the notion that the control of major companies should inevitably gravitate to London, and in his last weeks was actively promoting the concept of a Scottish Development Corporation (which was translated long after his death into the reality of the Scottish Development Agency). He was a bluff visionary of his time, with the build of a rugby forward.

Scotsman obituary

"It was characteristic of Hugh Stenhouse that he accepted the unenviable position of chairman of Govan Shipbuilders. There were many more glittering prizes which were freely open to him and which would have involved much less personal effort."

Stenhouse on Govan Shipbuilders

"The work force have a lot to grumble about. I want to fight for them now. I took this job because I saw my native city as a depressed area, and this applies to the whole of Clydeside. The people of this city are as good as anybody. I am quite happy to fight the Government. I want to fight for this yard on their behalf."

Stephen, Sir Alexander Murray
(1892-1974)
Shipbuilder, educated at Fettes College and King's College, Cambridge. He served in France during the first world war, won the MC, and was mentioned in despatches. As head of Alexander Stephen & Sons, Linthouse, Glasgow, he maintained a 200-year-old family tradition of shipbuilding.

Stevenson, Andrew King ("A.K.")
(c1887-1973)
Motor sport organiser, born in Kilwinning, Ayrshire. He was 12 when he saw his first car (in 1899). After leaving school, he joined a Glasgow firm of chartered accountants, one of whose partners was secretary of the Royal Scottish Automobile Club. Stevenson's first job was to address 120 envelopes to the members. He became the club's first paid official in 1904. From 1908, when he was given an 11.9 h.p. Arrol-Johnston open two-seater for club work, he delighted in going out at weekends, travelling all over Scotland to see what had to be done to make driving safer. He was appointed secretary to the club in 1942, a post he held until he retired 20 years later. During his long association he saw the clubhouse in Blythswood Square, Glasgow, expand steadily until it occupied one whole side of the square. For half a century, 1924-73, he was the official starter of the Monte Carlo rally and participated in the race on several occasions. He was honorary president of the Monte Carlo rally competitors' club. At home he organised the Scottish reliability trials. He was known as a cheerful character with an enormous zest for life.

Stevenson, D(avid) Alan
(1891-1971)
Lighthouse engineer, last member of the firm of civil engineers founded by his great-grandfather, Robert Stevenson, of which Robert Louis Stevenson was originally intended to be a partner. He was educated at Edinburgh Academy and Edinburgh University. During the first world war he carried out lighthouse work around the Scottish coast and the eastern Mediterranean and served as a captain in the Royal Marine Engineers. After the war he returned to the family firm, which he had joined for a short period before the war, and with his father, Charles A. Stevenson, was engineer to the Northern Lighthouse Board and the Clyde Lighthouse Trust, appointments held by successive members of the Stevenson family from 1808 until 1936 and 1952 respectively. In 1925-26, he surveyed lighthouses from Siam to Aden for a report to the government of India. He and his father were responsible for "the talking beacon" – a system enabling ships to plot their positions by synchronised radio and foghorn signals. First installed on the Clyde in 1928, it was later introduced in many parts of the world. He retired in 1952 to

study technical history. Among his books were *Lighthouse Tours of Robert Stevenson* and *The World's Lighthouses Before 1820*.

Stevenson, Dorothy Emily
Mrs J. R. Peploe
(1892-1973)
Author of novels and children's verse, whose father, D.A. Stevenson, was a first cousin of Robert Louis Stevenson. Born and brought up in Edinburgh, she married Major J.R. Peploe. Her first book, *Miss Buncle's Book*, was published in 1934, her last, *The House of the Deer*, in 1970; in her long writing career she published 40 novels.

Stevenson, Rev. Dr Jack
(c1903-73)
Church of Scotland minister, educated at Glasgow Academy, Glasgow University, and St Andrews University, ordained and inducted at Culter, Lanarkshire, in 1932. He became editor of *Life and Work*, the Kirk's magazine, in 1945 and held this post for 20 years. One of his chief interests was Scottish Churches House.

Stewart-Clark, Sir Stewart
(1904-71)
Sportsman, landowner and baronet, educated at Eton, who succeeded his father to the title in 1924. During the second world war he was a lieutenant in the RA. A versatile competitor, he represented Scotland at squash-rackets and was twice runner-up in the Scottish championships, played for East of Scotland at lawn tennis, and listed shooting, fishing, golf and billiards among his other sporting interests. He lived at Dundas Castle, South Queensferry. His son and heir, John Stewart-Clark, became a Conservative member of the European Parliament.

Storm, Lesley
Margaret Cowie
(c1904-75)
Playwright, a clergyman's daughter from Maud, Aberdeenshire, who was educated at Peterhead Academy and Aberdeen University. She wrote a dozen plays of which the psychological drama *Black Chiffon* (1949) and *Roar Like A Dove* (1957), a comedy set in a Scottish castle, enjoyed considerable success in London and went on to become staples of the repertory and amateur movements.

From Harold Hobson's review of *Black Chiffon*

"Alicia Christie, driven by her husband's jealousy into a peculiar emotional relationship with her son, steals a black chiffon nightdress on the eve of his wedding out of some vague feeling of jealousy of her future daughter-in-law, of whom nevertheless she thoroughly approves; and it is the minute examination of this mental illness which is the subject of the play's first act and a half. Now, I am not saying that mental illness should necessarily be excluded from the drama; I am merely suggesting that this is a new, fashionable, and regrettable way of dealing with it.

The proper way, to my mind, is shown by Miss Storm herself in the second half of the play. Once the illness is established, she asks what are her characters going to do about it."

Strathmore and Kinghorne, 16th Earl of
Timothy Patrick Bowes-Lyon
(1918-72)
Cousin of the Queen and nephew of the Queen Mother, who succeeded to the title in 1949 and lived at Glamis Castle. He served with the Black Watch until 1944, when he retired owing to ill-health. In 1958 he married Mary Brennan, an Irish nursing sister in Dundee, who renounced her Roman Catholic faith. A daughter born the following year died a few weeks after birth. Lady Strathmore herself died in 1967.

Stuart, James Gray
1st Viscount Stuart of Findhorn
(1897-1971)
Politician, third son of the 17th Earl of Moray. After leaving Eton, he became a captain in the 3rd battalion, the Royal Scots, and served in the first world war. Between 1923 and 1959 he was Unionist MP for Moray and Nairn. He was chief whip, 1941-45, and secretary of state for Scotland, 1951-57.

Essay by
R. D. Kernohan

The first in the line of Earls of Moray was the regent murdered in Linlithgow; the second the "bonnie earl", also slain and even more lamented. Their successors made less impact, except as better survivors.

James Stuart, eventually Viscount Stuart of Findhorn, was the third son of the 17th earl. He survived the first world war to become one of the best-connected, least spectacular, but almost unexpectedly effective of politicians. He blossomed as Churchill's chief whip and was a successful Tory secretary of state for Scotland, though he only partially diluted socialist policies. He delayed the impact of Scottish nationalism but helped set Scottish Conservatism in a mould which was also a trap.

The survivors of the generation so largely slain in 1914-18 never quite escaped the war. Sensitive souls were haunted by ghosts or worried about why they were spared. Even pragmatists like Stuart and Harold Macmillan (who married sisters, daughters of the Duke of Devonshire) had their outlook shaped by reflections on not being slain.

Tories divided into those, like Macmillan, who became reformers to head off revolution and those like Stuart who made do and mended with what survived of the old world.

Stuart was 17 in 1914 and went to war from Eton, commissioned in the Royal Scots. At 18 he was fighting in France and soon invalided home. He was back on the western front by 1916 and at 21 was a brigade-major with a military cross and bar.

After a jaunt as equerry to Prince Albert, the future George VI, he became Tory (strictly speaking, Unionist) MP for Moray and Nairn, a former Liberal seat he held for 36 years. His father ordered him into politics – so Stuart insisted – to claim a seat where a Lloyd George Liberal had previously scraped home with Tory votes. The response of the young candidate on topping the poll was reputedly: "This is bloody ridiculous".

The patrician was no pusher for office. His shrewdness, conformity and team-spirit did not even see him made a whip till

1935, though promotion was more leisurely then than now. Ministers lingered longer, with fewer reshuffles. And from 1929 to 1951 the Conservatives, when not in opposition, were in coalition – not only during the war but in the pre-war national government, a bargain by which Tories effectively ruled but conceded a disproportionate share of offices to Liberals and former socialists prepared to join them.

Even the brightest and best of Tories found promotion slow, and Stuart was not the most obvious among them. But he proved a good whip – listening, persuading, intimidating, and avoiding foolish measures against those (like Churchill) who refused to be intimidated. He also developed an effective political style of nonchalance, "carefully cultivated to disarm".

When Churchill in 1941 edged the Tory chief whip into higher office but away from influence he found a congenial replacement in Stuart, with whom he worked well as premier and then Opposition leader. Stuart opted out in 1948 but Churchill wanted him back after the narrow 1951 Conservative victory. He was to be secretary of state for Scotland and continued as first Tory "chairman of the party" in Scotland, an innovation Stuart did not promote too arduously but which created a structure closer to the Conservative one in England.

Historians with a modern perspective might therefore describe Stuart as leader of the Scottish Tories. But there would be an anachronistic incongruity in the description.

Stuart was a team-player prepared to be a team-leader, as he proved at the Scottish Office, but thought in traditional Tory terms of a "party in the country" mainly as backing for MPs. No-one ever accused him of demagoguery, though he deployed a neat turn of phrase – as displayed when a socialist demanded that he speak up: "I am sorry," said Stuart, "I didn't think anyone was listening."

In turning to him in 1951 Churchill set a pattern which affected Scottish Tories for decades. Just as administrative devolution was taken seriously but allowed to exclude consideration of legislative devolution (except when Heath briefly rushed in and backed out) administrative competence took precedence over political communication.

Stuart suited Churchill, who turned more than ever in old age to old friends. The alternative from the previous Opposition front bench was the articulate, even philosophical Walter Elliot, who might have guided the party in a different direction and given it a Lowland, urban emphasis. The style might also have changed, and subsequent history, if Stuart had done badly. But he succeeded.

The Scottish Office responded to someone ready to stay there (as Stuart did till 1957) and carrying weight at the cabinet table: good at assessing options and coming to decisions, but unlikely to intrude demanding ideology into future planning. Stuart was at his best in getting to the point of decision and construction for the Forth road bridge but showed his limitations in accepting the formula for low-quality, mass-produced, council-based, welfare-dependency house building by which Scotland shared in the commitment to "300,000 houses a year". What turned often into social and environmental disaster also contributed eventually to a political one for the Conservatives.

There was always a danger in accepting the Scottish Office's assessment of "good" secretaries of state; some marks were allocated for taking good advice and recognising the wisdom of civil servants. But Stuart did well, partly by bringing in another competent patrician as deputy: Alec Home. Churchill, who had old hesitations about Home as well as Elliot, conceded: "All right, have your Home sweet Home", and added a directive: "Go and quell those turbulent Scots, and don't come back till you've done it."

Home summed up Stuart: "He was apparently detached, work-shy and bored with life: nothing could have been more misleading." And the alliance worked in the effective link-up of St Andrew's House, Westminster, public opinion, and a range of organised Scottish interests. The turbulence seemed to subside and nationalism to recede. At Stuart's last general election in 1955 the Scottish Tories won 36 seats out of 71 and just over half the votes.

Times change. But James Stuart's capacity lay in adjusting and improving to meet the needs of his times. He was a skilful politician of an old style and *ancien regime*. He would accept that new ways are bound to be different, though not necessarily better.

From Sir Alec Douglas-Home's foreword to *Within the Fringe* [Stuart's autobiography, 1967]

"It is almost irreverent to suggest that anyone could 'handle' Churchill, but Stuart had a technique which was all his own. Here is a short extract following a proposal by the Prime Minister to appoint a certain person to office:
P.M.: 'Stop. You're not going, are you?'
Stuart: 'No. I'm only going to vomit. I'll be back in a minute.'
P.M.: 'Oh, so you don't like this?'
Stuart: 'Not much.'"

From Stuart's *Within the Fringe*

[1] "Afterwards I walked out into the Mall in my Privy Councillor's uniform to find my car when I was signalled by George Buchanan, the Glasgow left-wing ex-MP who had left the Commons to become Chairman of the Public Assistance Board after being an Under-Secretary at the Scottish Office in Attlee's Government. I had not seen him for a year or so and having always liked him I went over to see how he was faring. He ignored my greeting and said 'I never thought ye were such a bloody fool, Jimmy.' 'I'm sorry, Geordie,' I said, 'but what have I done wrong?' 'Och,' he said, 'to take on that job at the Scottish Office. Ye'll never make a bloody thing out o' that.'"

[2] "For myself, I have not been driven by ambition, which can break a man's health or sour his disposition or go to his head...So it cannot be said I ever reached to the stars. I have taken things as they came, and chance has played a big part in my life."

Sutherland, David Macbeth
(1883-1973)
Artist, born in Wick of a fish-curing family. After working briefly as a law apprentice, he left Sutherland for Edinburgh, where he found a job with a lithographic firm and studied at the school of the Royal Scottish Academy. In 1913 he joined the staff of the Edinburgh College of Art. He served with the 16th battalion, Royal Scots, during the first world war and was awarded the MC. After the war he returned to the college and married Dorothy Johnstone, a fellow painter and fellow member of the staff. He was the first holder of the Guthrie award for the most outstanding work by a young artist in

the annual RSA exhibition. He was elected an academician in 1936. Later he became head of Gray's School of Art, Aberdeen, where he did much to enhance the reputation of the painting school.

Sutherland, Mary Elizabeth
(1895-1972)
Pioneering trade unionist, agitator for women's rights and political organiser, born in Aberdeenshire of rural labouring stock, whose brother Alexander became editor of the *Scottish Farmer*. She won a scholarship to Aberdeen Girls' High School, combining her studies with nursing her sick mother, and went on to Aberdeen University in 1913. After graduating she qualified as a teacher, helping to organise the trainee teachers and pressing for a minimum wage. A year of teaching at her old school was followed by the first of her appointments in the Labour movement – organiser for the Scottish Farm Servants' Union, 1920-22. In this role she travelled widely throughout the country, encouraging women workers to join the union, and edited the union's journal. Later she joined the Socialist paper, *Forward*, in Glasgow, but deciding that organisational work rather than journalism was for her, left to become women's organiser for Scotland of the Labour Party, 1924-32.

She then went to London as the party's chief woman officer and developed into a highly competent administrator, addressing meetings, arranging conferences, and advising the party on issues affecting women workers, including factory act regulations. During the 1930s, influenced by her unsuccessful campaign to free a Russian dissident, she bitterly opposed the activities of crypto-communists within the Labour Party. In 1946 she became active in the National Institute of Houseworkers, set up by the Labour government to raise the status of domestic employment. She also took a prominent role in the Fabian Society, and vigorously supported British entry into the EEC, but was hostile to CND which she suspected of being communist-dominated. When she retired the vote of thanks to her at the Labour conference was rather lukewarm.

A close colleague wrote "Mary was an excellent chief as far as I was concerned. She never interfered, she never complained of one's work...but she was moody to a serious degree – one always had to wait to see what would be the state of her mind and her attitude the next day. I had holidays with her year after year and always knew in advance that there'd be some days that were almost a nightmare, but other days that would be delightful...She wrote extremely well – her written word was more effective than her speech because she had an impediment when addressing an audience. People who knew her earlier than I did say she hadn't had it when working with the Scottish Farm Servants' Union – I think those were happier days for her than her many years in Transport House where she became quite a loner."

T

Taylor, Dr Alexander Burt
(1904-72)
Registrar and scholar, son of an Orkney minister, born in Earlston

and educated at Hamilton Academy, Kirkwall Grammar School, and Edinburgh University. After teaching in Stirling and Falkirk he joined the government's schools inspectorate in 1933. Seconded to civil defence duties during the second world war, he was responsible for drawing up an evacuation plan for Scotland before resuming his civil service career as an assistant secretary at the Scottish Office, where he had responsibilities for the National Health Service and town and country planning. Between 1959 and 1965 he was registrar general for Scotland. He was a noted Icelandic scholar and an authority on early Scottish maps. In 1938 he published a new translation of the Orkneyinga Saga.

Thomson, Rev D. P.
(d 1974)
Evangelist, born in Dundee, who entered the ministry of the pre-union United Free Church of Scotland after military service in France and Salonika during the first world war. He left his first charge at Gillespie Memorial Church, Dunfermline, in 1935, to take up full-time mission work as evangelist to the home board of the Church of Scotland. He held this post for the next 30 years with a brief break during the second world war when he ministered to Trinity Church, Cambuslang. His drive and enthusiasm led to the foundation of St Ninian's lay training centre in Crieff.

Essay by R.D. Kernohan

The full name of David Patrick Thomson meant little to the range of Scots whom he influenced, inspired and (in a few cases) irritated. He was generally D.P. Thomson – very occasionally confused by those who got one initial wrong with his fellow Dundonians, the proprietors of Oor Wullie, but more often instantly recognised simply as "D.P.".

He was as impossible to classify as subdue. He was a minister, but not like most ministers. He was an evangelist, a "prisoner of grace" who liked the freedom to do things his own way. Yet it wouldn't do to say that D.P. Thomson was his own man, for that invited the pious but valid correction that, more than most Christians, he was seen to be Christ's man.

He was a zealot, but with a selflessness alien to most zealotry. He was a loner, yet a creator and mobiliser of teams and team-work. In another century he might have been driven to lead a secession or form a new denomination, but the 20th-century Kirk was comprehensive enough to accommodate him and let his vast energies go into an endless attempt to revive it and make its dry bones live. He also possessed its necessary arts of lobbying and persuasion – sometimes using the powerful but unspoken argument that if he got what he wanted he would then go away.

His major success was the creation of the St Ninian's lay training centre at Crieff in 1958. He was warden till he retired in 1966. But this was the outward and visible symbol of an influence expressed on and through people rather than institutions. The idiom of the age called him a "legend in his own lifetime". Today he would be recognised most readily as a great evangelical guru.

Although a prolific writer – probably too prolific – his main influence was through a power of personality to which even the spoken word was probably incidental. Until age slowed him down he was also able to work at a pace which left his disciples breathless. When he stepped out of one of his local mission headquarters it was said that "things slowed down to a gallop".

Thomson was always going to be a man with a mission, but its style and intensity were influenced by the first world war. He served as an officer first in France and then in Salonika before being invalided out of the army, but was the only one of three brothers to survive. This left him with "an awesome experience of some special purpose for which he had been spared". That found expression not only in a call to the ministry (after graduating at Glasgow University and training at the United Free Church College there) but in the desire to preach the Gospel to all who would listen and many who wouldn't.

He was organising secretary of a Glasgow University evangelistic union, then minister from 1928 to 1934 of Gillespie Church in Dunfermline, a UF church which in 1929 came into the reunited Kirk, and during the second world war minister of Trinity Church in Cambuslang. But for most of his working life he was an evangelist of the Church of Scotland's home board, variously regarded as apostle, occasional nuisance, saint, and "unofficial professor of practical training". He had a major role in the great success of the church's seaside missions, admirably matched to the social moods and trends of the time, and was a pioneer of lay and elder training in the church. But he also had an immense influence on large numbers of young ministers.

He was a great accumulator of books, especially on evangelical themes, and built up a notable library.

From Thomson's Men Christ Wants: evangelistic addresses [1950]

"There is another very prevalent misconception – that Christianity only appeals to men of certain types and temperaments, that there are natures for whom it can have no appeal, and to whom it can offer no real satisfaction. Men often say when I challenge them with the appeal of Christ, 'I'm not built that way.' Perhaps there is someone here saying that to himself tonight. My friend, let me assure you of this – in the Kingdom of Jesus Christ there is room and work for every variety of temperament and every form of gift. Was there ever a more varied company than that which Jesus gathered round Him during His earthly ministry? To go no further – look at the twelve apostles. There is Peter, volatile, hot-headed, impulsive. There is Thomas, with cool, keen, analytical mind, weighing every situation carefully, rashly prejudging no issue. There is John, the profound mystic, and James, the practical man of affairs. There is Andrew, the warm-hearted, big, brotherly soul, whom we have so happily adopted as our own patron saint. There is Simon the Zealot, member of the narrowest and most fanatical sect in Judaism; and Matthew, the large-minded man of the world, the servant of Imperial Rome."

From Thomson's The Road to Dunfermline: the story of a thirty-five years' quest

"There was a home to which I used to go, on week nights as well as Sundays. At its hospitable table, seven days a week, at every meal except breakfast – and, for aught I know, at that also – at least three extra places were always laid. These were for any stranger who might happen along. You had only to ring the front door bell and say you had come for tea, for dinner, or for supper, and you were made to realise that you could go as often as you chose, and could take whom you liked with you. It was the open door to the fellowship of the fireside as well as that of the common table. There, sitting next to one another, you might find the Admiral and the private, the daughter of a Maharajah and the junior clerk in a local bank. Long afterwards we were to embody that principle in our campaign work, and to realise that it brought an enrichment far beyond the price that had to be paid. The privacy of a group, whether family or team, had to be sacrificed, that the solitary and the stranger might find the earthly counterpart of that home above, where the gates are ever open, and where there is access from every side."

Thomson, Sir (James) Douglas (Wishart)
(1905-72)
Industrialist and politician, educated at Eton and Oxford, where he gained a blue for rowing. He succeeded his father as second baronet in 1935 and in the same year was elected Unionist MP for South Aberdeen, a seat previously held by his father. In 1946 he resigned the seat to devote himself to the family firm, William Thomson & Co., managers of the Ben Line. After the second world war, i which the fleet lost 19 ships by enemy action, the management faced a formidable task of reconstruction. Thomson succeeded in transforming the Ben Line into the second largest liner carrier of any nationality between Europe and the Far East and it became the first company to introduce ships capable of more than 20 knots on the Europe-Far East route. He resigned in 1970 owing to ill-health.

Thomson, James
(1888-1971)
Teacher and Gaelic scholar, born in Tong, Isle of Lewis. After graduating at Aberdeen University he taught briefly at Whithorn, served in the army during the first world war, and then became Gaelic master at the Nicolson Institute, Stornoway, helping to pioneer the language in secondary schools. From 1922 until 1953 he was headmaster of Bayble School, Stornoway, where one of his early achievements was to bring to an end the annual stone-battle between the boys of Bayble and Garrabost villages, and to substitute football matches.

Note by
Derick Thomson
(son)

My father had an important input to the growth of Gaelic consciousness in 20th-century Scotland.

His busy career involved a close involvement with the Church, with the Educational Institute of Scotland, with the Liberal Party and with the Lewis Association. He won the poetry competition at the National Mod in 1922, and the following year was the first to be given the Bardic crown. He contributed to the periodicals *An Rosarnach*, *An Gaidheal*, and *Gairm*, editing *An Gaidheal*, 1958-62. Earlier he edited *An Dileab*, an anthology of Gaelic verse for schools, and co-edited *Eilean Fraoich*, a collection of Lewis songs. A collection of his poems, *Fasgnadh* (Winnowing), was published in 1953, and his reminiscences of life in Tong about the turn of the century were written in the early 1950s and published in *Gairm*, 1997-98.

A quiet, dignified, and very efficient character, he could periodically relapse into uncontrolled laughter, recalling for example a fellow Lewis student at Aberdeen who jumped over the mat on a visit to a "posh" house there, exclaiming "I almost stood on it!".

Thomson, Sir John Mackay
(1887-1974)
Teacher and civil servant, born at Dunning, Perthshire, son of the Rev. Peter Thomson, DD, and educated at Trinity College Glenalmond, Edinburgh University, and Oriel College, Oxford. He was a master at Fettes College before a brief tenure as rector of Aberdeen Grammar School. In 1921 he entered the civil service as an inspector of schools, and between 1940 and 1952 he was secretary of the Scottish Education Department. He was knighted in 1946.

Thomson, J(ohn) Murray
(1885-1974)
Artist, born in Crieff and educated at Morrison's Academy and Edinburgh College of Art. In 1913 he was awarded a Carnegie travelling scholarship and completed his art training in Paris. An eye injury received in Germany during the first world war prevented him from painting for five years. Afterwards he became a noted painter of animals and birds. He was elected an academician of the Royal Scottish Academy in 1957.

Thomson, John S.
(c1909-73)
Entrepreneur and inventor, who served an apprenticeship as an engineer in the shipyards of the lower Clyde before opening a motor-cycle shop in Greenock in 1939. After the war he expanded his business interests, owning the largest garage in the district and holding numerous patents for cranes. He was reputed to be a millionaire. For 10 years he was an Independent member of Greenock Town Council and he tried on several occasions to win a Parliamentary seat. Not content with being chairman of the local senior football club, Morton, the cheerful extrovert was also for a time the club's manager. He delighted in the twin roles of crusader and rebel.

Tocher, Rev. Dr Forbes S.
(1885-1973)
Church of Scotland missionary, educated at the Universities of Aberdeen and Edinburgh, ordained at Boyndie Church, near his native Whitehills (Banffshire). In 1909 he left Scotland to work at the Ichang mission on the River Yangtze. He returned from China to serve with the Royal Field Artillery during the first world war and was awarded the MC. After the war he resumed his work at the Ichang mission and in 1927 negotiated the release of a sea captain taken prisoner by river pirates. For this bravery he was awarded the CBE. He was interned by the Japanese during the second world war. After his release in 1945 he became a parish minister in Banffshire.

Tod, Murray Macpherson
(1909-74)
Artist, educated at Kelvinside Academy, Glasgow School of Art, and

the Royal College of Art, London. He won a Rome scholarship in engraving. He was a teacher of art at Dalbeattie High School, but was struck down by muscular dystrophy while in his early forties. Nevertheless he continued to establish a reputation as an etcher and worked part-time as an assistant in the school of drawing and painting at Edinburgh College of Art.

Trotter, A.C. (Sandy) Trotter
(1902-75)
Journalist, a prominent figure in the Beaverbrook organisation, who began his newspaper career as a copy boy in his native Edinburgh. After early experience in Fleet Street he was appointed editor of the *Scottish Daily Express* at the age of 32 and stayed in the job for 25 years, resigning to become chairman of Beaverbrook newspapers in Scotland for a further 11 years. He played an active role in the wider community as a founder member of the Scottish Tourist Board, as a member of the Countryside Commission, and as chairman of the press and publicity committee for the 1970 Commonwealth Games.

Troup, Vice-Admiral Sir James Andrew Gardiner
(1883-1975)
Naval commander, born in Broughty Ferry and educated at Dundee High School and Ascham House, Bournemouth. He served in several wars. During the Boer war, 1899-1900, he fought at the battles of Colenso, Spion Kop, Vaalkrantz, and Tugela Heights, and was present at the relief of Ladysmith. In 1900 he was involved in the Boxer war. During the first world war he served on the Temeraire and Royal Sovereign in the grand fleet and was master of the fleet. He became, successively, captain of HM Navigation School, flag captain on HMS Revenge, director of the Tactical School, and director of naval intelligence.

Turnbull, Lt.-Col. Sir Hugh Stephenson
(1882-1973)
Policeman, from an old Borders family though born in India. His father, Maj.-Gen. P. S. Turnbull was honorary surgeon to the King. He was educated at Merchiston Castle School, Edinburgh, and at Sandhurst. In 1908, six years after receiving a commission, he had to leave the army because of a riding accident. He entered the police force with the Royal Irish Constabulary and at the age of 31 became chief constable of Argyll. During the first world war, he commanded the 7th Gordon Highlanders. He returned to the police and in 1920 moved to the Cumberland and Westmorland force as chief constable. Five years later he was appointed commissioner of police for the City of London. In 1931, after a visit to the United States to study traffic problems, he introduced automatic traffic signals in Britain – despite fierce opposition from Whitehall.

U

Ure, Mary Eileen
(1933-75)
Actress, born in Glasgow, whose great-grandfather was a lord

provost of the city. She was educated in Glasgow and at the Mount School, York. For three years she studied at the Central School of Speech and Drama in London, intending to return to Glasgow to be a drama teacher. In 1954, however, she made her professional debut at the Opera House, Manchester, and in the same year was highly acclaimed for her performance in Anouilh's *Time Remembered* at the Lyric, Hammersmith. The following year, in Moscow, she was Ophelia to Paul Schofield's Hamlet.

In 1956 she played Abigail in the first British production of Miller's *The Crucible* and Alison, the put-upon wife, in John Osborne's *Look Back in Anger*. Alison (complete with infamous ironing board) was to become her most celebrated creation: she played the part both on the New York stage and in the film version. In 1957 she married the author of the play, but the relationship with Osborne proved to be tempestuous and short.

Her classical roles included Desdemona in *Othello* and Titania in *A Midsummer Night's Dream*, both at Stratford-upon-Avon, and in 1961 she appeared with Robert Shaw in *The Changeling* at the Royal Court. Two years later she married Shaw. In an uncanny prelude to her death, she returned to the London stage after a long absence in a mediocre play called *The Exorcist*, in which she played a woman driven to sudden death by the unknown. The day after it opened at the Comedy Theatre, her husband found her unconscious in their hotel room and she died before reaching hospital.

From John Osborne's *Almost a Gentleman* [autobiography, 1991]

[1] "Mary was one of those unguarded souls who can make themselves understood by penguins or the wildest dervishes."
[2] "She took scant interest in her surroundings and, despite her eloquence about her mother's oatcakes, kippers and jams, scarcely cooked at all...She would leave the house every day after instant coffee and a slice of toast and reappear in the late afternoon...she always came back bubbling with happiness."
[3] "Kelvinist and Calvinist, schoolgirlishly light-hearted, she stood out in Manhattan like a Welsh miner at a bar mitzvah."
[4] "Mary was not much of an actress. She had a rather harsh voice and a tiny range."
[5] "It [Robert Shaw's death] didn't seem such a waste as that of Mary, whose destiny dragged her so pointlessly from a life better contained by the softly lapping waters of the Clyde."

W

Waddington, Professor Conrad Hal
(1905-75)
Biological scientist and a world authority on animal genetics, educated at Clifton College and Sidney Sussex College, Cambridge. During the second world war he conducted operational research in coastal command, and for two years was scientific adviser to the commander-in-chief. After a lecturing appointment in zoology at Strangeways research laboratory, Cambridge, he became Buchanan professor of animal genetics at Edinburgh University in 1947, a chair he held until his death. In 1972 he set up an experimental School of

the Man-made Future to study possible developments in human ecology and to provide a positive answer to what he saw as the self-destructive tendencies of modern societies. For six years he was president of the International Union of Biological Sciences.

Walker, Hon. Lord
James Walker
(1890-1972)
Judge, son of a solicitor, born in Wigtown and educated at Ewart High School, Newton Stewart, and the Universities of Glasgow and Edinburgh. Shortly after becoming an advocate in 1914, he served with the Royal Scots in Egypt and France. He was appointed Clerk of Justiciary in 1940, took silk in 1944, and joined the Scottish bench as a sheriff in 1949, becoming a senator of the College of Justice in 1954. His appointment brought the total number of judges in the Court of Session to 15 – the highest number for 120 years. He enjoyed the reputation of asking difficult questions with a deceptively benign smile. Chairman of the Scottish Law Reform Committee for 10 years, he acknowledged the need for adapting the law to the changing needs of society, particularly in matters of marriage and divorce. He made his last appearance on the bench in April, 1972, six weeks before his death at the age of 82.

Wallace, Alister Burns
(1906-74)
Plastic surgeon, educated at George Heriot's School, Edinburgh, Edinburgh University, and McGill University. In 1948 he became a consultant in plastic surgery to the army in Scotland and nine years later was appointed a consultant to the American army. From 1952 he received several grants for research in surgical metabolism, for the investigation of road and home accidents, and for the study of weight loss following extensive burns. He was founder and first general secretary of the International Society for Burns Injuries and twice president of the British Association of Plastic Surgeons. President Tito of Yugoslavia honoured him with the highest civilian award of the country in appreciation of the training given by him to young Yugoslav doctors.

Walton, Professor John
(1895-1971)
Botanist, son of the Scottish artist E. A. Walton, educated at Daniel Stewart's College, Edinburgh, and St John's College, Cambridge. He began his academic career as a lecturer in botany at Manchester University, and was botanist to the first Oxford expedition to Spitsbergen in 1921. In 1930 he became regius professor of botany at Glasgow University, retiring in 1962.

Watson-Watt, Sir Robert (Alexander)
(1892-1973)
Scientist and pioneer of radar, son of a joiner, whose encouragement by a woman teacher in Damacre Road Primary School, Brechin, fostered an early interest in scientific experiment. He was fond of devising household gadgets and took a particular interest in meteorology. From Damacre Road he went to Brechin High School

and to University College Dundee, where he graduated. In 1912, at the age of 20, he became assistant to Professor Peddie of the chair of natural philosophy at Dundee, and remained in this post for nine years. Later he found work in the Meteorological Office and the Royal Aircraft Establishment.

He was appointed superintendent of the radio department of the National Physical Laboratory and in 1938 was given the title of director of communication development. It was during this period that he conducted experiments in developing radar, which he had been thinking about for the best part of 20 years. In 1935 the director of scientific research at the air ministry asked him if he could devise a "death ray" for attracting and damaging enemy aircraft by means of radio waves. He replied that, although this was not practicable, the approach of an enemy plane might be detected and its position and speed ascertained by a radio echo from the plane.

After further mathematical calculations he was confident enough to prepare a memorandum outlining proposals for the use of radar in defensive and offensive operations. In effect this was the briefing for what was later called "the greatest advance [in communication] since the mariner's compass", which helped to save the country when the Germans launched their aerial attack on Britain. He was knighted in 1942. Watson-Watt married three times, his last wife being Air Chief Commandant Dame Katherine Jane Trefusis Forbes.

From Watson-Watt's *Three Steps to Victory* [autobiography, 1958]

[1] "Now I am fifty-six, five foot six, an unlucky thirteen stone, tubby if you want to be unkind, chubby if you want to be a little kind, fresh complexioned, organically sound and functionally fortunate, if fat, after a thirty-years war of resistance to taking exercise. I smile a lot because I feel that way, I talk of serious things, when I must, with a lightheartedness that does not spell levity – at least I hope it does not. I am objectionably silent and reserved in private conversations, because then I can never believe I have anything worth saying; objectionably fluent and talkative in public, because then I believe there is a lot that is worth saying again, that platitudes are worth repeating because they are true. A sixth-rate mathematician, a second-rate physicist, a second-rate engineer, a bit of a meteorologist, something of a journalist, a plausible salesman of ideas, interested in politics, liking to believe there is some poetry in my physics, some physics in my politics."

[2] "My creed as a scientific worker rests on an almost religious conviction about the goodness of measured facts, that all facts are good: they may be facts about bad things, but if they are facts they are good and valuable. I believe that the measured facts of basic science, the observed relations among them, and the tentative theories based on them, should be published for all to know. I know that this is the process from which the spectacular progress of science in the last two centuries has flowed. That spectacular progress has two quite independent aspects. On the one hand creative science as an artistic pursuit has greatly increased the stature of the human mind. It has made us rightly proud in the contemplation of the superb intellectual structure which has been built out of alert and exact observation, of imaginative and subtle speculation, and of exquisitely and elegantly ingenious experiment, devised to test and correct the speculation. I regard the release of

atomic energy as the highest achievement of the human intellect in history. And it is thus, as an aesthetic pursuit and as a humanity, that science should be taught to us all."
[3] "My greatest dread? The pleasures of retirement."

Weatherstone, Sir Duncan Mackay
(1898-1972)
Local politician and public servant, born in Edinburgh and educated at Daniel Stewart's College. After school he entered life assurance, retiring in 1961 as a senior manager of Scottish Equitable. He served in both world wars, winning the MC at the age of 20. In 1963, having been a Tory member of Edinburgh Town Council for the previous 13 years, he was elected lord provost. In this role he proved extrovert and outspoken, capable of infuriating local opinion, as when he asked the Beatles, who were attending a civic reception, for £100,000 to help the Edinburgh Festival. Three thousand Edinburgh ratepayers signed a petition objecting to his "begging" and demanding a public apology. He wanted to see inner and outer ring roads for Edinburgh and campaigned (unsuccessfully) for the demolition of Waverley station and the removal of the bus station from St Andrew Square. At a rally in 1964, before 2,000 schoolchildren assembled in the Usher Hall, he improvised a verse advancing the cause of road safety to the tune of "My Bonnie Lies over the Ocean", his favourite song. His eventful reign as lord provost came to an end in 1966, a year after he was knighted. Two years later, following the death of his wife, he re-married Elizabeth Evans, whom he had met on holiday in Jersey. She was 28, Sir Duncan 70. On 31 January, 1972, the couple committed suicide in their home. Their bodies were discovered by sheriff officers who forced their way into the house by smashing a pane of glass in the front door, while 20 people waited outside to attend a sale of Sir Duncan's goods by court warrant. A dress shop in George Street, Edinburgh, had obtained the warrant for a debt of £1,400.

Webster, Sir David (Lumsden)
(1903-71)
Arts administrator, born in Dundee, who left Scotland at the age of eight when his parents moved to Liverpool. He began his career in business, developing his musical interests as an amateur. In 1946 he was appointed general administrator of the Royal Opera House. He set up the first resident opera company at Covent Garden, acquired Sadler's Wells Ballet (which he developed into the Royal Ballet) and encouraged such protégés as Joan Sutherland and Geraint Evans. Throughout his regime from 1946 until 1970, Dame Margot Fonteyn was prima ballerina at Covent Garden.

Weir, Sir John
(1879-1971)
Physician, born in Glasgow and educated at Allan Glen's School and Glasgow University. He became Britain's foremost expert in homoeopathy, his interest in the subject dating from his time as resident physician and surgeon at the Western Infirmary, Glasgow. Much of his subsequent career was spent in London, though he never lost traces of his Glasgow accent. In 1923 he was appointed

physician to the Duke of Windsor, then Prince of Wales, and at once put his patient on a diet which banned cigars, allowed him only four cigarettes a day, and specified two small slices of cold beef for lunch. Between 1937 and 1952 he was physician-in-ordinary to King George VI, and was one of the doctors who signed bulletins before and after his lung operation. As physician to the Queen, 1952-68, he attended the birth of her four children. He had the reputation of being strict with his patients, constantly extolling the benefits of vigorous exercise. Weir once told how, after a consultation at Buckingham Palace, Queen Mary gave him a magnificent bunch of flowers to take to the homoeopathic hospital. He had them sent up to the wards. When he was doing the rounds later, he found a tiny six-year-old cockney patient standing beside the flowers. "Aren't they lovely?", he said to the child. "Wasn't it kind of the Queen to send them to you?" To which the patient replied: "Ow did she know I was 'ere?"

Welsh, Dr William Halliday
(c1879-1972)
Physician, athlete and rugby player, born in Edinburgh and educated at Merchiston Castle School and Edinburgh University. In his professional life he was a GP in Bridge of Allan. He broke the quarter-mile record in 1901 with a time of 50.3 secs. At the same time he played rugby for Scotland as a left-wing three-quarter and was a member of the side which won the international championship and the triple crown in 1901. After winning eight caps he retired from the game owing to injury. He served in the Royal Army Medical Corps in Salonika and Bulgaria during the first world war. Later he went big-game hunting in East Africa and Alaska.

Willis, Dave
David Williams
(1894-1973)
Comedian, born in Glasgow, who began his career at an early age as a "feed" to his elder brother at concerts. When he joined the Royal Flying Corps during the first world war, he volunteered to entertain the troops. He did so again during the second. Between the wars, and for long afterwards, he was much loved in Scotland as a clean comic with a gift for parody. His summer show, *Half-Past Eight*, once ran at the King's Theatre in Edinburgh for 32 weeks, a record for that theatre. He responded readily to good causes and an ambulance flag day was named in his honour.

Essay by
William Hunter

When holidaymakers went to coast resorts in the 1920s and '30s they did like to have their comics with them beside the seaside. While the laughter-makers filled shore pavilions, city theatres were left unprofitably dark and empty. Revues called *Half-Past Eight* were an effort by the Howard and Wyndham circuit to make it summertime everywhere. They were a variety of spectacle, sometimes lavish, and rat-a-tat comedy mixed with glamorous hoofing and even a dramatic interlude. Billing imported comedians (Jewel and Warris among them), they were a hit in Glasgow from 1933. At the King's Theatre, Edinburgh, they took longer to catch on. Only from 1937 did they become a hit with the hiring at starry fees of Dave Willis.

These were his golden days. He was No.1 comic after the death of Tommy Lorne (1890-1935).

Willis was built to be a clown, small and agile although less elegant than Charlie Chaplin, whom he copied. He became Scotland's Chaplin, except he was funny. He had long arms, short legs, and a big head. He was a Pictish droll. His chimpanzee act was life-like. He did Hitler. "I'm getting more like Hitler every day," he warbled until it was not funny any more. Mahatma Ghandi was not beyond a joke. Leading a goat, he sang: "Ye look like a galoot/In your wee dish cloot;/Ye'd look far better/In a plus-four suit." He could be a cheeky wee boy. Nessie became a monster source of hilarity. During the Hitler war his turn as an air-raid warden helped morale. "You'll no' get in ma shelter for it's far too wee" became a gritty ditty of defiance that entered folklore.

He was a lazy genius who abhorred rehearsal. He preferred to free-wheel it on the night. When he had perfected an act, he repeated it – endlessly swallowing a bowl-full of goldfish (actually pieces of carrot), disastrously hanging wallpaper and skittering about the stage on a pool of paste, helplessly looking for a light for his fag. Like other lazy geniuses, he was also hard-working. Along with other once-nightly shows, *Half-Past Eight* demanded all-day attendance every day to prepare for a change of programme on Fridays.

He worked three catchphrases, or two more than some other Scotch comics. "It makes you feel such a fool" he liked to keep saying in ticklish situations. Sharing a confidence with adoring audiences, he'd begin: "Wait till Ah tell you." Best-loved was 'Way 'way up a ky", which hardly meant anything. He retained it from a childhood cry of his son Denny Willis, later a comedian, when he spotted an aeroplane.

Determined not to fade away, he decided to be the youngest Scotch comic to retire, quitting aged 56. After his bankruptcy, he was seldom offered work and never anything big. He had a sad, aged clown's death in Peebles.

His patter went with him because it was not scripted. One surviving joke attributed to him was a small piece of business with his straight man, the accomplished Cliff Harley. "Feel that!" Dave Willis is said to have said, holding out his bowler hat. "It's felt." In print it perishes. Doing Hitler, he insisted: "I've always wanted to be a dictator. I was good at dictation at school."

Wilmot, Sir Robert Arthur
(1939-74)
Landowner and eighth baronet, educated at Eton, who succeeded to the title at the age of three when his father was killed in action at Alamein. In 1958 he was commissioned in the Scots Guards and served for six years, reaching the rank of captain. Latterly he ran an estate in Fife. On the day of his divorce, after he and his former wife had just had dinner, he was injured in a road accident and died three weeks later.

Wilson, Sir Garnet Douglas
(1885-1975)
Local politician and public servant, educated at the High School of

Dundee. He was lord provost of Dundee, 1940-46, and played a wider role in the public life of Scotland as chairman of the National Camps Association, Glenrothes Development Corporation, and the Scottish Special Housing Association. He was made a freeman of Dundee in 1972.

Wilson, William
(c1906-72)
Artist in stained glass, born in Edinburgh, who studied at Edinburgh College of Art and the Royal College of Art in London. One of his most important works is the bishop's window in the nave of Liverpool Cathedral, but he played an important part in the revival of stained glass in non-ecclesiastical settings, such as the windows of the entrance hall of the British Linen Bank's head office in Edinburgh. He went blind in 1961.

Wilson, William Combe
(1897-1974)
Surgeon, born in Burntisland, Fife, and educated at the Royal High School, Edinburgh. He served during the first world war as a private in the Argyll and Sutherland Highlanders and as a 2nd lieutenant in the Black Watch. After the war he graduated in medicine at Edinburgh University and held appointments in Edinburgh Royal Infirmary and the Royal Hospital for Sick Children, Edinburgh. During a Rockefeller travelling scholarship he researched surgery in Chicago. He returned to Edinburgh as a surgeon in the Royal Hospital for Sick Children, Edinburgh, and was director of the Edinburgh surgical research unit of the Medical Research Council. In 1939 he became regius professor of surgery at Aberdeen University, holding this post until 1962.

Wyness, Fenton
(d 1974)
Architect, conservationist, historian, antiquarian, artist and writer, an authority on the history of Aberdeen and Deeside. By his public work he helped to preserve for Aberdeen several buildings of historic and architectural value. His books included *City by the Grey North Sea* and *Royal Valley*, both published in the 1960s. He was a county commissioner of Scouts in Aberdeen and in 1973 received the movement's highest award, the silver wolf, to mark his 60-year association.

Y

Young, Professor Andrew McLaren
(c1914-75)
Art historian and scholar. A son of the manse, he was born in Southend, Argyll, but spent much of his boyhood in the West Indies. He was educated at George Watson's College and Edinburgh University. During the second world war he was commissioned in the King's Own Yorkshire Light Infantry and served in North Africa

and Italy. After the war he joined the staff of the Barber Institute of Fine Arts at Birmingham University. In 1949 he moved to Glasgow University's department of the history of the fine arts and in 1965 was appointed to the Richmond chair of fine art. An authority on Rennie Mackintosh and Whistler, he was curator of the university's art collection and closely involved in the building of the Hunterian Museum to house the collection.

Young, Professor Douglas Cuthbert Colquhoun (1913-73)

Classical scholar, author and poet, born in Tayport. Of the infant prodigy it was said that he could be found at the age of two seated in a small chair outside the garden gate of the family home in Merchiston, Edinburgh, reading aloud to passers-by from the book of Job. Part of his childhood was spent in Bengal, where he learned Urdu. At St Andrews University his fellow students – impressed by his height, black beard and omniscience – nicknamed him God. He lectured in classics for many years at the Universities of Aberdeen and St Andrews before emigrating to the United States, where he was professor of Greek at the University of North Carolina. It was a source of sadness to his admirers that a professorial chair in Scotland could not be found for this engaging polymath, whose published work included several books of poems and translations of Aristophanes into Scots.

He was always no less a figure of controversy than of academic brilliance. During the second world war he served a 12-month prison sentence for resisting conscription because of his Scottish nationalist principles, Young's stated principle being "that the Scottish people through a democratic Scottish government should have control of whatever war effort the Scottish people wish to make". He took Homer and Aeschylus with him to the cells. His chairmanship of the SNP, 1942-45, divided nationalists between those who argued that the party should close ranks behind the war effort and others who advocated a continuation of its pre-war policy. When Young was elected chairman by two votes over William Power, the preferred candidate of John MacCormick, the party secretary, MacCormick proclaimed, "I wouldn't now insult William Power by asking him to be chairman of this rabble", and started a breakaway movement which he called Scottish Convention. Douglas Young, meanwhile, came near to winning Kirkcaldy Burghs for the SNP in 1943. It is said that he died with Homer open in front of him.

Young on Scottish history	"The great mistake made by James VI in 1603 was to go to London. He should have governed the whole British Empire from Scotland."
Historian Tom Nairn's reply	"Unfortunately, this vein of delirium echoes the central uncertainty of Scottish nationalism only too accurately. When in doubt, take refuge in bombast."
From Young's *Scotland* [1971]	"In the long perspective of Scottish history, the present union with and under England, dating from 1707, may some day be thought of as just a curious piece of ancient history, like the Auld Alliance with France, which occupied about the same tract of history; or merely one of those dynastic accidents resulting from royal marriages, like the former Austro-Hungarian empire."

Personal memoir by
Ian Hamilton

A kent whaur Douglas Young leeved. He lived at Makar's Bield, Tayport, Fife. The address defined him, as sometimes addresses can. Translated by a Sothron it means The Poet's Shelter. Only a dullard would favour the latter name, and Douglas was never a dullard.

I don't know when he first came into my life. Probably when I was writing his name on an envelope when I was a schoolboy. In return for being a patriot I was permitted to address envelopes at SNP headquarters at 59 Elmbank Street. It was like writing a list of heroes.

Then he became a real hero. It was during the war and he was a conscientious objector for Scotland's sake, refusing to fight in England's battles. They sent him to Barlinnie for a year, and people used to play bagpipes to him outside the prison walls. "They'll do that for me sometime, dad," I said, but so far they've never had to. He wrote a pamphlet about his views called *The Freeminded Scot*. It nearly converted me, but not quite. Later he told me he had very much enjoyed Barlinnie. It was the only time he had had no responsibilities. "You can enjoy freedom in there," he used to say thoughtfully.

Somehow we became friends. I'm wee and to me he seemed seven feet tall. Maybe he was. When I got a real grown-up person's house in the New Town of Edinburgh he used to drop in on me on a Saturday morning. We would take a walk to the Botanics. This took us past Raeburn cricket ground. He would stop to watch the cricket over the wall while I stared into the masonry. It improves cricket to watch it through a stone wall. Then we walked on. I forget what we talked about but his students had set him a summer task. He had to translate *The Frogs of Aristophanes* into Scots. He called it *The Puddocks*. A copy is under my elbow as I write. All this was away above my head but I loved to listen to him. Douglas Young was a big long streak of joy.

Some of his poetry has stuck. I can never fish a river without recalling a fragment of a poem he wrote while lamenting his friends who were away in a war he couldn't join. "Casting the bright fleas into the dark spate," he laments and names his lost friends. All his poetry wasn't gloomy. Here's another for you. It may not be great stuff, but it's the poetry every Scot loves.

Last Laugh

The minister said it wald dee
The cypruss buss I plantit.
But the buss grew til a tree
Naething dauntit.

It's growan stark and heich,
Derk and straucht and sinister,
Kirkyairdie-like and dreich.
But whaur's the minister?

A ken whaur thon makar's fund his last bield. It's in aw Scotlan.

Bibliography

For the purpose of reviewing the lives and achievements of some of those included in the Dictionary of Scottish Biography, we have published short extracts from books either by or about them. A comprehensive list is given below, with the name of the author as expressed in the book, the name of the publisher, and the year of publication. We hope that this will prove useful to readers who wish to pursue research or a personal interest, though we should point out that very few of the books are still in print. Dedicated students are directed to their nearest reference library, failing which the Mitchell Library in Glasgow should be able to access the required volume.

Almost a Gentleman, John Osborne
   Faber and Faber, 1991
The American Political System, D.W. Brogan
   Hamish Hamilton, 1933
Art and Audacity, T.J. Honeyman
   Collins, 1971
The Atom of Delight, Neil M. Gunn
   Faber and Faber, 1956
The Bairns O' Adam: the story of the STUC, Keith Aitken
   Polygon, 1997
The Biggest Aspidistra in the World, Peter Black
   BBC, 1972
The Celtic Church in Dunblane, James Hutchison Cockburn
   Society of Friends of Dunblane Cathedral, 1954
Chosen Words, Ivor Brown
   Jonathan Cape, 1955
Compton Mackenzie: A life, Andro Linklater
   Chatto and Windus, 1987
A Cry from Europe, Annie I. Dunlop
   Kilmarnock Standard Press, 1939
David Astor and The Observer, Richard Cockett
   Andre Deutsch, 1991
A Dominie's Log, A.S. Neill
   Herbert Jenkins, 1915
Duncan Forbes of Culloden, C. de Bois Murray
   IPC, 1936
Dundee and the Reformation, J.H. Baxter
   Abertay Historical Society, 1960
The Elephant, the Tiger and the Gentle Kangaroo, Philip A. Stalker
   Ramsay Head Press, 1971
The English People, D.W. Brogan
   Hamish Hamilton, 1943
Food and the People, Sir John Boyd Orr
   Pilot Press, 1943
The Glory and the Dream: the history of Celtic FC 1887-1987, Tom Campbell and Pat Woods
   Grafton Books, 1987
Golfers' Gallery, Frank Moran
   Oliver and Boyd, 1946
Grierson on Documentary, edited H. Forsyth Hardy
   Faber and Faber, 1966
The Heart Is Highland, James A. Roy
   McClelland and Stewart, 1947

The Highland Jaunt, Moray McLaren
  Jarrolds, 1954
History of the Royal College of Physicians of Edinburgh, Professor W.S. Craig
  Blackwell Scientific Publications, 1976
How Scotland is Governed, C. de Bois Murray
  Art and Educational Publishers, 1947
Into the Wind, J.C.W. Reith
  Hodder and Stoughton, 1949
John Davidson, a study in personality, R.D. Macleod
  W. and R. Holmes, 1957
Law From Over The Border: a short account of a strange jurisdiction, Andrew Dewar Gibb
  W. Green and Son, 1950
The Life and Times of James Kennedy, Bishop of St. Andrews, Annie I. Dunlop
  University of St Andrews, 1950
Listening for a Midnight Tram, John Junor
  Chapmans, 1990
Lowland Lairds, James Fergusson
  Faber and Faber, 1949
The Lowlands of Scotland, George Scott-Moncrieff
  B.T. Batsford, 1939
The Man On My Back, Eric Linklater
  Macmillan, 1941
Medico-Legal Aspects of the Ruxton Case, John Glaister and James Couper Brash
  E. and S. Livingstone, 1937
Memoirs of a Modern Scotland, edited Karl Miller
  Faber and Faber, 1970
Memories, Tom Johnston
  Collins, 1952
Memory's Voyage, Marjorie Dalrymple
  Simpson Bell, 1963
Men Christ Wants: evangelistic addresses, D.P. Thomson
  Marshall Morgan and Scott, 1950
Modern Scottish Writers, W.M. Parker
  William Hodge, 1917
Motive for a Mission, James Douglas-Hamilton
  Mainstream, 1979
Music in my Heart, Horace Fellowes
  Oliver and Boyd, 1958
My Life with the Miners, Abe Moffat
  Lawrence and Wishart, 1965
Nursing Care of the Newly Born Infant, W.S. Craig
  E. & S. Livingstone, 1955
octobiography, Helen B. Cruikshank
  Standard Press, Montrose, 1976
Of Whales and Men, R.B. Robertson
  Macmillan, 1956
On Selfhood and Godhood, C.A. Campbell
  George Allen and Unwin, 1957
The Origin of the Earth, William Smart
  Cambridge University Press, 1951
The Philosophical Bases of Education, Robert R. Rusk
  University of London Press, 1928
Philosophical Lecture-Notes, C.A. Campbell
  Craig Wilson, 1945
The Pilots' Book of Everest, Marquess of Douglas and Clydesdale and Flt. Lt. D.F. McIntyre
  William Hodge, 1936

The Riddle of the Universe, W.M. Smart
   Longmans, 1968
The Road to Dunfermline: the story of a thirty-five years' quest, D.P. Thomson
   Publisher and year of publication not known
The Road Home, F. Marian McNeill
   Alexander MacLehose, 1932
Scot Easy, Wilfred Taylor
   Max Reinhardt, 1955
Scotland, Douglas Young
   Cassell, 1971
Scotland Bitter-Sweet, James Drawbell
   Macdonald, 1972
Scots Heraldry, Sir Thomas Innes of Learney
   Oliver and Boyd, 1934
The Scots Kitchen, F. Marian McNeill
   Blackie, 1971
Scottish Country, edited George Scott-Moncrieff
   Wishart Books, 1935
The Scottish Islands, George Scott-Moncrieff
   B.T. Batsford, 1952
The Scottish Office – and other Scottish government departments, Sir David Milne
   George Allen and Unwin, 1957
The Scottish Publishing Houses, R.D. Macleod
   W. and R. Holmes, 1953
Self-Subsistence for the Unemployed – studies in a new technique, J.W. Scott
   Faber and Faber, 1935
Should Auld Acquaintance, William Power
   George G. Harrap, 1935
Teach Yourself to Study Art, David Talbot Rice
   English Universities Press, 1955
They Converted Our Ancestors, John Foster
   SCM Press, 1965
Thorns and Thistles, Harry Whitley
   Edina Press, 1976
Three Steps to Victory, Sir Robert Watson-Watt
   Odhams Press, 1957
Too Long in this Condition, Fionn Mac Colla
   Caithness Books, 1975
Understanding the Scots: a guide for South Britons and other foreigners, Moray McLaren
   Impulse Books, 1972
The Voice of Labour – the Autobiography of a House Painter, James Clunie
   Privately published, 1958
The Way of My World, Ivor Brown
   Collins, 1954
Where Aloes Flame, R.H.W. Shepherd
   Lutterworth, 1948
The White Man's Dilemma: Food and the Future, John Boyd Orr
   George Allen and Unwin, 1956
With Winston Churchill at the Front, Captain X (Andrew Dewar Gibb)
   Gowans and Gray, 1924
Within the Fringe, James Stuart
   Bodley Head, 1967